POLITICS AS SYMBOLIC ACTION

POLITICS AS SYMBOLIC ACTION

Mass Arousal and Quiescence

MURRAY EDELMAN

University of Wisconsin

**Institute for Research on
Poverty Monograph Series**

ACADEMIC PRESS   New York San Francisco London

A Subsidiary of Harcourt Brace Jovanovich, Publishers

This book is one of a Series sponsored by the Institute for Research on Poverty of the University of Wisconsin pursuant to the provisions of the Economic Opportunity Act of 1964.

ACADEMIC PRESS, INC.
111 Fifth Avenue, New York, New York 10003

United Kingdom Edition published by
ACADEMIC PRESS, INC. (LONDON) LTD.
24/28 Oval Road, London NW1

LIBRARY OF CONGRESS CATALOG CARD NUMBER: 75-160519

PRINTED IN THE UNITED STATES OF AMERICA

For Laurie, Judith, and Sarah

ACKNOWLEDGMENTS

Before students succumb too far to the paradigm, the professionalism, and the other blinders graduate work too often imposes on them, they are lively, irreverent, and creative critics of efforts at political analysis. This book has benefited a great deal from the reactions of University of Wisconsin students who were exposed to tentative ideas they helped me to discard or to shape.

Some professionals evade the blinders too, among them the colleagues who helpfully criticized parts or all of the manuscript: especially Leonard Berkowitz, Barbara Dennis, Kenneth Dolbeare, Ann Jacobs, Henry Kariel, Michael Lipsky, Richard Merelman, Rozann Rothman, Judith Stiehm, and Betty Zisk. Linda Bemis, Bonnie Freeman, Barbara Lundin Kovarovic, and Lettie Wenner helped with the research.

The work was supported by funds granted to the Institute for Research on Poverty at the University of Wisconsin by the Office of Economic Opportunity pursuant to the provisions of the Economic Opportunity Act of 1964.

The author alone is responsible for the conclusions.

A part of chapter 2 is a revision of a paper that originally appeared in *The American Behavioral Scientist* 13 (November–December 1969), 231–46, published by Sage Publications, Inc. Chapter 5 is a revised and expanded version of a paper that originally appeared in *Psychiatry* 30 (August 1967), 217–28, published by the William Alanson White Psychiatric Foundation, Inc. Chapter 8 is a revised version of a paper that originally appeared in Gerald Somers (ed.), *Essays in Industrial Relations Theory* (Iowa State University Press, 1969). Each of these publishers has given me permission to use this material.

CONTENTS

Chapter 1

AROUSAL AND QUIESCENCE: AN INTRODUCTION

Political history is largely an account of mass violence and of the expenditure of vast resources to cope with mythical fears and hopes. At the same time, large groups of people remain quiescent under noxiously oppressive conditions and sometimes passionately defend the very social institutions that deprive or degrade them.

Collective acts that are violent or self-defeating are easier to accept if they are seen as atypical departures from a political process that is peaceful and rational. It is paradoxically comforting to believe that the race riots; the police riots; the destruction of six million European Jews; large-scale massacres in Indonesia, Armenia, Biafra, and elsewhere; avid support for despotic regimes; and those wars we do not like are the acts of moral monsters. What shocks and frightens us is the realization that such actions are banal.

The reassurance of labeling them deviant dominates academic political analysis as well as public opinion. Our most prestigious models of the political process see them as breakdowns of the polity, signals of the end of a period of system persistence, an unstable displacement of a pluralistic society by a mass society, or the temporary dominance of an irrational oligarchy acting without popular consent.

Not only the study of history but the study of the human mind makes it unfortunately clear that in ambiguous situations misperceptions about political threats and utopias, the identification of enemies and allies, and the means to achieve group goals appear predictably and systematically under some conditions. To regard such misperceptions as rare departures from a normal pattern reflects a deep-seated need for reassurance but clouds understanding of the conditions under which mass support for political violence and self-defeating policies occurs.

Widely shared perceptions and misperceptions about political threats and issues are crucial in political behavior. An exploration of the dynamics of their development and the conditions under which they change is a prerequisite to explanation of political arousal, violence, and quiescence. Such exploration should take account both of relevant knowledge of the psychology of cognition and what we can learn about the functions of specifically political perceptions in cognitive dynamics. This study suggests that political perceptions have distinctive characteristics that make them dynamically different from some other perceptions. They develop and are mutually reinforced in large collectivities of people, evoking intense hopes and fears, threats and reassurances. For some, religious cognitions are similar in this respect, though in the latter part of the twentieth century the polity is more widely influential than the church in such evocations.

This emphasis places at the center of attention the symbolizing ability with which man adapts his world to his behavior and his behavior to his world. Only man among living things reconstructs his past, perceives his present condition, and anticipates his future through symbols that abstract, screen, condense, distort, displace, and even create what the senses bring to his attention. The ability to manipulate sense perceptions symbolically permits complex reasoning and planning and consequent efficacious action. It also facilitates firm attachments to illusions, misperceptions, and myths and consequent misguided or self-defeating action.

To explain political behavior as a response to fairly stable individual wants, reasoning, attitudes, and empirically based perceptions is therefore simplistic and misleading. Adequate explanation must focus on the complex element that intervenes between the environment and the behavior of human beings: creation and change in common meanings through symbolic apprehension in groups of people of interests, pressures, threats, and possibilities. The understanding of the symbolic process is a long-range challenge for which symbolic interaction theory, structural anthropology, and phenomenological sociology have supplied a firm but embryonic grounding. Analysis of the links among political symbols and political behaviors is a facet of the challenge that can contribute both to an understanding of the functions of symbols and to a correlative understanding of change in political cognitions and actions.

Kenneth Burke makes the point:

> And however important to us is the tiny sliver of reality each of us has experienced firsthand, the whole overall "picture" is but a construct of our symbolic systems. To meditate on this fact until one sees its full implications is much like peering over the edge of things into an ultimate abyss. And doubtless that's one reason why, though man is typically the symbol-using animal, he clings to a kind of naive verbal realism that refuses to realize the full extent of the role played by symbolicity in his notions of reality.[1]

---

[1] Kenneth Burke, *Language as Symbolic Action* (Berkeley: University of California Press, 1966), p. 5.

THE INSTABILITY AND AMBIVALENCE OF POLITICAL COGNITIONS

That political cognitions are often ambivalent and highly susceptible to symbolic cues for change and that much of the impression of their stability is an artifact of measurement procedures, and perhaps of our anxiety about instability and irrationality, is increasingly recognized.[2]

Both popular and academic predilections about political wants, beliefs, demands, and attitudes have often diverted attention from fluctuation and focused attention upon stability. It is reminiscent of the celebrated observation that monkeys are placid when German psychologists observe them and active when American psychologists do. What an observer sees hinges in a subtle but compelling way upon his interests.

Americans have been taught to look upon government as a mechanism that is responsive to their wants and upon these in turn as rational reflections of their interests and their moral upbringing and therefore as stable and continuing. The American social scientist has been socialized to see individuals' political demands and attitudes as "inputs" of the political system; he has been encouraged, through comparative studies of civic culture, to identify different patterns of attitudes as characteristic of different countries, apparently over significant time periods; and he is being advised just how political socialization processes create particular cognitions and evaluations in children as they mature. The ready availability of opportunities for survey research on attitudes, moreover, places a premium upon the assumption that respondents' answers can be taken as "hard" data which have a clear, continuing, and systematic meaning. For some research and pedagogical purposes this assumption unquestionably is useful and valid.

Yet we have compelling evidence from a variety of kinds of observation that political beliefs, demands, and attitudes, far from being fixed and stable, are frequently sporadic in appearance, fluctuating in intensity, ambivalent in composition, and therefore logically inconsistent in pattern and structure. It is central to the explanation of political quiescence, arousal and violence both that attitudes potentially or actually have these

---

[2] In addition to the studies cited below see Carl Hovland, Irving Janis, and Harold Kelley, *Communication and Persuasion* (New Haven: Yale University Press, 1953); Samuel Eldersveld, "Experimental Propaganda Techniques and Voting Behavior," *American Political Science Review* 50 (March 1956), 154–65; Elihu Katz and Jacob Feldman, "The Debates in the Light of Research: A Survey of Surveys," in Sidney Kraus (ed.), *The Great Debates* (Bloomington: Indiana University Press, 1962).

unstable characteristics and that public policies and processes themselves serve as cues that evoke particular changes in the direction and intensity of political cognitions. If this is the case, public policies and processes must be recognized not only or chiefly as the resultants of individuals' demands but also as the paramount source of particular attitudes and demands, including those associated with mass violence.

The meanings to be drawn from political actions and rhetoric hinge partly upon which of these alternative models of the policymaking process a person accepts. The conventional assumption is that the individuals comprising the mass public hold relatively stable positions on public issues and that public policy represents a response to some aggregation of these positions. If this is an accurate view, it follows that political scientists should concentrate upon how sensitively and accurately and equitably political wants are aggregated and converted into policies—and that is what they have done for the most part.

The alternative model assumes that individuals' positions on public issues are mobilizable rather than fixed; that governmental activities are themselves potent influences upon change and mobilization of public attitudes; and that the significant "outputs" of political activities are not particular public policies labeled as political goals, but rather the creation of political followings and supports: i.e., the evocation of arousal or quiescence in mass publics. If *this* model is a fairly accurate one, it follows that political scientists and advocates of particular policies should recognize political maneuver as itself the end-point of the game; for in the process (rather than in the content of statutes, court decisions, and administrative rules) leaders gain or lose followings, followers achieve a role and a political identity, and money and status are reallocated, often to different groups from those formally designated as the beneficiaries of the governmental activity in question. The wide acceptance of a model that generates misleading interpretations of political activity is itself a compelling legitimation of the real payoffs of the system in status, money, and role definitions.

The instability of political cognitions is readily apparent to anyone who looks at its manifestations dispassionately. It would be self-evident if we were not cued to ignore it by (1) our socialization into the belief that enduring individual values shape the course of government policy and (2) the fact that opinion surveys and other reactive research instruments themselves create opinion and commitment among many respondents who are not opinionated before they are asked to state their views.

The most telling evidence lies in demonstrable major change in beliefs, in opinions, and in views of desirable public policy over both long and short time spans. One relevant form of research, illustrating the ambivalence and lack of cognitive definition and clarity characteristic of a high proportion of political opinions, involves the exploration in some depth of the bases of opinion responses on a particular issue. Leo Bogart cites research at Stanford in 1966 showing that a majority of the public at that time both supported the President's handling of the Vietnam situation (an escalation policy) and approved of de-escalation.[3] In 1964, 74 percent of the Minnesota public said it favored prayer in the public schools; but well over half of this same 74 percent of the respondents also said they approved of a Supreme Court ruling declaring it illegal to prescribe prayers for children to recite in the public schools.[4] Other research points to similar ambivalence or to inconsistency in opinion over time. Those who favor welfare programs more frequently oppose taxes to finance them than do opponents of the programs.[5]

Philip Converse found that for most of the population below the level of elites there is little consistency among political beliefs and opinions. Opinions are inconsistent with each other, and they vary *randomly* in direction during repeated trials over time.[6]

These conclusions are almost certainly partial statements or over-statements. In some situations and on some issues, sets of constrained beliefs do appear in any group of people, and we can learn something about the dynamics of their generation.

In part at least, opinion research findings reflect the pointlessness of trying to ascertain and measure the opinions of people about issues that have little salience or meaning for them except the salience created by the measurement effort itself. Bogart made the crucial point in his presidential address to the American Association for Public Opinion Research in May 1967:

> We think of public opinion as polarized on great issues; we think of it as intense . . . Because of the identification of public opinion with the measurements of surveys, the illusion is easily conveyed of a public which is 'opinionated'—which is committed to strongly held views. The public of opinion poll results no doubt acts as a reinforcing agent in support of the public's consciousness of its own collective opinions as a definable, describable force. These published poll data may become reference points by which the individual formulates and expresses his opinions. . . .

---

[3] Leo Bogart, "No Opinion, Don't Know, and Maybe No Answer," *Public Opinion Quarterly* 31 (Fall 1967), 332–45, 336.

[4] Minnesota poll, 1964.

[5] V. O. Key, *Public Opinion and American Democracy* (New York: Knopf, 1961), p. 158.

[6] Philip E. Converse, "The Nature of Belief Systems in Mass Publics," in David Apter (ed.), *Ideology and Discontent* (New York: Free Press, 1964), pp. 206–61.

Often what we should be doing is measuring the degrees of apathy, indecision, or conflict on the part of the great majority with the opinionated as the residual left over.[7]

One caveat is necessary. To analyze any complex transaction in discursive prose, its empirical facets must be considered separately and therefore out of context. At the same time it is a corollary of the model suggested here that psychological characteristics, social interaction, and political acts are alternative expressions of the same phenomenon; the conventional practice of conceiving them as separate entities, moreover, itself supports particular status relationships and modes of political behavior. In this sense the present formulation recognizes that the various processes here examined, including processes generated by the observer, are facets of a single transaction, as Dewey and Bentley use the term.[8]

This study is an effort to analyze this complex transaction, focusing on political arousal, violence, and quiescence, especially in the urban ghettos and among the poor. Its major objective is to identify and explore the systematic aspects of several related dynamic processes: (1) the processes of collective perception or misperception of threat and of initiation of collective action to deal with threat; (2) the processes through which groups with diverse interests coalesce into political allies; (3) the processes of symbol formation and of personality formation underlying collective threat perception and interest aggregation.

Empirically, these processes not only occur together but are the same process viewed from different perspectives. The kinds of analysis engaged in respectively by personality theorists, students of social movements, and students of the behaviors of political leaders and followers have all been useful, but none of these has gone very far in learning how the other facets of the process are dynamically linked to its own concerns.

It is through their power to merge diverse perceptions and beliefs into a new and unified perspective that symbols affect what men want, what they do, and the identity they create for themselves. In an important study of religious symbolism Mircea Eliade makes the point:

An essential character of religious symbolism is its *multivalence,* its capacity to *express simultaneously several meanings the unity between which is not evident on the plane of immediate experience.* . . . This capacity of religious symbolism to reveal a multitude of structurally united meanings has an important conse-

---

[7] Bogart, No opinion, pp. 335, 337.
[8] John Dewey and Arthur F. Bentley, *Knowing and the Known* (Boston: Beacon Press, 1960).

quence: the symbol is capable of *revealing a perspective in which
diverse realities can be fitted together or even integrated into a
"system"*. . . . One cannot sufficiently insist on this point: that
the examination of symbolic structures is a work not of *reduction*
but of *integration*. One compares and contrasts two expressions of
a symbol not in order to reduce them to a single, pre-existent expression, but in order to discover the process by which a structure
is capable of enriching its meanings.[9]

This book explores the multifaceted range of roles political symbols
induce people to play. Rather than taking it for granted that a man or
woman represents a stable set of political traits, beliefs, wants, and demands, we search for the conditions and the mechanisms that evoke change
or ambivalence in these respects. Stability over long periods of time now
appears as a special case, to be explained rather than assumed. The book
also examines the implications of both views of political man for public
policy: man as immovable object, who must be appeased or destroyed;
or man as capable of a range of potentialities that can be developed or
thwarted.

THE INFLUENCE OF GOVERNMENTAL
ACTIVITY UPON BELIEFS AND PERCEPTIONS

Government affects behavior chiefly by shaping the cognitions of large
numbers of people in ambiguous situations. It helps create their beliefs
about what is proper; their perceptions of what is fact; and their expectations of what is to come. In the shaping of expectations of the future the
cues from government often encounter few qualifying or competing cues
from other sources; and this function of political activity is therefore an
especially potent influence upon behavior.

To make this point is to deny or seriously qualify what may be the
most widely held assumption about political interactions: that political
arousal and quiescence depend upon how much of what they want from
government people get. *Political actions chiefly arouse or satisfy people
not by granting or withholding their stable substantive demands, but rather
by changing the demands and the expectations.* That central theme of this
book was apparently in Harold Lasswell's mind in 1935 when he wrote
that "sound political analysis is nothing less than correct orientation in the
continuum which embraces the past, present, and future. Unless the salient

---

[9] Mircea Eliade, *The Two and the One* (Harvill Press, 1965), pp. 201, 203.

features of the all-inclusive whole are discerned, details will be incorrectly located. . . ."[10]

The implication of this view, which is manifestly in accord with George Herbert Mead's postulate that by anticipating the future man creates his world, is that expectations influence perceptions and interpretations of ambiguous current facts; and that the two together determine attitudes. The range of cognitions that explain behavior therefore turns ultimately on what people can be led to expect of the future. Supporting the fundamental insight of Mead and Cooley, it is a view that is increasingly evident in current experimental social psychology. Thus Leonard Berkowitz, discussing aggression, notes that:

> Contrary to traditional motivational thinking and motivational concepts of Freud and Lorenz, many psychologists now insist that deprivations alone are inadequate to account for most motivated behavior. According to this newer theorizing, much greater weight must be given to anticipations of the goal than merely to the duration or magnitude of deprivation per se. The stimulus arising from these anticipations—from anticipatory goal responses—is now held to be a major determinant of the vigor and persistence of goal-seeking activity.[11]

Similarly, Jervis concludes from a study of misperception that "there is evidence from both psychology and international relations that when expectations and desires clash, expectations seem to be more important. . . . Actors are apt to be especially sensitive to evidence of grave danger if they think they can take action to protect themselves against the menace once it has been detected."[12]

Through what mechanisms do governmental acts influence political cognitions? What is the explanation of their influence? Insofar as people's hopes and anxieties are salient to politics they turn on status in society and on security from perceived threat. For the great mass of political spectators cues as to group status and security, and especially as to their future status

---

[10] Harold D. Lasswell, *World Politics and Personal Insecurity* (New York: McGraw-Hill, 1935), p. 4.

[11] Leonard Berkowitz, "Some Implications of Laboratory Studies of Frustration and Aggression for the Study of Political Violence," paper delivered at 1967 Annual Meeting of the American Political Science Association, Chicago, September 5–9, 1967, p. 7 (mimeographed).

[12] Robert Jervis, "Hypotheses on Misperception," *World Politics* 20 (April 1968), 461–62. See also Dale Wyatt and Donald Campbell, "A Study of Interviewer Bias as Related to Interviewer's Expectations of Own Opinions," *International Journal of Opinion and Attitude Research* 4 (Spring 1950), 77–83.

and security, can come chiefly or only from governmental acts. This is one of the few forms of activity perceived as involving all groups and individuals in society and as reflecting the range of public interests, wants, and capabilities. In an ambiguous but salient area of public affairs, therefore, political cues serve, in Lasswell's term, as "symbols of the whole"[13] in a way that the acts or promises of individuals or private groups rarely can. For some, religion no doubt serves this same function and did so even more powerfully in less secular times. For most, however, only government can evoke fairly confident expectations of future welfare or deprivation for large masses of people at home and of international détente or threat: can create the perceived worlds that in turn shape perceptions and interpretations of current events and therefore the behaviors with which people respond to them.

Though it is usually not approached from this perspective, some extant social science research specifies the kinds of cognitions that are regularly shaped and reshaped by political activity and publicized governmental policy. In each instance the central cognition affected is expectations; and in each instance public policy evokes cognitions in the degree that cues generated by existing social situations and role-playings are ambiguous or absent. In a long established and accepted caste society, status expectations are unambiguous and are cued and reinforced by daily personal interactions that make it clear who is superior and who subordinate. Where a status system is questioned and resisted, concomitant anxieties, doubts, aspirations, and ambivalence lend salience and potency to the expectations about the future generated by public policy.

Various forms of research have demonstrated the efficacy of political activity and public policy in influencing perceptions and expectations of relative status. Gusfield, Lipset, and Hofstadter have shown that public policies such as the Eighteenth (prohibition) Amendment derive their salience and their meaning less from their instrumental effects upon resource allocations than from the cues they generate that particular social groups occupy a changed status in relation to each other and will continue to do so.[14] Similarly, studies of governmental economic regulations have shown that these policies frequently convey little in the way of instrumental resources but do reassure anxious groups of their continuing or newly

[13] Harold D. Lasswell, *Psychopathology and Politics* (New York: Viking, reprint 1960), p. 183.

[14] Joseph R. Gusfield, *Symbolic Crusade* (Urbana: University of Illinois Press, 1963); S. M. Lipset, "The Sources of the Radical Right," in Daniel Bell (ed.), *The New American Right* (New York: Criterion Books, 1955), pp. 166–234; Richard Hofstadter, "The Pseudo-Conservative Revolt," in *ibid.*, pp. 33–55.

achieved status as protected groups.[15] Political activity and formally proclaimed policy therefore amount to authoritative signals and assurances, in ambiguous and anxiety-producing situations, that particular group interests will be taken into account; or, alternatively, that they will be ignored or suppressed.

Political activity also influences perceptions of who are adversaries and how they will behave. Legislation or administrative activity signalling that a group aspiring to a valued status has achieved it reassures that group that in the future its adversaries will be limited in their use of private bargaining tactics and other resources. In other cases, however, political action amounts to a signal that an adversary can be expected to escalate its hostile behavior: that no mutual recognition of limits has been established and that counter-escalation is appropriate.

Government creates and publicizes a North Atlantic Treaty Organization establishing a military defense against possible Russian aggression in Europe and so evokes and keeps alive an expectation that such aggression is likely and that countermeasures are justified and necessary. This action creates a perception that Russian hawks are dominant in the Kremlin (or that all Russians are hawks). Such policies as the Berlin blockade, the airlift, and the Truman doctrine reinforce these expectations of mutual threat in political spectators, who have no other basis for perceptions of the cold war or its likely future course.

Elites are just as likely as others to base their beliefs upon symbolic governmental cues. Though government officials and other elites make conscious efforts to manipulate mass opinion, these are not our chief concern. Far more influential are the mobilizations of both elite and mass political opinion that stem from their engagement with the same symbols. Sometimes governmental actions or language create distrust in official policy, and information from nongovernmental sources can reinforce or counteract official cues.

With respect to the salient issues of a person's future welfare, status, and survival neither past experience nor news reports of current developments can be clear predictors of what is to come. The same experience and set of facts can be interpreted by a group of people as meaning either that their legitimate interests are being protected or that the status and benefits due them are being denied or threatened. In a caste system assumed by all its participants to be divinely sanctioned, subordination and unequal benefits mean that the world is as it should be; in a polity with a norm of social equality the same facts come to mean deprivation and an incentive to

---

[15] Murray Edelman, *The Symbolic Uses of Politics* (Urbana: University of Illinois Press, 1964), chaps. 2, 3.

resistance. Does the large scale influx of black people into a northern city mean that the status, the livelihood, or the lives of white residents will ultimately be threatened, or does it signal one more phase in a continuing process of cultural diversification, economic progress, and political co-existence? Do large scale troop movements in a foreign country signal an intention to attack another country, an intention to protect it, or routine maneuvers? It is always the ambiguity, the uncertain and diverse possible implications of news, that creates the fears, hopes, and the search for authoritative cues that public policy often satisfies.

PLAN OF THE BOOK

The organization of the book reflects the need to examine both the empirically observable transaction and the analtyically diverse perspectives and processes that are integrated into it. Chapters 2 and 3 expound a general thesis regarding the conditions and processes that explain political arousal and quiescence, the escalation of political conflict, and the outbreak of violence. The remaining chapters develop the various facets of the thesis more fully, using data that illuminate the functions of particular symbolic forms and observations garnered from a range of diverse conflict situations. Chapter 4 explores the psychological component of the transaction, particularly the functions of emotion and of the search for a political role and identity. Chapter 5 focuses upon the functions of language forms in shaping cognition and action. In chapters 6 and 7 data and observations on militant and violent collective behavior of the poor and of their political adversaries are organized in the light of the book's general thesis and serve in turn to expand and refine the thesis. The next two chapters focus upon specific issue areas marked, respectively, by ritualization and by escalation of conflict. Chapter 8, a study of the links between industrial conflict and political conflict, examines the process through which organization of a disadvantaged group can eventuate in ritualized conflict and cooperation in both the political and the industrial spheres. Chapter 9 analyzes the process through which adversary economic and social interests in domestic politics are systematically linked both to the escalation of international conflict and to alliances and cleavages in domestic politics. The final chapter explores some implications for political behavior and for public policy.

Chapter 2

ESCALATION AND RITUALIZATION OF POLITICAL CONFLICT

THE POLITICAL DYNAMICS OF ESCALATION

That governmental actions help create common patterns of perception and belief does not in itself account for the manifest willingness of large numbers of people to sacrifice, attack, kill, or die en masse or to endure serious oppression en masse for extended periods of time. There are, however, evidences of the operation of complementary processes that coalesce groups with diverse concerns into a single political force and that infuse individual participants with the intense affect that comes from defense of one's own identity. The basic processes are most easily identified in the case of international conflict, and so a short analysis of that area precedes a more detailed examination of the escalation of violence in the urban ghettos.

The nation is taken as the unit of analysis in news accounts, histories, and most academic analyses of international conflict. It is the nation that is presented as an entity that comes into conflict with one or more other nations, and the public accounts of international negotiations and international organizations constantly reinforce this view that one national interest opposes others.

Within each nation, however, there are diverse and conflicting groups that are in disagreement about foreign affairs issues. Some industries, workers, and consumers benefit from restrictions on international trade and others benefit from the absence of restrictions. There are internationalists and isolationists, "hawks" and "doves"—themselves names for political coalitions with different reasons for the stands they take: religious, economic, professional, and others. Each of these groupings tries to win certain instrumental political gains in domestic politics: money, status, particular policy directions, and wide public support. Public support is manifestly critical for the other gains as well. How are followings mobilized?

One major way is through identification of a particular interest with the abstract, empirically undefinable "national interest" in terms of which we are socialized to think about international politics. People's perceptions regularly reflect their interests quite unconsciously as a function of a number of psychological mechanisms.[1] In doing so they mobilize and coalesce groups of people who share the same domestic concerns only mildly or not at all.

We can be more specific about the intriguing process through which hawks or doves widen their political support: i.e., about the escalation or de-escalation of conflict. Nothing helps the hawks in the Pentagon gain support as effectively as evidence that the hawks in the Kremlin have gained support, and vice versa. Hawks in rival countries therefore have an interest in observing, publicizing, and exaggerating the other's gains; such publicizing and exaggerating accordingly constitute a form of tacit though unintended cooperation. The same is true for the doves in rival countries. The governmental actions and policies of each nation thus represent the manifest, and usually the only, signal of what is to come. In this way public actions evoke and control the demands, fears, and expectations of mass publics. These demands, fears, and expectations in turn produce rich benefits for particular groups, most of them not typically thought of as intended outcomes of political processes: status and appropriations for the armed forces, contracts for manufacturers, jobs for their employees, and so on.

In this way a range of diverse group interests and anxieties in domestic politics come to be perceived in terms of a single political conflict between two countries. In the polar form of this identification, the countries are further reified into "national interests" pursued by monolithic planners or plotters. Regardless of the empirical verifiability of the belief about monolithic hostile plotting (the facts are typically ambiguous and unverifiable), these beliefs serve to mobilize mass publics behind particular concrete interest groupings. A latent political function of the translation of concrete interests into a vision of contending nations is therefore to create real and empirically observable benefits that are conventionally not recognized as the objectives of the political transaction or even as benefits, but rather as the "costs" of preparedness or war. Ritualistic engagement in

---

[1] Studies and discussions of the effect of motivation upon perception include: J. S. Bruner and C. Goodman, "Value and Need as Organizing Factors in Perception," *Journal of Abnormal and Social Psychology* 42 (1947), 33–44; J. W. Atkinson, "Explorations Using Imaginative Thought To Assess the Strength of Human Motives," in M. R. Jones (ed.), *Nebraska Symposium on Motivation* (Lincoln: University of Nebraska Press, 1954); George S. Klein, "Perception, Motives and Personality," in J. L. McCary (ed.), *Psychology of Personality* (New York: Logos Press, 1956), pp. 121–99; D. O. Sears and J. L. Freedman, "Selective Exposure to Information: A Critical Review," *Public Opinion Quarterly* 31 (Summer 1967), 194–213; Robert Jervis, "Hypotheses on Misperception," *World Politics* 20 (April 1968), 454–79.

mutual escalation (or de-escalation) based on mythical plots yields instrumental rewards that are conventionally defined as deprivations. Our language for conceptualizing such a phenomenon is inevitably simplistic and distorting. We cannot accurately speak of the "real reasons" for a militant attitude, for response reflects a complex of existential economic and social ties associated with a set of cognitions, each reinforcing the other.

The identification of discrete economic or other interests with international conflict creates valued self-conceptions and roles. Without international conflict, there is no role for hawks, for doves, or for the specific variations within each grouping, and there is none of the status and sense of efficacy and of significance that playing the roles creates. Self-conceptions are thereby created through acceptance of a general belief, or myth, about the course of events. The word "myth" signifies a belief held in common by a large group of people that gives events and actions a particular meaning; it is typically socially cued rather than empirically based.

In this example it is continuing international tension over long time periods and not a shooting war that is postulated as mobilizing mass opinion. So long as the war is a cold one, ambiguity about intentions and plans is maximal, and so is mass susceptibility to political cues about such plans. When a hot, shooting war with a major adversary begins, ambiguity about these things largely disappears, though this analysis remains pertinent in that it forces attention to the systematic links among domestic interests, the mobilizing of mass publics, and the outbreak of shooting wars. Even a shooting war, moreover, fosters ambiguity and confusion over the bases of cleavage and alliance among domestic political interests. Small wars and occasional shooting incidents associated with a cold war reinforce belief in the reality of threat from a foreign adversary.

It will be easier to recognize the crucial and general function of this social-psychological phenomenon if its central elements are specified before we consider other political examples. The elements listed here as analytically separate are of course mutually reinforcing facets of a single empirical process.

The translation of different concrete interests and anxieties into a general plan or plot involving far-reaching change or persistence in the social order and the fate of large collectivities of people is the key feature of the paradigm. In their respective ways, anthropological, psychoanalytic, and political observations all point to such identification as characteristic of anxious people. Ernst Cassirer points out in his encyclopedic study of mythical thought that in mythical thinking "every simultaneity, every spatial coexistence and contact, provide a real causal sequence"; and he notes Lévy-Bruhl's conclusion that in the primitive myths "nothing in the world happens by accident and everything by conscious purpose."[2]

Political myths fall into a small number of archetypical patterns, though they vary widely in detail. Either they define an enemy who is plotting against the national interest and may need to be exterminated; or they define a savior-hero-leader of a popularly or divinely sanctioned social order who is to be followed and obeyed and for whom deprivation, suffering, or sacrifice are gratifying. All sorts of specific political concerns are translated into these forms. Political examples of the identification of a particular group issue with a more widely salient but not necessarily related issue appear constantly; additional examples from the field of race relations are considered below.

In its political manifestations the translation process exhibits some specific common features already suggested in general terms. The protagonists in the mythical conflict are sharply personified into leaders or oligarchies, though empirical research typically reveals a high measure of drift in policymaking or unplanned incrementalization of small decisions that makes long-range planning minimal and the function of leadership a limited one. The top policymakers are also perceived in the myths as monolithic and resolute, even though they are in fact divided into factions or diverse group interests and are typically ambivalent and susceptible to influences for change. Finally, acceptance of the mythic formulations is associated with frustration, fear, or anger, emotions that inhibit the empathy and the sharing of others' feelings that facilitate understanding of their problems and their internal conflicts.[3] This phenomenon is manifestly linked to the previous one, for so long as it is recognized that one's potential adversary is internally divided and not monolithic (in perceptions, aspirations, intensity of feeling, and political interests; indeed, in the whole range of affect and cognitions), political negotiation with him is possible and encouraged. It is then apparent that he can be influenced.

It is therefore not the substantive nature of a particular political issue that determines whether a translation into myth will occur, but rather the mode of cognizing or of apprehending *any* issue. The polar opposite modes are, on the one hand, tentativeness in reaching conclusions and systematic care to check hypotheses against empirical observation and, on the other hand, apprehension through social suggestion, generating beliefs not susceptible to empirical check or revision. In the second mode, what

---

[2] Ernst Cassirer, *The Philosophy of Symbolic Forms* 2 (New Haven: Yale University Press, 1955), 45, 48.

[3] For an explanation of emotion as a factor in political cognition see chap. 4.

is manifest and observable is denied and repressed, often through meta-phorical ambiguity; for it is not socially sanctioned. What is mythical and unobservable is publicly affirmed and believed, for it evokes social support.

In the field of race relations the talk and the affirmation of goals is in terms of liberty and equality on the one side and in terms of the prevention of social disorder or disruption of the natural or God-given social scheme on the other side. Neither of these ostensible goals, which evoke a powerful emotional response, specifies a condition that is objectively definable in the sense that there can be a consensus that it has been achieved. The function of these "goals" is precisely, and only, what they observably do in the present, not what they connote for a never-attained future. They evoke political support and opposition; and their semantic ambiguity, coupled with their socially supported teleological connotations, is precisely what makes them potent condensation symbols.

At the same time the maneuverings in the political battle that is os-tensibly over these goals do produce contemporary and observable benefits of various kinds; but they are not the benefits about which people boast, or even consciously recognize, with equanimity. Both white supremacists and civil libertarians win political followings and money in the course of their political maneuvers. As part of the same "transaction," policemen, blacks of various political stances, white sympathizers with the civil rights cause, and white opponents of that cause all achieve a valued role and a self-con-ception or identity. The need to protect that identity helps explain the emotional intensity with which these roles are defended, once they are assumed.

The escalation of such a political conflict wins for police forces a widely supported role as defender of law and order, increases the prestige and political influence of the police vis-à-vis other municipal agencies, evokes public support for expansion of the force, its weapons, and its wage scales, elevates the status of top police officials, and gives policemen greater authority over others. For policemen it thus creates a new and valued self-conception. In the same way escalation of the civil rights issue has won for blacks and their sympathizers such partly symbolic political benefits as an antipoverty program, voting rights they had formerly not enjoyed even in legal theory, and the mayoralties of some important cities. Probably more important, it has brought these groups new roles and causes that have manifestly become major sources of self-respect and of a new self-conception, whether they take the form of black power or of identification with other ideologies. These benefits for both sides increase as the civil rights issue escalates, though that empirical fact is incompatible with the symbolic definition of the issue and is therefore conventionally disregarded.

In an escalating political conflict over race relations issues, therefore, the ostensible political adversaries do observably help each other win important political benefits; and there is a clear disparity and incompatibility between the conventional definition of the issues in terms of symbolic goals and the empirical conflict over instrumental values that are in fact allocated. At the same time groups conventionally defined as political allies are manifestly in conflict over these same political benefits of money, status, and social support. The American Civil Liberties Union, SNCC, CORE, the Urban League, the NAACP, the Southern Christian Leadership Conference, and other groupings symbolically allied as sympathetic to Negroes and to the egalitarian position manifestly compete with each other for political support, funds, influence, status, and even the escalation or de-escalation of the race conflict—over all the instrumental outcomes of the race relations issue, as distinguished from its expressive or symbolic outcomes. In the same way the oligarchies of a range of groupings symbolically aligned on the other side are in evident conflict for the instrumental benefits: the John Birch Society, the Ku Klux Klan, the White Citizens' Councils, the ideological moderates of various hues who want to preserve law and order against anarchy, the groups that want southern support in congressional logrolling, and so on.

This model is incompatible with commonsense notions of what is involved in political conflict, for the commonsense notions mirror the very ambiguities and myths which serious analysis must recognize for what they are. The model is wholly compatible, however, with the empirically observable outcomes of political conflict. The chief use of the model is to identify the function of each element in the transaction. The abstract and remote symbols conventionally cited as defining the issues and the goals can now be recognized as serving the function of eliciting wider political support for the various groups involved in the conflict. Adversary role playing serves to bring valued benefits to the adversaries; and the most valued of these have little to do with the publicized symbolic goals; rather, they take the form of the achievement of an identity which will be cherished and defended. Formal allies, on the other hand, are observably in conflict with each other for such instrumental values as status, resources, and political support. The very escalation or de-escalation of the conflict, as signaled by current public policy developments, amounts empirically and instrumentally to gains by some political allies at the expense of others. The escalation of racial conflict therefore means gains for black militants at the expense of the Urban League and white liberal types and for citizens councils at the expense of moderate conservatives; while de-escalation means the converse. As emphasized above, such "gains" basically involve transfers of political support and not only material resources.

This model thus makes apparent the functions served by politically communicated ambiguities and confusions regarding issues, alliances, and lines of cleavage.[4] By focusing attention upon the occasions of shifts in political support and opposition, it clarifies the links between resource allocations, token and real, and such shifts.

Each of the chief dynamic elements that contribute to quiescence or violence in race relations has already been introduced into the analysis; now we can consider their interaction in a particular social context.

One historically important element is a myth of a symbiotic social order in which blacks have a subordinate role and whites a superordinate one based upon their respective abilities or legal rights or divinely ordained status or the popular will. As long as it is accepted, this myth contributes to quiescent acceptance of the Negro's subordinate status by all who are involved; belief in the myth is reinforced by Jim Crow ordinances and statutes and court decisions. In recent decades it has been attenuated through conflict with other cognitions.

Probably the central dissonant cognition has been a norm of divinely (or popularly) ordained equal rights regardless of race or color, together with perception of progress in achieving that norm. Both these cognitions have very largely been created by public policies. These include, historically, the Declaration of Independence and Reconstruction legislation but chiefly an unprecedented concentration of egalitarian policies beginning roughly with the World War II Fair Employment Practices Commission and including the white primary cases, the *Brown* decision, and the civil rights laws of the late fifties and sixties.

It should be emphasized that all the mythical formulations into which people translate public issues rely upon a major premise that cannot be observed or verified empirically: the public will at some past time, divine will, a dark plot of which any political opponent can arbitrarily be assumed to be a part. Crane Brinton noticed, for example, that opponents of revolutions consistently attribute them to conspiracies and proponents to a spontaneous public uprising.[5]

So far as the egalitarian norm is concerned, there is obviously a con-

---

[4] Striking examples appear in a study of the aftermath of American political assassinations by Rita James Simon and the writer. After every major political assassination a wide range of groups with diverse concerns perceived the assassination as somehow tied to their own adversaries, which included, for example, advocates of suffrage for women, Jews, Negroes, Communists, rightists, and African nationalists. "Presidential Assassinations: Their Meaning and Impact on American Society," *Ethics* 79 (April 1969), 199–221.

[5] Crane Brinton, *The Anatomy of Revolution* (New York: Random House 1952), pp. 77–85. Brinton also notes that Marxist writing constitutes an exception, for it is Leninist doctrine that tight planning and dedicated cadres make revolutions.

flict between the myth expressed and reinforced in the civil rights laws and
the myth of socially or divinely ordained inequality. In accepting one or
the other of these beliefs, each individual accepts a self-conception, role,
or identity to be cherished and defended.

There are systematic reasons why individuals in particular social
statuses choose one or the other view and therefore one or the other self-
conception. An affluent middle class white, not threatened in his employment or his social status by Negro competition, is free to respond to the
cognitive cues of egalitarian public policies. Indeed, his own social success
and his self-conception are the more impressive if he and others believe
that opportunity is equal or growing more so, and his insulation from the
Negro ghettos screens out evidence inconsistent with that belief. This
group has few benchmarks to rely on other than expressive public policies,
and it has considerable status incentive to accept the egalitarian myth and
shape its perceptions accordingly.

Working class, low status whites live in a world of different pressures
and different perceptions. They see themselves as threatened in their employment and their social status by Negro competition; the case studies
of racial conflict repeatedly show an association between the emergence of
economic competition from blacks and anti-Negro sentiment and behavior.
This group is less isolated from observation of living patterns in the ghettos.
It translates its economic and social anxieties into the terms of the myth of
threat from hostile, alien, or subhuman forces, and it perceives life in the
ghetto as evidence of immorality, lack of intelligence, or alien attributes in
blacks. The divinely and legally ordained social order of inequality upon
which civilization depends is perceived as threatened by a plot that must
be stamped out. Given this existential situation and its translation into a
legitimizing myth, working class whites are likely to reject the egalitarian
norm, though they do interpret the enactment of egalitarian public policies
as evidence of Negro social advancement, for that perception fits neatly
into a belief that a desirable social order is being threatened.

Much the same set of fears and of observations explains the dominant
reaction of white policemen to blacks and to the poor generally and their
acceptance of the same cognitions as the lower class whites, of whom they
are a part. Anxiety about Negro resistance to their authority and fear of
physical attacks upon them further reinforce such cognitions in policemen.

For Negroes the changes in the southern economy and social order
that led to their migration to a northern city are early cues that the myth of
their subordinate but protected status in a stable social order is no longer
believable. The enactment of civil rights laws and the proclamation of
egalitarian public policies are symbols that they can expect equal treatment
and that policymakers view them as deserving equal treatment. At the

same time, these policies cannot effectively convey to the Negro living in a ghetto a perception of significant advancement toward that happy state of affairs. His experiences in virtually every waking moment are unambiguous evidence that he is not progressing, that he remains subordinate, and that many of the whites he encounters expect to exploit him and degrade him. Insofar as these whites are policemen or other local officials, their actions and policies effectively counter the largely empty rhetoric of national civil rights policy. Other local public policies further emphasize to the ghetto black his low place in the social order and his alienation from a community. Urban renewal programs uproot people from the neighborhoods they know, force them to live among strangers, and teach them that their interests are ignored in social planning. Public assistance programs define relief recipients as potentially or actually immoral, devious, and parasitic. Such blatant conflict between the self-conceptions and expectations conveyed by different public policies inevitably generates further alienation, fear, and anger.

Some public policies therefore create for blacks a belief in their right to equal treatment, while at the same time daily experiences and other governmental actions signal the absence of progress toward that goal. Survey data on white and Negro beliefs regarding Negro progress in the years after World War II show that Negroes in the ghettos believe they have failed to share in progress or that their situations have grown worse in strikingly higher proportions than is true either of whites or of Negroes outside the ghettos.[6] Actual conditions plainly incompatible with the promises of publicized policies make a major impact when they are physically experienced, but are likely to be overshadowed by those promises or screened out of perception when they are not experienced. The studies also show that the higher status black ghetto residents are even more likely than those with lower status to believe in the necessity of violence to achieve civil rights objectives. The former group presumably finds the egalitarian norms of the civil rights laws more salient and the unambiguous evidence of their absence in the ghettos more frustrating.

These cognitions and behaviors create among large groups of whites as well as Negroes both a stake in a belief in race conflict and conflicting myths that rationalize it for militants on both sides. Policemen and other working class whites sometimes translate their fears of economic and social encroachment by Negroes into a myth of a black conspiracy against the established order, and in the process of acting out their own militant roles in that scenario these groups protect their self-conception of a superior group defending the social order and at the same time win other benefits,

---

[6] See Louis Harris Poll reported in *Newsweek* (August 22, 1966).

such as freedom to discriminate against blacks, to exploit them, and to dramatize their superior social status through harassment and other such gestures. In creating and acting out the myth of a manichean confrontation between the forces of law and order and the threatening blacks, the more militant groups also bolster their own political positions vis-à-vis white groups with more moderate stances.

The mirror image of this translation of a set of fears and aspirations and interests into a myth occurs among blacks. Here, too, it creates cherished roles and self-conceptions, wins political support for militant groups, and in some measure yields other tangible benefits such as loot from plundered stores, minor concessions from frightened businessmen, and so on. As suggested earlier, perceptions that the militants on one side are gaining support evokes support for militants on the other side. The middle class white liberals, whose symbolic egalitarian policies without much accompanying tangible implementation fuel the militancy on both sides, are now themselves bound in some degree to be drawn into the more militant camps. Perhaps the fundamental change effected by the emergence of this pattern of cognitions is movement from perception and expectation of a stable order, with limits on role and status differences, to perception and expectation of an uncertain state of affairs in which an outside group threatens roles and statuses outside the context of an overarching order that can limit the threat. Given this pattern, a precipitating incident can easily touch off violent action.

This account oversimplifies; it understates ambivalence in order to permit description of the dominant mechanisms through which cognitions are created. Certainly these mechanisms act upon indivduals with varying impacts; neither increasing polarization nor de-escalation could occur if ambivalence in cognitions were not a universal attribute.

RITUALIZATION OF POLITICAL CONFLICT

All politics involves group conflict, but not all conflict escalates. The premises of this chapter furnish a basis for specifying the conditions under which political conflicts become stabilized within fairly narrow limits, as virtually all continuing conflict does at times.

In every area of conflict involving large populations there are likely to be periods in which anticipations of unlimited oppression or suppression of legitimate demands contribute to escalation, to militance, and sometimes to violence. In the latter part of the nineteenth century American workers had reason to fear employer exploitation uninhibited either by empathy for workers or by governmental regulation. Troops and police frequently helped suppress worker resistance and organizational efforts, and the socialist doctrine embraced by the labor leaders and movements of the day fed employer anxiety. There were comparable escalating stages in the political conflicts between railroads and farmers and between trusts and consumers; in each case the very fact of escalation reinforced the intensity with which the actors fought against major threats to downgrade their status.

In all these areas the inability to foresee limits on the conflict and the consequent anxiety on both sides eventually led to a common interest, supported politically by concerned groups not directly involved, in establishing routines for conflict resolution. The routines, in fact, did not inhibit the adversaries from using their unequal economic and other resources against each other, though they formally purported to do that. They did, however, create an expectation that acceptable limits would be observed: that industry would not be socialized, that workers could strike to support wage demands, that consumers' interests would be protected by an official agency established for the purpose. The economic effects of the new institutions were typically minimal; their psychological effects were crucial.

The result was not the elimination of the conflict of interests, but its ritualization. Governmental procedures ostensibly established to make policy in fact produced predictable results in line with relative bargaining power; and policymaking procedures whose outcomes are known in advance amount to ritual and not to decisionmaking. They constitute an acting out of the underlying conflict and a legitimation of the terms on which it is currently resolved.

Like all ritual, this political form of it chiefly influences states of mind. It facilitates social interaction, mutual role taking, and a sharing of perspectives among leaders; it thereby encourages cooptation. For unorganized consumer groups, the cooptation takes place between regulatory agency staff members and representatives of the regulated industry. Ritualization also encourages acceptance of a myth by the masses of political spectators: a myth of protected status and of policies based upon an objective standard of equity rather than relative bargaining resources. Given such a context of ritualized relationships, the use of bargaining weapons no longer produces escalation. What does arouse anxiety about renewed escalation is deviation from the prescribed rituals.

SYMBOLIC CONFLICT
AND MASS IMMOBILIZATION

Two forms of conflict are identified in this analysis as something rather different from what they appear to be in the sense that they chiefly influence states of mind rather than affect current instrumental benefits. One of these

is conflict over abstract or remote objectives that lack unambiguous empirical referents. The other is ritualized conflict. The preceding discussion suggests a common political function. They immobilize large groups of people
who might otherwise be expected to use their political resources in common
for an instrumental objective.

Symbolic conflict between communism and free enterprise (or between
reactionaries and radicals or other ambiguous labels for ideologies) makes
the great mass of liberals reluctant to side with either on concrete issues for
fear of helping the other. In consequence mass support for civil rights, for
aid to the poor, and for effective business controls is weakened and often
reduced to tokens or less, as in the McCarthy years of the fifties. Labor-
management conflict over wages induces consumers to accept substantial
price and utility rate increases.[7]

Electoral conflict between political parties in a two-party system
offers another example. Sometimes the conflict is a ritualistic engagement
between very similar adversaries who are reduced to disagreeing on how to
deal with Quemoy and Matsu (an issue never heard from after the 1960
campaign) or on the wording of a pledge to do away with prohibition.
Sometimes it is a symbolic engagement between clearly different but highly
ambiguous ideologies, one of which may be so unpopular that it has no
chance of winning endorsement, as in the 1964 and 1936 elections. Usually
the conflict combines both forms. In either case it engages the interest of a
large segment of the population and legitimizes the electoral result and the
succeeding administration. In neither case does it offer a reliable or major
means of influencing instrumental payoffs through subsequent legislative,
administrative, and judicial decisionmaking; but it does permit group influence in these processes to operate without significant interference by
mass publics who are affected by the decisions.

As a polar case, wars—cold or hot—induce mass publics to accept
and support higher taxes and prices, restrictions on free expression, com-
pulsory military drafts, and sometimes large numbers of deaths at home or
abroad.

The politically significant observation in every example is that the
symbolic or ritualized conflict enables specific groups in conflict over instrumental rewards to use their respective bargaining resources free from
interference by mass publics who may be affected. The chief winners of
instrumental payoffs are therefore those groups with the greatest resources
in money and the means of imposing economic or political sanctions. The
chief losers are those who, like the poor and the enlisted men, lack either of
these and are also deprived of political support from mass publics of which

---

[7] See chap. 8 for an examination of ritualization of industrial conflict.

they are a part. This effect is not typically a form of deliberate manipulation. It is an unintended consequence of a change in cognitions effected by public policies, and it influences the cognitions of both elites and mass publics.

ORGANIZATION AND VIOLENCE

Among people who are content with existing status and power relationships it is a common assumption that when those with lesser status organize, they represent a threat to the established order, and that so long as they are not organized, they are impotent or loyal. This view is apparent in the reactions of employers to the idea of union organization of their workers and in the reaction of those who identify with established political parties to the organization of a new party appealing to a low status sector of the population. The view is also consistent with the myths considered above.

It is not consistent with empirical observation of the impact of the organization of low status groups, however. The relationships among continuing organization, leadership, and sharing or conflict in social goals unquestionably constitutes one of the most common and most subtle sources of confusion in the analysis of social action, and especially political action, for perception in the mythic forms is involved here, too. The popular assumption seems to be that organization is the independent variable which lends power to a movement and provides a setting in which leadership can operate effectively. Frequently no distinction is made between the existence of leadership and the existence of organization.

The studies of protest movements indicate that the distribution of social support rather than the presence or absence of stable organization is the critical variable. Where support for the established order of power and status relationships is strong and the expectation is widespread that the existing elite will continue as an elite, protest organizations serve one or both of two possible functions, neither of them consistent with the conventional view.

They serve most frequently as a channel of communication of elite perspectives and values. Labor unions, political parties, and social organizations geared to an ongoing social and political system soon arrive at a position in which their continued existence and function depend upon the maintenance of the system. They create in their members an expectation of influence in the system: an expectation that is realized to the extent of their bargaining resources and that is kept potent to the extent of their symbolic resources. Unions typically move from an ideological tie to socialism and a vision of the overthrow of private business to an ideological and economic tie to business and the existing political order, so that they come to serve partly as a channel through which wage restraint policies and production maintenance policies (especially in wartime) can be encouraged; and the dramatizing of collective bargaining helps induce consumers to accept higher prices. Political parties typically evolve into loyal oppositions. In the degree that organizations serve this function, they facilitate the acceptance by their mass memberships and sympathizers of one form of myth discussed earlier: the belief in a benevolent established order in which they have a valued role.[8]

The functioning of a continuing organization also facilitates the maintenance of a particular and relatively uniform set of expectations in the rank and file membership by encouraging them to reply on their leaders to find the means of achieving the abstract goal that engages them. The organization therefore makes leadership easier than otherwise; for ritualistic organizational procedures continuously reinforce the confidence of the mass membership that their goals are being pursued. These procedures, moreover, become an adjunct of the larger pattern of ritualistic procedures through which the symbiotic relationship with other, more powerful organizations is expressed. Internal union procedures geared into union-management bargaining illustrate the point, as do the activities of the NAACP.

Hobsbawm's account of the tie between the preindustrial mob and the ruler in Western European cities of the nineteenth and early twentieth centuries furnishes the perspective for a more specific statement of the linkage between adversary use of the bargaining resources of the two groups and their symbolic alignment. The preindustrial city mob was a "permanent entity," certainly closer to a continuing organization than to an amorphous and ephemeral crowd:

> . . . the "mob" was not simply a casual collection of people united for some *ad hoc* purpose, but in a recognized sense, a permanent entity, even though rarely permanently organized as such. It sometimes was, though the forms of permanent organization of the *plebs*—apart from artisan gilds—remain to be investigated. . . .[9]

A "combination of wage-earners, small property-owners, and the unclassifiable urban poor," the city mob retained the loyalties of its members and at the same time demonstrated the extent of its bargaining resources through two forms of expression: loyalty to the king as symbolic represent-

---

[8] Philip Selznick's analysis of cooptation represents one useful way of describing the process: *TVA and the Grass Roots* (Berkeley: University of California Press, 1953), pp. 217–46.

[9] E. J. Hobsbawm, *Primitive Rebels* (New York: Norton, 1959), p. 111.

ative of justice in society, and periodic rioting, often precipitated by rising prices or unemployment. The upper classes or nobility, and sometimes the Jews, were often regarded with hostility, but on the ground they had "betrayed the king." This pattern of behavior reveals rather clearly the basic elements and dynamics of permanent organizations claiming to function as protests against established social institutions: loyalty to the established role structure and to the role established for the masses within that structure; anxiety and resentment that others in the structure will betray it or not play their parts; and a mechanism, such as the riot, through which the resentment is expressed and the elite reminded that they must make minor concessions in line with bargaining resources on both sides.

To this list of basic elements must be added one other. The mob sometimes engaged in real revolutions, rationalized on the ground that the ruler had not done his duty to the people. It is significant, however, that rebellion was possible for the city mobs because, as Hobsbawm puts it, "living in cities and capitals, it had a far more precise conception of what 'government,' 'power' and the 'seizure of power' meant than peasants in remote villages,"[10] and the rebellions occurred "because the 'mob' was empiricist, and Church-and-King regimes were on their way out."[11] In short, the perception that social support for the established order was decaying and that power could be seized was a necessary condition for genuine revolt, an observation that supports the generalization that social support is a more critical variable than organization.

Further insight into the dynamics of protest, cooptation, and revolt is gained from examination of other cases in which the protesting group has been unorganized or very loosely organized and of cases in which support for the established order is ambivalent. As already noted, absence of organization means absence of a channel for effective communication and for establishing an accepted basis for coexistence. A group that regards itself as denied the status to which it is entitled and which has no stable organization and leadership that can be perceived as serving its interests will certainly express its anxiety in some fashion. Where the protesting group perceives weakness, ambivalence, or a falling off of support for the elite, anger is likely to predominate over fear, and overt violence against the established order is likely when a suitable precipitating incident occurs.

When members of the protesting group perceive the established order as entrenched and generally supported and its own resources for superseding it manifestly inadequate, attacks on the symbols of its own degraded status are predictable, as are attacks on weak groups perceived to be on

---

[10] Ibid., p. 122.
[11] Ibid., p. 123.

the margins of the elite or benefiting from the established order without sharing in its resources for exercising power. Such activities by young people today, while ineffective in changing status relationships, represent a searching for identity, according to Erikson:

> Today this problem faces us most painfully on that frontier where leaderless and unguided youth attempts to confirm itself in sporadic riots and other excesses which offer to those who have temporarily lost, or never had, meaningful confirmation in the approved ways of their fathers, an identity based on a defiant testing of what is most marginal to the adult world. The mocking grandiosity of their game names ("Black Barons," . . . "Saints"), their insignia, sometimes even tattooed into the skin, and their defiant behavior clearly indicate an attempt to emulate that which gives other people the background of a group identity: a real family, nobility, a proud history—and religion.[12]

The same searching for a role in a society which reassures Negroes they are created equal and then degrades them and, in the urban ghettos, denies them a community as well as an identity, produces other characteristic behaviors: attacks on small storekeepers and especially on Jews, and destruction of the physical ghetto environment, both of which symbolize their degradation. The ghetto fires that are frequently set by lone arsonists, even when there is no collective violence, are one manifestation, as are the riots that consist of fire setting, looting, and harassment of stray whites who happen to be caught in the middle of them. All of these represent attacks on the weak and on the self; they flow from the frustration and fear that are channeled by lack of organization of the deprived and by general support for the elite.

Consideration of the conditions that trigger mass violence, once these conditions are present, throws further light on the social psychological dynamics at work. The *Report of the National Advisory Commission on Civil Disorders* makes some observations that are also evident in the news accounts. It notes that the precipitating incident is typically trivial and the response to it out of all proportion in its scale of violence.[13] Approximately 40 percent of the triggering incidents in the riots the Commission examined involved "allegedly abusive or discriminatory police actions," about 17 percent harassment or violence by whites against blacks, and about 22 percent black demonstrations or protest meetings. A wave of riots occurred

---

[12] Erik Erikson, *Young Man Luther* (New York: Norton, 1958), pp. 114–15.

[13] *Report of the National Advisory Commission on Civil Disorders* (New York: The New York Times Co., 1968), p. 118.

following the assassination of Dr. Martin Luther King in April 1968, after publication of the *Report*.

Incidents similar to most of these, though of course not to the assassination of a charismatic figure, occur every day in every American black ghetto. In themselves, therefore, they cannot be regarded as decisive. A particular response to them occasionally invests them with a meaning that *is* decisive: they occasionally become a signal to frustrated ghetto residents that if violent action begins, many will join it and a still wider range of people will give it moral support. The *Report* documents the fact that the triggering incidents occurred at times and places where large numbers of people were present or could gather quickly; and that they followed a series of similar harassing or frustrating incidents over a period of several weeks.

An individual will hesitate to initiate violence for which he can be held responsible unless he believes others will join and support him. In this context the precipitating incident serves that function, furnishing the final component to the sequence of necessary conditions. Typically somebody in the crowd hurls a rock or otherwise exhibits defiance. If there is supportive action from others, participation snowballs and spreads. There is no organization or generally recognized and accepted leadership to restrain it, start it, limit it, or stop it. Recognition that it cannot overturn the established order does direct it inward or toward marginal groups, as already noted. The appearance of additional police and soldiers is likely to reinforce the frustration and anger and therefore the range and intensity of participation. Thus the National Commission found that:

> In nine disturbances—involving a wide variation in the intensity of violence—additional control forces were brought in after there had been serious violence which local police had been unable to handle alone. In every case further violence occurred, often more than once and often of equal or greater intensity than before.[14]

Consider next what we know of the occasions of violence where there *is* serious question that the elite are widely and strongly supported. For clear cases it is of course necessary to look to countries that have experienced successful revolutions. In these instances as well, the protesting groups display a lack of overall organization and of stable and generally accepted leadership in the early stages of the revolutionary process. Crane Brinton found that in the English revolutions of the 1640s and of 1688, and in the American, French, and Russian revolutions, the initial forays against the established order displayed much the same pattern. Here are excerpts from his description of the assault on the Bastille:

---

[14] Ibid., p. 126.

. . . there is every evidence that once the dismissal of Necker got these various groups excited, what followed was in a sense spontaneous mob action. . . . Actually it is clear that in Paris in those days there was not one mob, but at least several dozen. People came out in the street because their neighbors were already out. They paraded up and down, shouting and singing, stopping now and then for another drink, or to hear another street-corner orator. Self-constituted leaders of little groups certainly supplemented any planned action. The decision to march on the Bastille seems to have been taken independently in several quarters. No one knows for sure who first had the brilliant idea of going to the Invalides Hospital to secure small arms. The rioting seems to have died out less because the Bastille fell than because the rioters were tired out. Three days is a long time to be riotous, drunk, or both.[15]

Brinton then declares, "What holds for the taking of the Bastille holds for the general preparatory work and the first stages of revolutions as we have discussed them. . . ." The Russian case is especially interesting. It is part of the myth of Leninist history that a small conspiratorial cadre planned events, a form of myth usually adopted by opponents rather than advocates of revolution. The record, and even Trotsky's own *History*, however, leave no doubt that many different groups, with diverse leadership, played upon widespread disaffection to create the incidents that initiated the revolution of October 1917.

Effective planning and conspiratorial organization are indeed significant factors in the genesis of riot and revolution, but as myth influencing attitudes and opposition, not as behavior influencing events. The intriguing conclusion from these diverse cases is, rather, that lack of effective organization and the absence of planning are so consistently associated with the beginnings of domestic violence. It is as though the absence of a well organized resistance movement keeps the elite unaware of the seriousness of the threat it faces and also makes it impossible to negotiate a viable pattern of cooptation and concession that will maintain tensions at a non-explosive level.

If events demonstrate wide support for the rebels, stronger organization and widely accepted leadership emerge, but the analyst must recognize that these developments reflect an assessment of the relative social support for the rebels and the established order more clearly than they influence that balance. Gradually participants in the resistance see themselves as having achieved a significant role: fighter in a war for liberty and equality. It is revealing that in a survey of opinion regarding the Watts riot of 1965, Negro respondents who had favorable attitudes toward the

---

[15] Brinton, *The Anatomy of Revolution,* p. 84.

riot called it a "rebellion" or used some other word denoting a planned movement toward a social goal and disliked the connotations of the word "riot."[16]

Police and Guardsmen representing the established order *are* tightly organized, of course. As already noted, the threat a disaffected group poses to their authority and status and sometimes to their livelihood as well, is translated into a mythic plot against a good society which it is their role to defend. The disaffected group is perceived as potentially violent and as inferior or subhuman, and so harassment, demeaning treatment, and efforts to force the low status group to act out the elite's definition of its inferior role become endemic.

For police, as for armies, violence is precipitated by a formal order to engage in it, not by a subtle anticipating of the impact of aggressive cues on potential allies. Once the order is given in a riot situation, however, police behavior leaves no doubt that more is involved psychologically than obedience to a superior officer's command. There have consistently been the clearest manifestations of intense frustration, anger, and a belief that physical punishment of the rioters is a noble deed. For the police the individual rioters symbolize the threat, and there is an eagerness to attack them. This posture contrasts with the pattern of assaults against property and against the setting of degradation that chiefly marks the behavior of the rioters. This contrast in behaviors further supports the hypothesis suggested here about the respective functions of organization and of relative support.

---

[16] M. Tomlinson, "Negro Reaction to the Los Angeles Riot and the Development of a Riot Ideology" (mimeographed).

Chapter 3

INFORMATION AND COGNITION

Political beliefs and perceptions are very largely not based upon empirical observations or, indeed, upon "information" at all. More than that, non-empirically based cognitions are the most resistant to revision based upon observations of the world, and accordingly they have the most potent influence upon which empirical observations and social cues are taken into consideration and which ignored.

Neither of these two propositions is either self-evident or examined in political science literature, though a prima facie case for their validity will occur to any political scientist who considers the question. Yet, if they are valid, they bear fundamentally upon our understanding of political perceptions and expectations, for they deal with the dynamics of change in such cognitions and with the psychological conditions under which alternative cognitions emerge.

Information theory offers several conceptual distinctions that encourage analysis of the relationship between information and meaning. Political analysts have not adequately explored the implications of an axiom of information theory: Meaning is basically different from information and incompatible with it. Meaning is associated with order—with a patterned cognitive structure that permits anticipation of future developments, so that perceptions are expected and not surprising. A belief, for example, that ghetto riots are incited by radical agitators or a belief that riots reflect aggressive individual traits indigenous to blacks (or to policemen) gives meaning to the riots and precludes surprise when they recur.

Information involves complexity or lack of order: inability to foresee. Unlike meaning, it is transmitted; and what is transmitted is complicating premises. To a believer in the conspiracy theory of riots, an empirical study that concludes there was no plot is complicating and unanticipated. The believer must either retain his belief and the meaning it confers or abandon it. The case offers a political illustration of the proposition that information destroys meaning. Notice that this proposition does not depend upon an assumption that the conspiracy theory is demonstrably invalid. Any datum that can be anticipated does not have to be transmitted, whether it is valid or not. If it is anticipated and still transmitted, it is redundant and therefore not information—not complicating or surprising. By this test one is not giving a person information in telling him that a senator from Mississippi opposes a civil rights bill, but may be giving information in telling him that the senator bit a dog.

To define information as complexity or the unpredictable makes it a measurable quantity. One can learn which items receptors can anticipate and thereby in principle segregate the segments of messages that are unanticipated and therefore informative from those that are anticipated and uninformative. To a telephone engineer such quantitative study of the degree to which messages are redundant is critical, for it makes possible the transmission of only the nonredundant portions of messages and thereby improves efficiency.

To a political scientist it is the other end of the information-meaning dipole that is ordinarily critical: the study of the generation of meaning, with and without the transmission of information. Either emphasis presupposes the identification of both the informative and the redundant phases of messages. Which of these is which hinges upon the perceptive capacities of the receptor if *political* information and meaning are in question. That the letter *u* always follows the letter *q* in English has nothing to do with the perceptions of the receptor, and so a teletype engineer could mechanically generate the *u* after every *q*. Which publics perceive a plot behind every reported instance of mass urban violence can, however, only be learned from empirical inquiry into the phenomenological perceptions of diverse publics.

Information theory warns us, then, to avoid the tempting pitfall of assuming that messages "mean" the dictionary definitions of their contents to those to whom they are addressed. Instead, we have to learn from examination of the phenomenological responses of people to political events and language which signals reinforce meanings already held (and so are redundant), which change or destroy existing meanings (and so are informative), and which are ignored or not perceived (and so are cognitively subordinate to accepted perceptions).

Perceptions of order and pattern and predictability emerge as selections from a background of uncertainty regarding future and current developments in remote and otherwise unobservable places. The attention of participants is of course focused upon their own orderings of events; but a social scientist needs to recognize that political beliefs, perceptions, and expectations are overwhelmingly not based upon observation or empirical evidence available to participants, but rather upon cuings among groups of people who jointly create the meanings they will read into current and anticipated events.

There can be no signal without noise, no figure without a ground;

political signals and configurations emerge through the exchange and mutual creation of symbols that amount to abstractions from a background of other possible meanings that remain "noisy": unordered and uncertain. The uncertainty about political signals inevitably involves anxiety about possibilities of great and intimate concern, from war through poverty. By the same token, the orderings that afford meaning and some measure of certainty are made necessary by the uncertainties and anxieties that constitute their background. The particular meanings that are consensually accepted need not therefore be cued by the objective situation; they are rather established by a process of mutual agreement upon significant symbols. This process is itself systematic, of course, and this study is an effort to identify some of its systematic elements. That the process is basically one of selection is, however, fundamental. People can use only an infinitesimal fraction of the information reaching them. The critical question, therefore, is what accounts for the choice by political spectators and participants of what to organize into a meaningful structure and what to ignore.

Moles[1] offers a set of dipoles that describes the tension between meaning and information upon which our explanation of cognition and behavior builds:

Order	Disorder
Predictable	Unpredictable
Banal	Original
Redundant	Informative
Intelligible	Novel
Simple	Complex

In any particular instance, what is informative hinges upon the extent of common knowledge of the transmitter and the receptor. What they know in common is redundant; it is not, or need not be, transmitted; and it is meaningful. What they do not know or expect is informative. It must be transmitted if it is to have a cognitive impact. To say that it is received is to say that it has in some degree changed prior meanings. A measure of quantity of information therefore boils down to a measure of unforeseeability. Clearly, the greater the number of alternative possibilities, the greater the unforeseeability. Engineers have concluded that "a measure of amount of information must be a logarithmic measure of the number of alternative possibilities."[2] The proposition necessarily holds generally,

---

[1] Abraham Moles, *Information Theory and Esthetic Perception* (Urbana: University of Illinois Press, 1968), p. 208.

[2] Wendell R. Garner, *Uncertainty Structure as Psychological Concepts* (New York: Wiley, 1962), p. 12.

though there are evident variations in the feasibility of applying it, and political information typically involves difficulties in its precise application.

In these terms a symbol can be understood as a way of organizing a repertory of cognitions into meanings. As Moles puts it:

> A symbol is a constant mode of grouping subelements which is known *a priori;* a rule defines a set of collections following the rule. Each is the mark of intelligibility which opposes information. . . .[3]

If a political leader symbolizes ability to cope, his followers perceive his specific acts, redundantly, as evidence of that ability and may be oblivious both of information calling that meaning into question and of the frequent impossibility of proving either his competence or his incompetence. Put another way, symbols make messages assimilable by reducing their originality, the degree to which they complicate cognitions, and the degree to which they lessen ability to predict.

That established beliefs and perceptions are valued and interfere with the reception of information inconsistent with them[4] suggests the possibility of some exciting forms of political inquiry: the manner in which political actions themselves help generate particular cognitions, both in mass publics and in policymakers; examination of the ordering of cognitions into hierarchies of consonant subcognitions; the implications of consonance and of dissonance in cognitions for *change* in beliefs and perceptions; the functions of public discussion and controversy in catalyzing or inhibiting cognitive changes.

SEMANTIC AND ESTHETIC INFORMATION

The phenomenological approach to information theory, as developed in the work of Moles, incorporates a distinction between semantic information and esthetic information, the former dealing explicitly with the

---

[3] Moles, *Information Theory,* p. 63.

[4] There is a fairly extensive social science literature that explores selective perception and the predilection of an individual to ignore data in systematic fashion. See especially M. Brewster Smith, Jerome S. Bruner, and Robert W. White, *Opinions and Personality* (New York: Wiley, 1956); Carl Hovland et al., *Communication and Persuasion* (New Haven: Yale University Press, 1963).

Walter Lippmann, *Public Opinion* (New York: Macmillan, 1922). These studies say little, however, about the specific influence upon political cognitions of mass opinions and polarization or of governmental actions as stimuli for cognitions.

state of the external world, the latter in fact, though not by intention, determining states of mind.

The utility of this distinction for political analysis deserves consideration, for the impact upon behavior and policy of political information of the "esthetic" kind has frequently not been recognized. The propositions suggested below about the generation of cognitions by governmental action itself refer chiefly to information that influences states of mind: emotional postures respecting various other people and groups; though a great deal of political information also consists, of course, of explicit propositions about the state of the external world.

Moles takes some pains to explicate the precise character of the distinction:

> The semantic viewpoint asks a question about the state of the external world, about its material evolution. . . . They [orders relaying semantic information] prepare acts, forms of action, and in general, semantic information has a clearly utilitarian, but above all *logical* character. It sticks to acts and to meaning. At the level of language it obeys the laws of universal logic: It is logical in the sense that all the receptors of the message accept its rules and symbols; it becomes universal. In other words, it uses the statistical part common to all men of the sociocultural matrix. . . .
>
> *Esthetic* information does not have the *goal* of preparing decisions; it has no goal properly speaking. It does not have the characteristic of *intent;* in fact, it determines *internal states*. . . . Thus the viewpoint is not at all utilitarian . . . Esthetic information is specific to the channel which transmits it; it is profoundly changed by being transferred from one channel to another. . . . esthetic information is randomized and specific to the receptor, since it varies according to his repertoire of knowledge, symbols and *a priori* structurings, which in turn relate to his sociological background. It is very poorly known and difficult to measure.[5]

By these tests political scientists have conventionally studied political information of a semantic kind: allegations of pressure groups about the impact of a proposed bill upon their members and others, assertions that a candidate for office will pursue particular policies, warnings that a particular form of welfare measure will detract from the incentive of its recipients to work. Such information prepares forms of action, obeys the laws of universal logic, and is interpreted by those who receive it in accordance with the rules and symbols common to their sociocultural matrix. Because the intent of such information as an influence upon actions is clear, its assertion evokes debate, skepticism, and efforts to verify it.

Police beating up bearded or black demonstrators, by contrast, is not

---

[5] Moles, *Information Theory*, pp. 131–32. The term *esthetics* is appropriate here insofar as it refers to the study of the laws of perception.

a conscious effort to create a particular *cognition* in an audience, but does in fact create different perceptions in different receptors according to their various repertories of knowledge, symbols, and a priori structurings, and serves to influence the attitudes of these people toward the demonstrators and toward the police, i.e., to create states of mind. Similarly, much of this book, and particularly this chapter, is an effort to analyze the manner in which information not intended to prepare particular decisions or forms of action and not logical in its organization and mode of presentation nonetheless is perceived by receptors in ascertainable ways according to their diverse repertories of knowledge and prior cognitive structurings. Because the process is neither intentional nor logical, beliefs and perceptions created in this way are more resistant to debate and opposition, and especially to doubt and ambivalence within the individual who holds them, than are those based upon semantic information. Every message is bound to have both semantic and esthetic content; but the analytic distinction leads to some nonobvious observations.

GOVERNMENTAL GENERATION OF COGNITIONS

If esthetic information is a key element in the structure of political cognitions, it is clearly of crucial importance to learn as much as possible about the dynamics of their generation. Which forms of political cues convey or reinforce which meanings in mass publics? The rationalist bias with which we are socialized to interpret political events makes a serious examination of this question difficult at first, but any observer of public affairs who can temporarily suspend his conventional assumptions is likely to recognize the following suggestions as conservative conclusions about the conditions under which large publics reach particular political beliefs and perceptions in ambiguous situations. Whether any particular cognition is valid is, of course, a separate question and must be ascertained by other kinds of research with which political scientists are more familiar, and which frequently cast doubt upon the validity of the cognitions in question. The issue here is how people come to hold particular cognitions, whether or not they are valid. Clearly, the beliefs and perceptions of mass publics and policymakers have more substantial political and social consequences than the conclusions of social scientists about their validity. The perceptions and beliefs examined here deal with the central issues affecting political consensus or dissensus, conformity or rebellion.

The following catalog lists forms of belief and perception generated chiefly by governmental actions or rhetoric.

A. Generation of the perception of popular participation and influence in policymaking.
1. Voting. Both elections of candidates and referendums on issues are potent cues of this perception. The manifest attention is upon who or what wins or loses, but a latent function of voting is to cue a belief in popular participation.
2. Hortatory language. That people are urged to take particular political positions conveys the signal that it matters what they think or do, regardless of the persuasiveness of the argument on a particular issue; though the manifest emphasis is upon the merits of particular positions.[6]
3. Legal language. In its popularly perceived form legal language purports to reflect in a highly precise, unambiguous way the will of the elected representatives of the people and to require administrators and judges to carry out this will rather than their personal predilections or values. The manifest emphasis is upon the content of particular legal provisions.[7]
4. The dramaturgy of publicized consultation of interest groups by public officials.
5. The dramaturgy involved in *expressing* opposition to established (or Establishment) policies. That minor parties exist and that dissent is expressed are taken as evidence that dissent can be influential; radical and dissenting groups therefore help bolster wide support for the regime. Sometimes a government takes pains to publicize its alleged incorporation of dissenting views within its own ranks, as when the Johnson Administration repeatedly referred to Undersecretary of State George Ball as a dove on Vietnam whose views were regularly taken into account.
B. Generation of the perception that particular groups are hostile and evil.
1. The publicized organization and subsequent escalation of defense pacts or police actions against them. Hostile speeches, gestures, arrests, and similar acts force political spectators either to perceive the targets of these actions as malevolent or to perceive the government as deceptive. In the absence of other cues the great majority will predictably resolve such dissonance in favor of the official regime, already bolstered by the cognition considered in (A). In the measure that it is formally defined as the object of "defensive"

---

[6] Cf. Murray Edelman, *The Symbolic Uses of Politics* (Urbana: University of Illinois Press, 1964), pp. 134–38.
[7] Ibid., pp. 138–42.

action, the perception is created that the target group is itself organizing for aggressing, conspiring, and escalating.

Actual attacks upon the target group are especially potent in
creating a perception of their hostility and their guilt. The generation in bomber and FAC pilots in Vietnam of a belief that the
people they were bombing were Viet Cong where the empirical evidence was either wholly lacking or contradictory exemplifies the
phenomenon,[8] as does the conviction of policemen and of a majority of political spectators in the Chicago police riot of August
1968 that the demonstrators the police beat up and arrested were
militant subversives.

2. Rituals of trial. That some people are arrested and formally tried
   while others are not itself evokes a presumption of guilt; psychologically, the formal insistence upon a presumption of innocence
   until the accused is found guilty very likely reflects an effort to
   repress or mask this phenomenon. The utility for regimes of show
   trials even where there is no question the accused will be found
   guilty is further evidence that trials play a major part in the bolster-
   ing of public perceptions that those the government accuses of vice
   are probably guilty.

C. The generation of the perception that political leaders can cope and
will cope in the public interest with issues that concern and baffle mass
publics.

1. A dramaturgy of self-assurance and confidence in attacking a personified enemy. People who are both anxious and uncertain how to
   cope with perceived threats want to believe that their leaders know
   what they are doing and so will accept a dramaturgical presentation
   of such ability on its own terms. This form of cuing is apparently
   especially effective if the issue is portrayed as an attack upon a
   personified enemy rather than as an effort to deal with complex
   economic trends or an unplanned incrementalization of small decisions, with nobody responsible for their cumulative effect.[9]

2. Artistry on the part of the leader in the employment of an accepted
   rhetorical style, especially when the rhetoric is banal in content.
   Where public anxiety is intense, rhetorical proficiency reinforces
   other dramaturgical signals that the incumbent of a high public
   office is an uncommon man who can cope. Unlike fresh or controversial *content* in speeches, the stylistic element does not raise
   questions of policy agreement or disagreement for debate and criti-

---

[8] Jonathan Schell, *The Military Half* (New York: Knopf, 1968).

[9] Edelman, *Symbolic Uses of Politics,* pp. 73–84.

cism. Where the content is banal, the very banality is taken as a signal of conformity to widely accepted values, further encouraging public support for the leader.[10]

By contrast, consider the modal response of audiences to political speeches that are highly innovative and unexpected in both style and content. Such speeches, by definition, contain both esthetic and semantic information. The information produces anxiety, for it conflicts with beliefs that order the world for the individual; and so it is resisted. The rhetoric of Black Panther leaders exemplifies this genre, and its impact upon most listeners is like a kick in the teeth. For those who already accept the vision of the future the Black Panther movement holds, the substance of these speeches is of course banal, and their impact no doubt like that of Roosevelt and Kennedy on the vast majority of *their* audiences, enlarging the charisma of the leader and solidifying his followers' support.

D. Generation of perceptions that particular groups are friendly and benevolent.
  1. The publicized organization of alliances and joint action. An especially revealing example was American joint action and alliance with West Germany shortly after the bitter fighting of World War II and the revelation of the deliberate destruction by the Germans of six million people in extermination camps.
  2. The metaphoric definition of the target groups as like "us" in values and modes of behavior.

For American military public relations officers to refer to hapless Vietnamese troops as "rangers" is to associate them with some romantic American military and western traditions rather than with a counterbelief in their sullen resistance to their own government and in their reluctance to fight for it.

Some less obvious examples are more revealing, though also more speculative. The talk and the emphasis over many years upon the desirability of Negro-white integration evokes in audiences a picture of group differences they are asked to ignore. In effect, the normative, ethical content of these speeches conflicts with the perceptions they generate, and that tension in turn contributes both to ambivalence and to group conflict. When avowed opponents, on the other hand, discuss each other's tactics and strategies, they are stressing a crucial respect in which they are alike. Military strategists thus come to respect their opposite numbers in a hostile foreign country, even while other information may lead the general public,

---

[10] See chap. 5.

including the military strategists in another role, to perceive them as aggressive and escalating. Many years of discussing Russian-American strategy after World War II has gradually led to increased perception of Russians as essentially engaged in the same game as we, and therefore more like us. To put it another way, we have come in some degree to perceive Russians and Russian policy-makers as complex people subject to some of the same cross-pressures and interests as we, rather than perceiving them as embodiments of the malevolent conspiracy myth.

Recent developments in race relations in America have thus far exemplified a different pattern or, on an optimistic assumption, an early stage of the same pattern. In the talk among the most aroused whites about black miltants, and vice versa, the emphasis is not upon similarities in strategies, but upon dark plot and escalation without limit. The meaning conveyed is therefore that the others are essentially alien and are simple embodiments of a myth of malevolent conspiracy.

Rhetorical suggestion, it appears, is a function neither of the conscious intent of the speaker nor of the particular phrases employed, but rather of an implication about future roles and future scenarios.

3. Elite status is itself accepted as evidence that those who enjoy it have the talents and perform the services that justify it. Very large subsidies to the affluent (as to the managements and stockholders of shipbuilding concerns, airlines, commercial farms, oil companies, etc.) generate and reinforce the perception that these companies are serving the national interest and so deserve some compensation for part of the alleged risks they are running. Far smaller subsidies to the poor are perceived as evidence that the latter are parasitic, wasteful, lazy, or immoral.

E. Generation of perceptions that particular kinds of actions are evil. The dynamics are essentially the same as those for generation of perceptions that particular people are malevolent. The most revealing cases are those in which a particular kind of behavior does not in itself necessarily harm others, but nonetheless comes to be widely perceived as immoral or threatening: prostitution, gambling, liquor or marijuana consumption, advocacy of unpopular policies or polities. To formally label them as illegal generates widespread perception of them as evil. People want to perceive them that way in order to conform to others' cues, and they perceive almost any ambiguous data as evidence of what they want to believe.

Language forms are relevant here too. Publicity to alleged bargaining among representatives of groups with adversary interests may give rise to suspicions of elite plotting at the expense of the unrepresented masses.[11]

Governmental acts are not, of course, the only influences upon political cognitions; but they are the only type whose impact is systematically overlooked or undervalued. Because we are socialized to see governmental acts as reflections of people's cognitions and not as causes of them, and because it is not the official or deliberate intent of governmental acts to influence what people perceive and want, the influence of cues such as these is systematically overlooked. They constitute esthetic information.

Other social cues also shape cognitions: cues from family, school, and peers, as the socialization studies say. These studies also furnish evidence of the systematic tendency toward consonance and reinforcement among these various agents of socialization. If the socialization researchers were socialized to raise questions about the influence upon cognitions of the government itself, their data would establish the conclusion that the nongovernmental influences serve chiefly to reinforce the governmental ones.[12] Dissonant cues apparently come from family or peers only where, as in the ghettos,[13] Appalachia,[14] or the communities of upper middle class college students in the late sixties, there is unambiguous evidence in everyday life that official policy hurts the group in question; protest movements and revolutionary parties can play on these cues. Even in these cases, the school continues to promote beliefs consonant with the governmentally cued cognitions.

THE HIERARCHICAL STRUCTURE OF POLITICAL COGNITIONS

Symbolization imposes some degree of structure upon a repertory of cognitive elements. It gives the elements a form which, in Moles's words, "expresses the ascendancy of the intelligible over the perceptible." The

---

[11] Edelman, *Symbolic Uses of Politics*, pp. 145–49.

[12] Fred I. Greenstein, *Children and Politics* (New Haven: Yale University Press, 1965); David Easton and Jack Dennis, *Children in the Political System* (New York: McGraw-Hill, 1969); David Easton and Robert Hess, "Youth and the Political System," in S. M. Lipset and Leo Lowenthal (eds.), *Culture and Social Character* (New York: Free Press, 1962); Robert Hess and Judith Torney, *The Political Development of Attitudes in Children* (Garden City, N.Y.: Anchor Books, 1967).

[13] Edward S. Greenberg, "Children and Government: A Comparison across Racial Lines," *Midwest Journal of Political Science* 14 (May 1970), 249–75.

[14] Dean Jaros, Herbert Hirsch, and Federic J. Fleron, Jr., "The Malevolent Leader: Political Socialization in an American Subculture," *American Political Science Review* 62 (June 1968), 564–75.

characteristics of particular cognitive structures are critical to the kinds of beliefs and perceptions that are generated. Especially in point is hierarchical structure: the power of some cognitive elements to dominate others. The hierarchical characteristics of political cognitions must be inferred from observation of people's attachment to some beliefs, their resistance to others, and the predetermination of some by others.

Cognitions that purport to deal with first causes of future developments and therefore are least susceptible to empirical verification are (1) at the top of the hierarchy, (2) most directly associated with the emotions of fear, anger, dominance, and submission, and (3) associated with a reference group patterning such that conformity to the dominant cognitions (rather than success in action) is rewarded and lack of conformity punished.

It is self-evident that a belief that God ordained a caste system, that it is the burden of the white man to reshape the culture of nonwhites to conform to his own, that it is the destiny of a political leader to lead the forces of righteousness in an inevitably successful war against the forces of darkness, or that a silent majority supports a course of action that is widely and bitterly attacked are cognitions that cannot be proven false by the everyday experiences of those who hold them. Performing as they do the basic function for the anxious human being of giving meaning to his life and to the confusing events around him, assuring him of divinely willed or inevitable status and of close attachment to a movement that is just and destined to succeed in exterminating evil, such myths create valued self-conceptions and political roles that are highly resistant to incompatible or complicating information. The very remoteness of a cognition of this kind from the possibility of empirical verification gives it a potency testable cognitions cannot achieve.

A basic cognition in the form of a myth of a destined future or a remote past or a first cause in turn generates many reinforcing beliefs and perceptions about more immediate and more detailed matters. Thus in the context of a controversy over zoning policy, upper middle class homeowners are likely to perceive the lower middle class, the workers, and the poor as inferior and alienated types who would ruin a "nice" neighborhood; but in the context of a debate over welfare policy many of the same prosperous people perceive the same less prosperous people as well provided for and content in a symbiotic society which provides adequately for all.[15] What lends intensity and valence to the cognitions of the affluent in both contexts is, of course, their self-conception as playing a crucial

---

[15] For this example I am indebted to Judith Stiehm, "General Welfare Stood on Its Head" (mimeographed).

role in a benevolent social order. Like everybody else, they then find it easy, and necessary, to generate consonant beliefs and perceptions about specific public issues that are impervious to empirical disproof but serve a crucial function in reinforcing the myths that give the affluent their identities. To examine the cognitions of people about any public issue is to become aware of the facility with which the mind generates perceptions and beliefs that round out a consonant cognitive structure.

Such perceptions and beliefs cannot ordinarily be verified even by those in the midst of the events with which they purport to deal. That gunfire in a riot signals sniper activity is believed or disbelieved chiefly on the basis of assumptions the observer brings with him, rather than because of what he sees.[16] The same is usually true of beliefs about plots; about the intentions of a group defined as outsiders, aliens, or hostile; and about what will serve the "public interest." It is not simply that most political spectators have to take the word of more direct participants. Even the direct participants rely upon nonempirically based cognitions when their self-conceptions are at stake.

In an experiment subjects were shown a picture of two passengers on a subway: a white man in working clothes holding an open razor and talking to a Negro. The subjects who saw the picture described it to a second person, who described it to a third, and so on through a sequence of six or seven subjects. In more than half the trials the razor was ultimately reported in the hand of the Negro; sometimes he was described as "brandishing" or "threatening with" it.[17]

A key condition of the domination of cognition by a political myth is the disposition of the anxious mind to take perceptions of present constraints as immutable: to avoid exploration of alternative possibilities. If governmental policies generate in a susceptible public a belief that a foreign nation is hostile and aggressive, then reports of day-to-day events are selectively perceived as further evidence for this basic belief even though the same or other events are susceptible to an alternative interpretation. Nor is there exploration of the alternative possibility of exploiting internal ambivalences and schisms in the foreign country to yield a different posture; the foreign country is not perceived as internally complex and maneuverable, but as presenting inflexible support for hostile action. The

---

[16] A careful study of sniping in the urban riots of 1967 concluded that virtually all allegations of sniping were based upon invalid perceptions. See "Sniping Incidents—A New Pattern of Violence," *Riot Data Review*, No. 3, Lemberg Center for the Study of Violence, Brandeis University (February 1969) (41 pp., mimeographed).

[17] Reported in Otto Klineberg, *The Human Dimension in International Relations* (New York: Holt, Rinehart & Winston, 1964), p. 42.

perceptions of the present that generate anxiety and fear are therefore the perceptions least likely to be questioned. To some degree empirical social science methods themselves reflect and help perpetuate this orientation in the present by taking individual attitudes and perceptions as "hard" data rather than as flexible, ambivalent, and contingent.[18]

Such fixation upon a particular perception of allies and adversaries frequently produces self-defeating positions on current public issues. Working-class whites angered by the high taxes they are assessed perceive their tax money as wasted by lazy or immoral welfare recipients, but do not question the highly regressive tax structure. Those who are poorer than themselves make a more visible, vulnerable, and status-providing enemy than the affluent, who are the real beneficiaries both of regressive taxes and of the largest subsidies from the public treasury. This latter perception, however, requires a kind of exploration of alternatives that attachment to political myths discourages.[19] The dominant current belief both creates supporting perceptions and blocks receptivity to incompatible information.

Because commitment to a dominant mythic cognition is socially cued and spread, public policies are potent vehicles for the cuing and the dissemination, through the devices examined earlier and no doubt through others yet to be identified. Cognitions based upon reality testing, on the other hand, are by definition arrived at through individual assessment of the available empirical evidence. The disposition of individuals to arrive at their perceptions and beliefs in this rational fashion cannot be cued by governmental actions, though these may facilitate it by minimizing threat perceptions. Uninhibited susceptibility to change in any cognition on the basis of empirical evidence is very likely also associated with anticipation of reward for verifiable success in action (rather than for conformity to the widely held beliefs of other people). Some kinds of governmental agencies do reward their staff members largely on the former basis, though it is doubtful that conformity to widely held beliefs ever goes wholly unrewarded. Polar examples of agencies that encourage commitment to reality testing in this way are research organizations and those whose objectives are perceptible and unambiguous (e.g., building dams or stopping soil erosion).

---

[18] Henry Kariel explores this point in "Expanding the Political Present," *American Political Science Review* 63 (September 1969), 768–76.

[19] See Richard A. Cloward and Frances Piven, "The Poor against Themselves," *The Nation* (November 25, 1968), pp. 558–62.

THE POLITICAL FUNCTION
OF PUBLIC CONTROVERSY

This view of the respective functions of meaning and information in building cognitions has as a corollary a nonobvious conclusion about the political function of public controversy and debate. For one thing it suggests that the most cherished, deeply rooted, and intensely held political beliefs are neither cued by explicit appeals to adopt them nor actively debated within the subcultures in which they are held. They are cued by the *form* of political actions far more potently than by rhetorical exhortation, and they serve too vital a function for the personality to be questioned in public debate. The belief that the opposition in an internal or external war is malevolent and morally inferior; the belief of the racist in white supremacy; the belief of a fervent follower in his leader's charisma: all these represent cognitions that are not controversial within the subcultures they dominate. Seriously to debate their validity would be an admission of the possibility of error and would be fatally damaging to resolute action in accord with them. There may be ritualistic reaffirmation of such beliefs or prayerful or ironic definition of nonbelievers as misguided.[20] These, however, are the only forms of public discussion of their beliefs in which believers engage, and they both amount to defining and solidifying the inner circle of the righteous and refusal to consider evidence.

Those who do engage in public controversy, on the other hand, are likely to have strong beliefs about which course of action is right and which is wrong; but the very fact that they seek an exchange with their opponents and with the uncommitted is a signal that they are seeking a politically viable resolution of the issue and that such a resolution will be accepted, whether or not it is favored. The occurrence of serious public debate between proponents and opponents is therefore also a signal that the issue is not worth fighting and dying or killing for. Though debate may sometimes achieve some mutual sharing of cognitions among opponents, and sometimes catalyzes interest in those who were formerly apathetic, those are clearly not its chief functions. Opponents almost always remain divided over values and the optimum direction of policy after the debate is over.

Public controversy over an issue functions to help participants in the debate accept an outcome that deviates from their beliefs about the optimum policy. It offers an opportunity for the interested individual to rationalize his acceptance of an outcome he does not like (or to expect such

---

[20] Schell (*The Military Half*) offers revealing examples of resort to both these devices in the leisure and mealtime talk of Vietnam pilots.

rationalization of his opponent) on the ground that acceptance is necessary to social adjustment and coexistence.

The forms of hortatory political rhetoric therefore may be taken as signals of the particular function the rhetoric is serving in the process of political role formation. Ritualistic reaffirmation of beliefs and prayerful or ironic definition of nonbelievers as misguided are signals that these beliefs are unquestioned, dominant in the hierarchy of cognitions, and generators of consonant subcognitions. Serious discussion with opponents of the premises of political arguments signals readiness to deviate from established norms in the interest of political viability and social adjustment.

The three mechanisms postulated here as alternative avenues through which meaning and information influence cognition and behavior, turn out to parallel the three functions of political opinions identified empirically by Smith et al.: reality testing, externalization of tensions, and social adjustment.[21] This parallel increases the confidence one can have in the model offered here, though Smith et al. did not offer a hypothesis comparable to that offered here about their dynamics.

This hypothesis about the political function of public controversy carries some implications for the evaluation of political activism. Active advocacy of a political position cannot be regarded as either an index or a cause of strong or extremist or effective views and behavior, but rather as a catalyst of concessions on an issue on which views are already largely crystallized. The really intense political advocate acts without tolerating or encouraging controversy about his action, without recognizing that any alternative course of action is tolerable, and therefore without acknowledging that a political issue exists or entering into a dialogue about it.

THE CONDITIONS OF MASS CHANGE
IN POLITICAL COGNITIONS

In neither of the forms of interaction just considered do large masses of people rapidly change their basic beliefs or perceptions. Rapid change in widely held cognitions does sometimes occur, however, and under conditions that reveal something important about the dynamics of such change.

The common and striking instances occur in identification of a nation's enemy or potential enemy. Between August 1939 and July 1941 Russians and Germans changed their perceptions of each other twice, see-

---

[21] Smith et al., *Opinions and Personality*.

ing the other country first as the enemy, then as an ally, then as an enemy again. Very soon after bitterly fighting each other in World War II, the United States and West Germany became allies in 1945–46; the United States and Russia switched in the opposite direction at the same time. World history abounds in similar neat examples.

Equally rapid and widespread change in cognitions about the major domestic political issues does not occur. Beliefs about the rights, abilities, and the proper political and social status of blacks have changed substantially over the last hundred years, but the change has been extremely slow, and in a large fraction of the population it has hardly occurred at all. The same pattern of slow change, strongly resisted by a large proportion of the population, holds for basic cognitions on such other major issues as labor relations and welfare policy.

Rapid change in beliefs and perceptions respecting an important domestic issue occurs only when the issue is noncontroversial, though it may occasion anxiety. The fairly sudden emergence in the late sixties of widespread concern about the threat of environmental pollution is an example.

This historical record suggests a conclusion that seems paradoxical but is understandable in the light of pertinent psychological theory: *only mass cognitions that are noncontroversial are easily changed.* When a belief is not widely or significantly challenged, there is no diverse range of cues on the issue; some one source of cues enjoys a monopoly. In the case of a political belief the monopolistic source is usually the government. This pattern manifestly holds for an unchallenged belief about a foreign enemy or ally, just as it does for an unchallenged belief that pollution of the environment endangers life.

When a political belief is challenged, those who hold it are forced to examine it and to defend their position. They may do so, as suggested earlier, by avoiding serious discussion with adversaries while holding fast to the belief because it provides them with a needed self-conception. They may engage in public debate on the issue and even accept an outcome they do not like as a concession in the interest of public order, while retaining their belief. Some may become convinced they have been wrong and change their belief; but if the issue is controversial, a significant proportion of the population remains unconvinced, by definition.

In the case of a consensually held cognition stemming from a monopolistic source of information, however, none of these psychological mechanisms or outcomes occurs. Because the belief is not challenged, there is no need to justify or rationalize it. It is held because the only available cues disseminate it and because other people, similarly cued, reinforce it. By the same token it is readily changed when the only source of cues issues different signals. A belief that a particular foreign country is hostile is not necessary to maintain a self-conception because in this case it is the form and not the content of the belief that is critical. Identification of a different country as the enemy serves the same function for the self or for reality testing. Hence there is little resistance to a change in the content of the cognition, and the new one is just as easily and just as completely reinforced by consensus.

THE DETROIT RIOT OF 1967

That cognitions unrelated to observation and impossible to verify are generated and serve a major function in political behavior is itself an empirically observable proposition. This form of empirical scrutiny is readily possible in a nonreactive way through attention to people's speeches in the course of their actual political engagements. Although it is of course desirable ultimately to learn as much as possible about the frequencies, intensities, and ambivalences of such cognitions, the initial and really critical question is whether and in what circumstances large numbers of people do arrive at perceptions and beliefs in common without the possibility of observing their referents empirically, verifying their validity, or even receiving reports from others who can engage in such observations and verification.

Even a rough review of the course of development of behaviors on a major political issue from this perspective yields revealing findings and hypotheses. The perceptions of the Detroit riot of 1967 voiced by the people who were involved in it illustrate the point. In the nature of the case it is impossible even in principle to assemble the "universe" of such perceptions and therefore to know what proportion of the total these represent (though one can imagine various unpersuasive strategies for postulating such a universe and working indicators of its contents). The considerations discussed in the early parts of this chapter suggest that there are more meaningful questions and possible conclusions about political behavior and cognition to be drawn from this kind of listing:

1. Referring as they do to allegations of threatening actions and malevolent motivations, plans, and plots, these cognitions were largely of a kind that evoke counteraction and escalation and broaden public support on both sides.
2. The various involved groups create and spread among themselves a great many specific cognitions that are not empirically based but that are crucial to behavior in that they rationalize

joint actions, rationalize self-conceptions, and catalyze similar processes in opposition groups.

3. To a marked degree different cognitions emerge within different interest groupings; but the nonempirically based ones are systematically alarmist.

4. Empirical studies of the events refute the widely and intensely held perceptions and beliefs. Later or concurrent studies consistently lead to drastic downward revisions in reports about casualties, property damage, sniping, and plotting on both sides and show specific cognitions to have been false.

5. Dominant patterns of perception and belief give rise to an unknowable number of more specific cognitions in the form of legends or tales that amount to a detailed filling in of the pattern.

In the degree that such a pattern and its legendary infrastructure emerges and is accepted, meaning dominates information. To the student, therefore, the critical observations are the character and range of acceptance of the pattern and of deviations from it and the empirical and nonempirical bases of cognitions.

Examples of specific perceptions come from "Profiles of Disorder" recounted in the *Report of the National Advisory Commission on Civil Disorders*. These are the most exhaustive and most carefully checked accounts of the course of events in the riots available to us. A description of the methods and checks employed by the Commission staff in assembling these profiles appears on pages 108 and 577–78 of the *Report*. From the account of the Detroit riot these examples of specific perceptions are identified for particular groups of receptors:

Typical perceptions of the black community:
The killing of a prostitute in the 12th Street area at the end of June had been at the hands of a Vice Squad officer.

The newspapers were deliberately downplaying the murder. A Negro youth had been shot at by snipers. Many persons sympathized with the idea of a rebellion against the "system."

Typical perceptions by police and National Guardsmen on duty in the riot areas:
Police Commissioner: "If we had started shooting in there . . . not one of our policemen would have come out alive. I am convinced that it would have turned into a race riot in the conventional sense."

A National Guardsman, believing he had heard shots from the front, fired a shot at the building.

Reports of heavy sniper fire at particular locations poured into police headquarters, and officers were dispatched to rout out the snipers.

General perceptions:
Police and residents seemed apathetic and often aloof to the situation.

Looting was becoming organized.
The young people seemed to be "dancing amidst the flames."
Perceptions of Cyrus Vance, former Deputy Secretary of Defense and presidential representative in Detroit, and Lt. General John L. Throckmorton, Commander of Task Force Detroit:
They observed no looting, and fires were coming under control. They decided that the use of federal troops was unnecessary.
Use of loaded weapons was unnecessary.

A reading of the full account of the Detroit riot in the *Report,* or even a perusal of newspaper accounts, makes it obvious that this list of perceptions typifies hundreds of others generated during the riot, which is to say that the perceptions did follow patterns that conformed to, and further reinforced, meanings already held and serving important functions for those who held them. The perceptions of the blacks and those supporting them and the perceptions of the law enforcement officers and those supporting them intensified and broadened support for each other. Equally revealing were the perceptions of the officials like Vance and Throckmorton, who were outside the battle but whose prestige depended directly on the speed with which the rioting could be ended. Their perceptions, in striking contrast to the others, were of lessening tension that justified de-escalation. That such disparate and incompatible sets of perceptions should grow out of the same situation is clear evidence that the perceptions were largely based upon something other than facts.

Once one is alert to the influence of nonempirically based perceptions and beliefs, their pervasive presence as a factor in political cognition and behavior on all controversial issues becomes evident. A major influence upon welfare policy, for example, is the conviction that the poor do not deserve much help because: (1) they are lazy and will not take jobs available to them; or (2) they are not really so poor or deprived anyway; or (3) they are a lesser breed and their poverty reflects the social order ordained by Providence, which man upsets at his peril; or (4) they are subversives and to encourage them will foster revolution. Myth can be expected to appear as a component of cognitions respecting every controversial political issue, for these always involve conflict and strain.

THE CONDITIONS OF RECEPTIVITY
TO MYTHIC CUES

Not everyone accepts the myths, there are variations in degree of commitment among those who do, and widely accepted myths eventually come to be regarded as illusions. What are the conditions of receptivity to mythic cues?

It appears that those who can be expected to benefit substantially in status or money from belief in a myth are especially susceptible: they are inclined to translate their interests in status and money into the terms of a myth that defines their behavior as serving the public interest. It is hard to find any other premise to explain the marked tendency of police to perceive plots among blacks and the poor when empirical studies cannot find them; the marked tendency of aspirants for leadership of black militant organizations to perceive white plots for genocide; the marked inclination of military brass and armaments contractors to perceive aggressive plans and capabilities in their counterparts in rival countries; and so on.

For the poor and those with low status the case is more complicated, but it is likely that the same dynamics are operative. Both Lipset's conclusions regarding working class authoritarianism[22] and the findings of sociologists who challenge his thesis[23] are in point here. It is hard to deny that lower income groups and the poor are frequently highly susceptible to ethnocentric appeals and to political myths even when they are demonstrably hurt disproportionately by the policies and the leaders they support. There is good survey evidence, on the other hand, that they are frequently not susceptible to such appeals, apparently when unambiguous evidence is available to them that they will be disproportionately hurt (as in the Selective Service policy during the Vietnam war).[24] This complex set of reactions certainly reflects the complex of tangible and symbolic cues and threats to which the poor and the working class are subjected. When, as frequently happens, low income whites fear damage to their existing status and income from a specific group, such as blacks migrating into an area in large numbers, they are highly susceptible to a myth justifying suppression of the group perceived as a threat. The poor and the working class, on the other hand, are in a position to experience more directly than the middle class the arbitrary character of many governmental acts; they are disproportionately susceptible to the draft, to death in war, and to police harassment. Such cues apparently create dissonance and the ambivalence the debate about working class authoritarianism reflects.

The corollary of this view is that the conditions that lessen or minimize susceptibility to belief in political myth are: a social and economic position such that widespread belief in the myth will be harmful or self-defeating, and a context encouraging individual observation rather than

---

[22] Seymour Martin Lipset, *Political Man* (Englewood Cliffs, N.J.: Prentice-Hall, 1962), chap. 4.

[23] See S. M. Miller and Frank Riessman, "Working Class Authoritarianism: A Critique of Lipset," *British Journal of Sociology* 12 (September 1961), pp. 263–76.

[24] James W. Davis, Jr., and Kenneth M. Dolbeare, *Little Groups of Neighbors* (Chicago: Markham, 1968).

mass response to others' cues; these conditions hold in some measure and in some contexts for everyone. They hold in a rather special way for scientists, whose specialized competence is to substitute fact for myth in the fields of their professional concerns and who are therefore directly threatened by a political environment with a stake in retaining the myth. Though there is very likely some transfer of this bias to fields other than those in which a scientist is professionally trained, the transfer is far from complete —witness the notorious susceptibility of natural scientists to myths about society and politics, and even the susceptibility of social scientists to myths about social concerns in areas where they do not work professionally.

Semantic information, esthetic information, cognitive structures, and political controversy certainly influence each other and under various conditions dominate each other, though different conditions establish different orders of dominance. This chapter is an effort to suggest some of the functions of each of them in the determination of political behavior, and especially to suggest some of the conditions under which esthetic information becomes hierarchically dominant.

Chapter 4

MYTH, EMOTION, AND SELF-CONCEPTION

Individual participants in a controversial mass movement frequently cling to their roles in it with some passion. Can we explain the concurrent evocation of similar emotion and similar role choices in large masses of people in such circumstances, and in what degree is the process systematic? In what sense are the individual phenomenon and the group phenomenon linked?

Mead pointed to symbol formation through role taking as the behavioral basis of both phenomena. The shared beliefs and perceptions of a group and the individual's definition of himself are reflections of the same process: the formation of significant symbols that hold common meanings for all who are engaged by them. The formation of the self and the social interactions of the group are therefore the same process seen from different perspectives.

The myth, an unquestioned belief held in common by a large group of people that gives events and actions a particular meaning, is a particularly relevant form of symbol in the emergence of mass political movements. When we recognize the functions it serves for the group and for its individual adherents, we can define the systematic ties between individual role attachment and common adherence to a controversial political movement.

MYTH AND IDENTITY

Jerome Bruner, relying on psychoanalytic theory, has made the point that in choosing belief in a particular myth a person chooses a particular role and identity for himself:

> It is not simply society that patterns itself on the idealizing myths, but unconsciously it is the individual man as well who is able to structure his internal clamor of identities in terms of prevailing myth. Life then produces myth and finally imitates it.[1]

---

[1] Jerome Bruner, "Myth and Identity," in Henry A. Murray (ed.), *Myth and Mythmaking* (New York: Brazillier, 1960), pp. 282–83.

Erik Erikson also sees a link between myth and identity, further suggesting that it comes to be perceived as self-created:

> By accepting some definition as to who he is, usually on the basis of a function in an economy, a place in the sequence of generations, and a status in the structure of society the adult is able to selectively reconstruct his past in such a way that, step for step, it seems to have planned him, or better, he seems to have planned *it*. In this sense, psychologically we *do* choose our parents, our family history, and the history of our kings, heroes, and gods.[2]

Charles Morris complements these positions:

> The general significance of mythical discourse lies in the fact that it informs the interpreters in a vivid manner of the modes of action approved and disapproved by some group (or in the extreme case, by some individual). It thus makes available to the interpreter information concerning an important body of appraisals which he may utilize in his behavior whether by way of agreement or disagreement.[3]

Bruner and Erikson stress the close and necessary connection between severe anxiety and attachment to a myth that establishes a socially supported identity and suggests a collective course of action to allay the anxiety. Both the empirical world in which people feel threatened and a fantasy about causes and what to do are involved, and "the art form of the myth connects the daemonic world of reason by a verisimilitude that conforms to each."[4] For those who do feel threatened because of a gap between what they are taught to believe they deserve and what they are getting, attachment to a myth replaces gnawing uncertainty and rootlessness (what Erikson calls an "ego-chill") with a vivid account of who are friends, who are enemies, and what course of action must be pursued to protect the self and significant others. It channels individual anxieties and impulses into a widely shared set of expectations and a widely shared scenario to guide action. It frees the individual from responsibility for his unhappy or threatened place in society and prescribes a clear and widely supported program for protecting his identity. To consider political examples of this phenomenon is to recognize the force of Bruner's observation about myth. "Its power is that it lives on the feather line between

---

[2] Erik Erikson, *Young Man Luther* (New York: Norton, 1958), p. 111.
[3] Charles W. Morris, *Signs, Language and Behavior* (New York: Brazillier, 1946), p. 135.
[4] Bruner, "Myth and Identity," p. 279.

fantasy and reality. It must be neither too good nor too bad to be true, nor must it be too true."[5]

Each of these expectations also evokes a specific political role and self-conception for those individuals who accept the myth in question: the patriotic soldier whose role it is to sacrifice, fight, and die for his country; the policeman or National Guardsman whose role it is to save the social order from subhuman or radical hordes; the consumer whose role it is to respect the state which protects him; the slave or low class or caste person whose role it is to accept his deprivations and perform menial functions in a docile way. In every instance the degree of attachment to the political myth and to the role it creates and the fervor with which the role is played depend upon (1) the degree of anxiety the myth rationalizes, and (2) the intensity with which the particular expectation that forms the central premise of the myth is held. Public policy is a paramount factor in creating both cognitions.

In their political behavior since at least the Civil War the American poor have offered a revealing example of the potency of myth in creating a particular identity and thereby promoting submissiveness and docility in the face of deprivation. Americans are taught at home, in the schools, and in pervasive political rhetoric that America is the land of equal opportunity; that there is equality before the law; that government accurately reflects the voice of the people, but does not shape it; that political and economic values are allocated fairly. Given such opportunity, those who are poor are inclined to attribute their unhappy condition to their own failings and inadequacies. Poor people are bound to be troubled by this logical inference and widely held belief. They are reinforced in their feelings of guilt by the affluent and their legislative representatives, who attribute their own success and others' failure to personal worth or lack of it. They are further reinforced by a host of governmental practices that define the poor as unworthy: social worker investigations of their habits, morals, and ambition; means tests; evictions for debt; arbitrariness in the award of welfare benefits; denigration in the schools and in contacts with bureaucratic agencies of the folkways, dress, social skills, and stock of knowledge of the poor. The poor are therefore inundated with cues from reference groups and from government defining them as personally inadequate, guilty, dependent, and deserving of their deprivations; and they manifestly accept the self-definition, at least ambivalently.

In consequence the poor have typically been meek, acquiescent in their role and status, and grateful for the welfare benefits they receive: benefits whose very meagerness further defines the worth of the recipients.

---

[5] Ibid.

The American poor have required less coercion and less in social security guarantees to maintain their quiescence than has been true in other developed countries, even authoritarian ones like Germany and notably poor ones like Italy; for the guilt and self-concepts of the poor have kept them docile. That such violence as has occurred has been localized, sporadic, limited to small groups in special circumstances, and rarely perceived by participants as a movement for purposeful institutional change but rather as despairing protest, is further evidence for this conclusion. The Black Panther Party is an effort to break with the historic pattern of cognition and behavior, but is also evidence that the break has not occurred.

Myth and deprivation also feed and sustain each other in shaping the lives of many people who are not economically poor and who are often affluent. Consonant cues from schooling, from governmental actions, and from social groups teach people to equate material wealth and hierarchical status with the good life and to remain oblivious to the real impoverishment of their everyday lives: to the narrow bounds within which they define their roles and self-conceptions; the blinders that prevent realization of their intellectual and social potentialities; their inability to be playful except as a desperate adjunct and confirmation of their roles as businessmen, bureaucrats, and elites; the anxieties that reinforce their rigid role playings. Government constantly shapes and reflects the myths by which the well-to-do and the aspirants to their roles live, both through the substance and through the style of its acts. It does so when it subsidizes the affluent far more generously than the destitute. It does so in its ceremonies and awards of status symbols. Deprivation is universal; beliefs about it and adjustments to it are socially cued.

EMOTION AS A CATALYST OF POLITICAL RITUAL AND POLITICAL VIOLENCE

In view of the manifest association between emotion and political action and support, it is surprising that social scientists have generally offered quite limited explanations of the tie between the two. Usually these explanations have taken the form of declarations that some particular emotion, such as fear or anger or joy, has been the cause of some observed political behavior. This kind of statement, especially popular among journalists, is almost always an evasion rather than an explanation, as Arthur Bentley made clear long ago.[6] It takes an unobservable state of

---

[6] Arthur F. Bentley, *The Process of Government* (Granville, O.: Principia Press, 1908; reprint 1949).

mind as an independent variable and therefore conveys information only about a tautology (anger caused the crowd to riot), avoiding systematic analysis of the relationships among actions.

If it is dubious social science to be satisfied with the assumption that an emotion is a cause, it is vital to learn as precisely as possible what functions emotions serve in political behavior. Pertinent studies in role analysis, studies of language and the symbolic processes, and psychoanalytic theory encouragingly point to consistent or identical conclusions. The hypotheses suggested here applying these propositions specifically to political behavior cannot be blamed on the writers cited in the discussion.

It is convenient to start with an observation from role theory. People differ markedly in the range of "others" who become significant for them and whose roles they can freely take. Sarbin notes that "the more roles in a person's behavior repertory," the better his social adjustment, other things remaining the same, and he suggests that the absence of role-taking skills contributes to the development of paranoid disorders. In play, a child hopefully learns to shift from role to role. Lack of the skill and the imagination to do so retards socialization, and culture myths and folk tales help the child acquire the necessary skill and imagination.[7] Similarly, in Mead's terms, the ability to be self-critical (and therefore tentative, skeptical, and curious) is a function of the number of roles ("me's") a person can take or of his internalization of a generalized other.

Many forms of political interaction, including most law enforcement activities, the interactions between policymakers and constituents, and those among competing elites involve mutual role taking.[8] Each party observes from the other's perspective and so comes to understand, and in some measure to share, his aspirations, fears, strengths, and weaknesses. Each accordingly limits his own demands in line with a perception of what is feasible and will reassure the others. Unequal bargaining resources are expressed in behavior and in instrumental benefits, but so also are the limits evoked through mutual role taking. The evocation of limits reassures people, especially where there can be no unambiguous assessment of the balance of bargaining resources and payoffs, as in public policies purporting to regulate business in the interest of consumers and in antipoverty programs.

For those individuals who are adept and effective at the politicking such flexible role taking involves, the very exercise of their talents brings with it a play of feeling and an exhilaration which reinforces their ability

---

[7] Theodore Sarbin, "Role Theory," in Gardner Lindzey (ed.), *Handbook of Social Psychology* 1 (Reading, Mass.: Addison-Wesley, 1954), 226–27.

[8] Murray Edelman, *Symbolic Uses of Politics* (Urbana: University of Illinois Press, 1964), chap. 3.

to do it well: empathetically to take the roles of others, to understand them and therefore to reassure them, while making demands within acceptable limits. In the operations of a resourceful and sensitive politician or labor mediator we can see such talent at work, and the memoirs and statements of such people leave no doubt that gratifying affect is involved.

The psychological literature offers more general support for the hypothesis that feeling complements comprehension as an aspect of such role taking. Sarbin's references to its origin in children's play is one clue. Studies of speech disorders, language pathology, and their relation to psychosis and neurosis also point to a close linkage among affective contact and the abilities to symbolize, to abstract, and to socialize or integrate into society.[9] In his study of the emotions Plutchik declares:

> Many authors have noted that neurosis and psychosis are characterized by a decrease in affective manifestations and that there is generally a restriction or narrowing of the range of emotional responsiveness.[10]

Neurosis and psychosis are, in one sense, names for inadequacy in socializing and integrating into society.

Generalizing from such studies, Church writes:

> Feelings are the substrate and the raw material of cognition as opposed to reflexive action, and our human capacities for thought are no greater than our human capacities for feeling. It may well be that capacity for feeling, whether innate or generated out of early parent-child relations, is the essential variable in intellectual differences. It is only those with strong feelings who can resist the secondhand formulations of experience handed down from their progenitors and can work to thematize reality afresh for themselves. Certainly, it is possible to be retentive without great feeling, but learning without the understanding that emotion gives is barren and perhaps even dangerous.[11]

As a concomitant of mutual role taking and the exchange of significant symbols, feeling is part of understanding: an adjunct and a necessary condi-

---

[9] Cf. Silvano Arieti, "Some Aspects of Language in Schizophrenia," in H. Werner (ed.), *On Expressive Language* (Worcester, Mass.: Clark University Press, 1955), pp. 56–57; Joseph Church, *Language and the Discovery of Reality* (New York: Random House, 1961), p. 161.

[10] Robert Plutchik, *The Emotions* (New York: Random House, 1962), p. 158. See also Silvano Arieti, *Interpretation of Schizophrenia* (New York: Brunner, 1955).

[11] Joseph Church, *Language and the Discovery of Reality* (New York: Random House, 1961), pp. 202–3.

tion of the very process of sharing perspectives that makes it possible for politicians and leaders of clientele groups to enter into a symbiotic pattern of action.

Cassirer makes the same point when he analyzes the feeling accompanying the experiencing of a work of art. Art offers a form of understanding and not simply emotion. "Art gives us order in the apprehension of visible, tangible, and audible appearances. . . . The infinite potentialities of which we had but a dim and obscure presentiment are brought to light by the lyric poet, by the novelist, and by the dramatist."[12] To be able to achieve such apprehension, we must be able to feel. For the same reason the most sensitive practitioners of the social art of developing a large repertory of roles are those who best understand the potentialities of the range of others who are significant for them. As they do so, they reassure both followers and adversaries and contribute to the ritualization of conflict. The visible, publicized process of role taking in politics becomes a ritual which chiefly functions to shape a myth of a symbiotic social order in which the weak are protected. In this case the myth contributes to political quiescence for masses and to political craftsmanship for leaders.

In his book on aggression in animals Konrad Lorenz suggests that conflict may itself help generate the mutual understanding and feeling that creates a bond: "Doubtless the personal bond, love, arose in many cases from intra-specific aggression, by way of ritualization of a redirected attack or threatening."[13] The observation is strikingly analogous to our observations about the ritualization of political conflict and resulting immobilization of affected publics. Here is one major form in which feeling is integrally involved in political behavior, and it serves not as an emotional diversion from thought or rational action, but as a necessary aid to comprehension.

Another form of emotion, generated under other conditions, serves a different political and psychological function. In this second form, as in the previous one, feeling is a concomitant of belief about relationships with others; but now it grows from, and complements, a belief that others constitute a threat that cannot be limited through political negotiation. Rather than empathetic mutual role taking which enlarges understanding of the range of viable potentialities, such emotion catalyzes engagement with a particular myth and limits the individual to a particular self-conception.

The crucial distinction is that between personal interaction involving a sharing and exchange of diverse perspectives, and belief in a particular

<hr>

[12] Ernst Cassirer, *An Essay on Man* (Garden City, N.Y.: Doubleday Anchor, 1956), pp. 213, 215.

[13] Konrad Lorenz, *On Aggression* (New York: Bantam, 1967), p. 209.

course of future development, where the belief is based upon cues from a remote source and lent intensity by disparate individual anxieties. In the second case there is not the constant check of direct interaction with people who might have adversary interests. Adversaries are not perceived as complex social beings whose perspectives can be shared, at least in part, but rather as objects embodying a particular abstract function: aggression, evil, domination, obedience, and so on. They do not exist for mutual role taking, but to serve the function in the mythic scenario that their inherent nature requires of them, just as the perceiver sees himself as an entity with a fixed function in the same scenario.

The perception of others and of self as objects rather than as complicated and ambivalent and vacillating human beings involves different kinds of emotion and a different function for emotion. The political myths portray scenarios of manichean struggle or of a stratified social order in which all must play their parts and keep their place in order to be protected. Rigid expectation that a particular scenario in one of these forms will be played out seems to evoke the emotions associated with hostility and anxiety: anger, fear, hate, triumph, acceptance, acquiescence. These contrast both in quality and in function with the feelings associated with creativity, exploration, and discovery. They inhibit search and flexibility, and they keep attention centered upon a particular vision of the world and upon the particular roles for individual actors specified in the myth. They catalyze banality by encouraging people to fulfill expectations of how others have to behave, and this response in turn signals threat (or domination or submissiveness) to the others, who are reinforced in *their* expectations and behavior patterns. So, as Bruner suggests, life copies myth.

The person who, by virtue of such social cues, comes to perceive himself as limited to a single role also sees himself as an object rather than as a complex person of many potentialities; and so he comes to need a myth which legitimizes his role and gives him a function. He therefore accepts the myth and the self-concept inflexibly: the black or the Indian untouchable as fulfilling a cosmic design through his inferior status; personal wealth as defining the self and its value; physical beauty as defining the self and its worth (as in some apparently unhappy sex goddesses who see themselves as objects). Thus does perception of the self as an object limited to a particular role encourage self-hatred and consequent attachment to a rationalizing myth.

Social psychological studies of aggression contribute some additional hypotheses regarding the dynamics and function of emotion as a component of the manichean form of myth. In these scenarios some group is defined as conspiring to overthrow the social order with which the perceiver identifies or as thwarting his rightful claims to a particular status;

in either case there is a perception of frustration. Berkowitz makes the following insightful observation about the frustration-aggression theory that grew out of the work of Dollard and Miller at Yale:

> Dollard and his collaborators had not faced the important theo-retical problem of "fear." Fear-producing situations are frus-trations according to their (and our) definition of this latter term, but what is there about these obstructing situations that yields stronger fear than anger reactions? The answer is, fearful events signify noxious consequences; in such circumstances the individual anticipates either physical or psychological damage to himself. It is hypothesized that fear increases more rapidly than does anger as these anticipated noxious consequences increase in magnitude. The low "power" of the frustrated individual relative to that of the frustrating agent is another important aspect of the fearful situ-ation. The more vulnerable or less powerful he feels, i.e., the less able he is to control or punish the frustrator for the injury he has received, the more fear predominates over anger.[14]

Berkowitz also emphasizes a related proposition in the Dollard-Miller theory. The latter declare that the stronger the thwarted drive, "the stronger the resulting instigation to aggression," and so " 'threats' are more likely to produce overt hostility than are 'deprivations.' "[15] Here, again, the perceived relative power of the frustrated individual and the frustrating agent is crucial.

The experimental work of Dollard, Miller, and Berkowitz has been done with individuals in laboratory situations, while the political scientist is concerned with explaining the aggressive behavior of groups and masses. The ties suggested here among public policy, mythical belief, and mass responses offer a means of doing that. The myths governmental actions evoke create perceptions of the nature and the strength of the frustrating threat for large numbers of anxious people who can have no other, equally persuasive, cue from direct observation as to what to expect.

Where the myth evoked in this way portrays an adversary group as dominant or all-powerful and another group as rightfully subordinate, Berkowitz's formulation suggests that there will be fear and presumably acquiescence. This observably occurs in many political relationships, though it is often tempered by another myth promising some measure of pro-tection or a reward in an afterlife. In such cases the continuing tension between fear and reassurance typically results in quiescent acceptance of existing status relationships.

Often, however, public policy evokes a belief in broad support for

---

[14] Leonard Berkowitz, *Aggression* (New York: McGraw-Hill, 1962), p. 50.
[15] Ibid., pp. 49–50. The quotes are from Berkowitz.

the aspirations of a threatened or frustrated group for improvement of their status, or it evokes a belief that a superordinate group is maintaining and enjoying its privileges unfairly or unjustly. In this instance the Berkowitz formulation suggests that anger will predominate over fear, making overt hostility and aggression more likely. This proposition is useful for students of collective behavior that is either quiescent or aggressive because it focuses attention upon the dynamic reasons that deprivation may not be perceived as threat or that maintenance of a long-standing status relationship may come to be perceived as threat. In both instances the acts and the rhetoric of public officials serve to create the same perceptions or expectations in large groups of people, so that the key variables in the psychologists' frustration-anger-aggression theory are influenced in politically relevant situations by cues emanating from the government.

The emotions of anger and fear seem empirically to impede the kind of free exploration of possibilities noted above as characteristic of some political interactions. In his book, *The Emotions,* Plutchik suggests that the primary emotion dimensions form bipolar factors or axes. He names them as, "destruction versus protection, incorporation versus rejection, reproduction versus deprivation, and orientation versus exploration."[16] This formulation lends support to the empirical impression that the emotions evoked by threatening situations impede the feelings associated with mutual role taking and acceptance.

A common political expression this syndrome takes is the personification of perceived sources of threat. The person who worries about displacement from his social status or his job or feels powerless to cope with impersonal economic developments or many bureaucratic decisions that add up to a threatening trend feels little solace if the blame falls upon impersonal social processes or developments. Hence the appeal of a conspiracy myth in which guilty leaders and their dangerous dupes are identifiable and *ad hominem* aggression is possible, and hence also the appeal of a hero-leader who can be perceived as knowing how to cope with these frustrating developments while most do not. Neither the enemy nor the benevolent leader in these situations can be viewed as a human being with complexities, ambivalences, and a potentiality for empathy. They are perceived as embodiments of a particular role. That perception in turn creates a rigid self-conception and a banal mode of behavior on the part of the perceivers. Often there is explicit expression of a belief that such personifications are not really human: that Negroes perceived as threats to the social order are subhuman, for example, or that a leader is partially divine or receives divine inspiration. These mythic themes facilitate and rationalize aggression

---

[16] Plutchik, *The Emotions,* p. 108.

without limit or subordination without limit, just as exploratory role taking informed by feeling *places* limits on courses of political action and encourages tentativeness. Lorenz calls attention to a pertinent anthropological observation:

> The dark side of pseudo-speciation is that it makes us consider the members of pseudo-species other than our own as not human, as many primitive tribes are demonstrably doing, in whose language the word for their own particular tribe is synonymous with "Man." From their viewpoint it is not, strictly speaking, cannibalism if they eat fallen warriors of an enemy tribe.[17]

By virtue of pseudo-speciation, to kill enemies is not perceived as murder in advanced societies and to degrade people defined as inferior is not perceived as oppression.

Both patterns of political behavior identified here function to provide a loyal following for leaders and aspirants to leadership. Leaders therefore often have an interest in encouraging acceptance of the myths and in accepting them themselves; motivation is not irrelevant to perception.

The two patterns of behavior should not be understood as dichotomies; it is unlikely that they ever occur empirically in any individual in pure form, though there are close approximations. Response to every political issue involves some mix of them, though the proportions vary greatly both in different individuals and for different issues. The inevitability of their concurrent appearance is one more example of the ambivalent nature of individual response to political issues.

On the civil rights issue, for example, both whites and Negroes must in varying degrees look at status differences, discriminatory practices, and segregation from the point of view of the other, recognize his aspirations, fears, shame, inertia, and so on for what they are, and in some degree share these attitudes. At the same time the same individuals in some measure fear and resent what these others may do to them and their future status. Empathetic feeling and sensitive exploration of possibilities coexist with anger and fear, in some mix that is relatively unstable. Ambivalence and anxious uncertainty help make the cues stemming from public policies the potent symbols they are, capable of mobilizing broad support or opposition.

This analysis offers a basis for formulating more specific hypotheses regarding the conditions of stability both in personality traits and in cognitions. The dimensions usually used to define personality include: authoritarian-submissive, extroverted-introverted, tough-minded–tender-minded

---

[17] Lorenz, *On Aggression,* p. 45.

friendly-hostile, weak ego–strong ego. All of these denote relationships with others: tendencies to yield to others, dominate them, take them into account, ignore them, placate them, and so on. But now we recognize that in the ambiguous but highly salient area of political expectations, particular patterns of personality characteristics reflect particular patterns of cognitions: i.e., beliefs about future political outcomes and how they can be influenced and therefore particular political values or policy positions. A belief, for example, that the poor are inferior to others mentally or morally and susceptible to mobilization by outside agitators becomes associated with tough-mindedness and authoritarianism and also with distaste for public policies to raise the status of the poor. The three observations, about the cognition, about the personality traits, and about the policies, amount to the same observation reported in different vocabularies. They are usefully conceived as part of a single transaction rather than as causes or effects of each other.

Similarly, submissiveness and a belief that others are all-powerful and need to be placated are complementary and mutually reinforcing. A belief that others can be influenced through personal understanding and sharing of perspectives and benefits fosters, and is fostered by, a strong ego and tender-mindedness. Personality characteristics, belief systems, and values or policy positions are therefore interrelated through dynamic process which we can in part identify and analyze. If this is true, the conventional perception of them as wholly or largely independent of each other is itself a source of illusions in perception and in expectations and a catalyst of support for mythic cognitions.

Once a pattern of cognition, self-conception, and congruent behavior becomes established, several of the social psychological processes already noted contribute to its stability while others tend to upset it. It is manifestly crucial both to knowledge and to control to be able to identify the respective processes and their impact. Selective perception that reinforces a self-conception and a cherished political role contributes to stability, as do the feelings that accompany the enactment of the role. Political acts and public policies may reinforce such selective perception, and occasionally they encourage the ambivalent to change their perspective radically: to define some previously ignored group as a source of threat or to recognize the possibility of accommodation with a group previously perceived as a threat.

Chapter 5

METAPHOR AND LANGUAGE FORMS

Metaphors and myths are devices for simplifying and giving meaning to complex and bewildering sets of observations that evoke concern. Political events and trends are typically complex and ambiguous, and they become foci of anxiety. This chapter considers some observations suggesting that metaphorical and mythical modes of viewing the political scene are central to the shaping of political values, attitudes, and perceptions, and sometimes to personality formation. It concentrates upon some hypotheses about the mechanisms through which these language forms help promote conformity to organizations, movements, and leadership, though they are also central to arousal and rebellion.

It is hard, in politics, to know what causes what and which group interest has won the last battle, let alone the last war. Worse, inner anxieties are displaced onto public objects so that overt enemies can be blamed and social supports created. Political events can thereby become infused with strong affect stemming from psychic tension, from perceptions of economic, military, or other threats or opportunities, and from interactions between social and psychological responses.

These political "events," however, are largely creations of the language used to describe them. For the mass of political spectators, developments occur in a remote arena where there can be no direct observation or feedback. The bewildering political universe needs to be ordered and given meaning. People who are anxious and confused are eager to be supplied with an organized political order—including simple explanations of the threats they fear—and with reassurance that the threats are being countered.

Language forms perform a crucial function by creating shared meanings, perceptions, and reassurances among mass publics. By applying some generally accepted propositions about language forms as symbols to some common observations about political opinions and behavior, important theses can be derived about this function of language.

Serious work on language as a dynamic influence upon social relationships, as distinct from language as an index of attitudes and perceptions, has been done by anthropologists, social psychologists, and students of symbolism.[1] A central theme in this literature is the power of myth and metaphor to intensify some perceptions and screen others out of attention. Language does not mirror an objective "reality," but rather creates it by organizing meaningful perceptions abstracted from a complex, bewildering world:

> . . . one cannot grasp the true nature and function of linguistic concepts if one regards them as copies, as representations of a definite world of facts, whose components are given to the human mind *ab initio* in stark and separate outlines.[2] . . .

> Whatever has been fixed by a name, henceforth is not only real, but is Reality. . . . We find a relation of identity, of complete congruence between . . . the name and the thing.[3]

The reality that is linguistically created is not random or accidental. It is the constraint under which the process of creating meaning operates that makes it peculiarly relevant to political behavior, for concepts become meaningful when they are related to people's affective demands:

> Whatever appears important for our wishing and willing, our hope and anxiety, for acting and doing: that and only that receives the stamp of verbal "meaning." . . . Only what is related somehow to the focus point of willing and doing, only what proves to be essential to the whole scheme of life and activity, is selected from the uniform flux of sense impressions, and is "noticed" in the midst of them—that is to say, receives a special linguistic accent, a name.[4]

---

[1] Among the general studies I have found most useful are: Weston La Barre, *The Human Animal* (Chicago: University of Chicago Press, 1954), pp. 163–207; Edward Sapir, *Culture, Language, and Personality* (Berkeley: University of California Press, 1960); Bronislaw Malinowski, "The Problem of Meaning in Primitive Languages," in Charles K. Ogden and I. A. Richards (eds.), *The Meaning of Meaning* (New York: Harcourt, Brace, 1959), pp. 306–36; Toshihiko Izutsu, *Language and Magic* (Keio Institute of Philological Studies, 1956); Benjamin L. Whorf, "Science and Linguistics," in Sol Saporta (ed.), *Psycholinguistics* (New York: Holt, Rinehart & Winston, 1961), pp. 460–68; Norman O. Brown, *Life against Death* (New York: Random House, 1959), pp. 68–73; Ernst Cassirer, *Language and Myth* (New York: Harper, 1946); Susanne K. Langer, *Philosophy in a New Key* (New York: New American Library, 1959), chap. 5; Jerome S. Bruner, "Myth and Identity," in Henry A. Murray (ed.), *Myth and Mythmaking* (New York: Brazillier, 1960), pp. 276–87.

[2] Cassirer, *Language and Myth,* p. 37.

[3] Ibid., p. 58.

[4] Ibid., pp. 37–38.

This chapter considers language as a central facet of a more inclusive process through which people's cognitions are generated, powerfully reinforced, or changed. Other facets of the same process are actions that escalate or ritualize conflict, concomitant emotions, and the formation of self-conceptions, each of which has been examined in earlier chapters. Although each of these phenomena is experienced separately, and is analyzed separately, they are dynamically integral and reinforcing, just as Mead demonstrated that significant symbols (meaningful communication), self, mind, and acts are aspects of a common social transaction. That all these facets create and reinforce the same cognition helps us understand the potency of the social cuing and the ease with which it sometimes dominates testable reality. Only human beings among living creatures can use symbolic language. Language forms are a critical element in the shaping of beliefs; they do so in ways we do not consciously experience and so are nonobvious.

The basic argument, then, is that internal or external conflicts and passions catalyze attachment to a selected range of myths and metaphors which shape perceptions of the political world.[5]

FACTUAL PREMISES IN POLITICAL METAPHORS

Thought is metaphorical and metaphor pervades language, for the unknown, the new, the unclear, and the remote are apprehended by one's perceptions of identities with the familiar. Metaphor, therefore, defines the pattern of perception to which people respond. To speak of deterrence and strike capacity is to perceive war as a game; to speak of legalized murder is to perceive war as a slaughter of human beings; to speak of a struggle for democracy is to perceive war as a vaguely defined instrument for achieving an intensely sought objective. Each metaphor intensifies selected perceptions and ignores others, thereby helping one to concentrate upon desired consequences of favored public policies and helping one to ignore their unwanted, unthinkable, or irrelevant premises and aftermaths. Each metaphor can be a subtle way of highlighting what one wants to believe and avoiding what one does not wish to face. Sapir and later anthropologists and psychologists following his lead have noticed that cultures differ significantly in their namings of distinctions, and that people's per-

---

[5] To avoid misunderstanding of the implications of the thesis, let me say that I regard it as misleading and irrelevant to label this process of creating perceptions and meanings as "irrational." It is more to the point to say that it is inevitable, that it has systematic effects upon political attitudes and behavior, and that a beginning can be made toward specifying those effects.

ceptions of the world and their ability to remember distinctions vary with this difference in fineness of coding—that is, in naming.[6]

Metaphor is, therefore, an instrument for shaping political support and opposition and the premises upon which decisions are made. It also can inject affect into the responses to political acts. Beginning with Freud's study of wit, his closest approach to a theory of language, the psycho-analytically oriented students of language have called attention to the prevalence of repression and taboo in metaphor and in language generally.[7] This conclusion may help explain the seemingly disproportionate emotional response to some definitions of public issues and to challenges to the accepted definitions.

To some people any evocation of certain issues is apparently a metaphor for repressed anxieties. For some, a reference to fluoridation seems to connote a poison plot. Limits on access to firearms apparently connote impotence and perhaps castration. Capital punishment seems to evoke in some people highly gratifying sadism and the abolition of capital punishment an intolerable restriction on the gratification. These are examples of recurring political issues that consistently arouse peculiarly intense emotional concomitants in some. They are revealing in that they make it clear that language is not an independent variable but a catalyst in the shaping of perception; for those whose ego needs require a particular metaphoric evocation, even "straight" language is metaphoric. More often, people can potentially see an issue in several alternative lights, and the language form itself evokes some one of the potentialities.

Commonly accepted assumptions about political reality and political cause and effect often consist of simplified or distorted perspectives embodied in metaphors; once one is alert to the hazard, each day's reports of political speeches, statements, and news events bring new and impressive examples. A politician more persuasively conveys a particular picture of reality when he simply assumes it in the terms he uses rather than asserting it explicitly. He may talk about the defense of freedom against Com-

---

[6] See Sapir, *Culture*, p. 36; Whorf, "Science and Linguistics." For an account of experimental research supporting this conclusion, see Roger Brown, *Social Psychology* (New York: Free Press, 1965), pp. 332–49.

[7] Sigmund Freud, *Jokes and Their Relation to the Unconscious* (New York: Norton, 1960). Norman Brown, for example, suggests that language is diseased in that it is the resultant of repression of the pleasure principle (as expressed in the lalling instinct in children) and the reality principle. In their emphasis upon language as a misleading medium, such students reach the same conclusions as the linguists and philosophers. See Brown, *Life against Death*, and La Barre, *The Human Animal*, p. 171. See also Heinz Werner, *Die Ursprünge der Metapher* (Drückert, 1919); Charles Morris, *Signs, Language and Behavior* (New York: Prentice-Hall, 1946), esp. pp. 210–11.

munist aggression from the north in Vietnam, conveying a picture of a gallant, freedom-loving people united in their resistance to a foreign invader. This is the model of reality that legitimizes American military action in Vietnam. To doves, on the other hand, Vietnam evokes a vision of historic disunity and recent civil warfare among the South Vietnamese, a general lack of concern with either the democratic or Communist ideologies as such, intense war weariness, and anti-American sentiment.

Similarly, references by high officials to encouraging turns in "the tide of battle" in Vietnam convey the image of a World War I trench battlefield on which it is possible neatly to plot military advances and retreats. A countermetaphorical view highlights the complex, quickly shifting guerrilla occupations and tactical withdrawals, often on a diurnal cycle; the kaleidoscope of localized wins and losses; the inability to know who is winning what for how long. In this view the one thing there clearly is not is a "tide." It therefore becomes all the more important to bolster civilian and soldier morale and political support by talking as though there is, and as though it has "turned." In contrast, opponents of the war describe the military action by concentrating on the bombing and napalming of apolitical women and children.

For the mind avid for benchmarks in a complex area, a vivid instance, real or hypothetical, supplies meaning and is readily taken as typical. When he is self-consciously acting in the role of scientist or in the role of adversary, a person raises questions about the typicality of such a case and looks for evidence; but he systematically avoids doing so when, in the role of spectator, he lacks counterevidence or any other guides to the situation and wants meaning rather than skepticism. This accepting response is greatly facilitated when the typicality of a particular perspective is simply assumed in a term or phrase. If an instance is explicitly asserted to be typical or salient, the very assertion brings it to the conscious attention of the audience for consideration and perhaps for argument, skeptical revision, or dismissal. Any political speech, then, evokes its most compelling cognitions in a large part of its audience (and in the speaker himself) through the metaphoric views it takes for granted rather than through those it explicitly asserts and calls to people's attention.

Such implicit metaphors recurring in the speech of political activists and spectators constitute behavioral evidence of norms. They might well be a particularly useful form of evidence when, as is often the case, governmental routines and pressure group activities systematically but ritualistically suggest that other, more widely acceptable norms, are shaping public policy. Overt signs of pluralism in policymaking, for example, may have to be interpreted in the light of evidence of deep-seated and widely held norms that systematically defeat some groups and strengthen others.

The metaphors are necessary to the self-conceptions and self-justifica-
tions of speaker and empathetic audience. Without them the dissonance
between beliefs about the world and beliefs about appropriate political
action becomes disturbing. This is typically not conscious deception. It is
more deep rooted, based on social role taking.

With respect to controversial issues in domestic politics, metaphors
also play their part in marshaling political support. Negroes riot in the
urban slums, and at once explanations are offered, beginning with the
McCone Report[8] on Watts, suggesting that the basic trouble is a combination of rural-bred, disoriented, and potentially violent black masses and outside agitators cunning at sabotaging the efforts of police and social workers
to maintain order and improve conditions. The McCone Report highlights
such phrases as "a devastating spiral of violence," "marauding bands," and
"the thin thread that enforces observance of law." To see the riots in this
light is to ignore pertinent political and economic characteristics of the real
world of the city slums. It is to focus attention upon alleged Negro character
traits and to blind oneself and one's audience to exploitation of Negroes in
housing, financing, retail sales, and employment, and to harassment and
violence against Negroes by nervous and frightened policemen. Again, it is
a question of which metaphorical world one inhabits. It is not chance that
the two worlds diverge as they do: The world of the McCone Report justifies the continuation of governmental favors to those with political bargaining power, and the world of its critics justifies a challenge to existing power
structures.

VALUE PREMISES IN POLITICAL METAPHORS

In the examples cited so far, metaphors achieved their effects chiefly
through shaping seemingly factual premises. A particular setting peopled
with characters with designated traits made a particular strategy for
achieving a desired future seem appropriate.

Political metaphors also create and filter out value premises. They
highlight the benefits that flow from a course of action and erase its un-
fortunate concomitants, helping speaker and listeners to conceal disturbing
implications from themselves. Making it easy for people to read their wish-
ful thinking into an ambiguous phrase in a a policy pronouncement may be
the most venerable political device extant. Ambiguous terms in a threatening context create a world from which painful, inconvenient facts are
excluded and in which self-serving courses of action are justified.

---

[8] Governor's Commission on the Los Angeles Riots, *Violence in the City*
(State of California, 1965).

The fashionable phrase "American presence" performs such a function. It suggests a friendly interest in a foreign land. But it usually means the stationing of military forces as a threat to indigenous political groups or to those in neighboring countries. References to "strike capacity"—which can be translated as power to kill people—provide another example of the metaphoric erasure of disturbing value premises.

The device is just as common in domestic politics. "Parity" has long evoked an image among political spectators of a fair distribution of costs and benefits among farmers and consumers; but it has legitimized a system of generous government subsidies to large commercial farms, little or no help for small family farms, and no effective protection for consumers. But who can oppose "parity"? It encourages quiescence among the mass public as effectively as it provides self-justification for the material beneficiaries of farm policies.

The "war on poverty" suggests massive mobilization against a universally hated enemy, and thereby helps win political support. It gives people the gratification of seeing themselves support a crusade against evil. It just as effectively enables them to ignore other values implicit in the program that are dominant in the metaphors of some of its critics: that major beneficiaries, so far, have been affluent recipients of public contracts; that the resources committed to the war have been too small to harass the enemy, much less win the war; that the war on poverty has become embroiled in political infighting and sometimes stalemated in city after city.

Arguing the need for "law and order," President Nixon made the following statement in a speech in South Dakota in 1969: "To those intoxicated with the romance of violent revolution, the continuing revolution of democracy may seem unexciting."[9] Like the other metaphors cited here as examples, the figures of speech in that sentence evoke a particular world for an audience whose anxieties have already made them eager to reconstruct the world in that image. Dissenters, violators of the property laws, and black and student demonstrators become transformed in this reconstructed world into "intoxicated" potential or actual violent revolutionaries. A regime perceived by some as repressively reinforcing the status quo and unresponsive to widespread demands for change becomes transformed in this reconstructed world into one that is so responsive ("democracy") that it is continuously revolutionizing itself. The essence of metaphor is that a part evokes a new whole. Political metaphors can vividly, potently, and pervasively evoke changed worlds in which the remedies for anxieties are clearly perceived and self-serving courses of action are sanctified.

In some measure, alternative metaphors compete to define particular

---

[9] *Vital Speeches* 35 (1968–69), 548.

political issues; but the metaphorical view that is officially disseminated usually enjoys a significant advantage. It is the first definition of the issue most people receive. In the degree that the mass public is anxious, it is eager to be reassured and to share the widely held view; the myth of the official leader as protector against enemies (analyzed later in this chapter) further encourages acceptance of the official view. The metaphor thus serves as a powerful legitimizer of established policies, helping forestall protests.

Once accepted, a metaphorical view becomes the organizing conception into which the public thereafter arranges items of news that fit and in the light of which it interprets the news. In this way a particular view is reinforced and repeatedly seems to be validated for those whose attitudes it expresses. It becomes self-perpetuating.

Political opposition frequently rallies around a competing metaphorical definition, of course. For those who accept it, this definition similarly becomes a continuing bulwark of conformity to the position of the group in question. Metaphors thus help all kinds of groups to believe that their political beliefs and loyalties are rational and to maintain them.

Occasionally, changes occur in the view that is most widely accepted. Such widespread change in the accepted metaphor usually seems to occur fairly quickly, as a result of a dramatic event: a Montgomery bus boycott, a stockmarket crash, a Pearl Harbor, the publication of *Uncle Tom's Cabin,* or the success of a Sputnik. A new source of threat, a new vision of future opportunities, or exposure to empirical evidence creates a new metaphor to focus perception and passions, and therefore creates the basis for a new political leadership and a new orthodoxy. Each of the events just listed signaled the culmination of a complex set of trends that had been in the making for a long time; the very fact that many people began to see them as politically significant only after a dramatic or shocking event occurred is further evidence of a rigidity in political opinion and attitude, encouraged by metaphorical viewing of the political scene. Such rigidity supports conformity to accepted positions and obliviousness to data suggesting the need for a change in orientation. It does so in part because the established view is infused with affect; the stability of counterviews reinforces the perception of threat and therefore, in circular fashion, increases the conformity on both sides.

LANGUAGE AND SOCIAL IDENTIFICATIONS

So intimately integrated are language and thought, so completely and subtly do they shape and signal each other, that language can be utilized as a sensitive empirical indicator of values and of social, organizational, and status identifications. Bureaucratic jargon is an especially revealing example of this linkage. It is often noticed, in jest and in despair, that the sentences in which staff members of large administrative organizations pretend to communicate with each other and with their clientele consist very largely of stale, stylized, and stereotyped phrases, clichés, and pseudotechnical terms for common referents. Such jargon is a remarkably inefficient medium for conveying facts, ideas, or instructions—so inefficient and ambiguous in its extreme forms that it approaches total meaninglessness. Why, then, is it so endemic in large organizations that it has become a symbol of them?

Part of the answer, certainly, is that bureaucratic jargon systematically communicates something necessary to the stability of status relationships and objectives of bureaucracies. Its ubiquity is not accidental, but functional. It conveys the message that its author has adapted himself to the goals and values of a particular organization and its leadership—that he is conforming and presents no risk of doing anything that will upset the established order or question its basic value premises. Through his stylized language form he is broadcasting the message that just as his words are banal, so his ideas are banal. His performance will be predictable and conventional; his loyalty and his support of authority are not in doubt. To the degree, moreover, that the audiences of messages in this language style take them straight, without irritation, blush, or protest, their acceptance signals the same meaning.[10] Hannah Arendt noticed that Adolf Eichmann expressed himself largely in clichés.[11] It seems reasonable, in the light of the considerations discussed here, that this linguistic inadequacy of Eichmann's was systematically related to his uncritical willingness to adapt himself to the goals of the bureaucratic organization of which he was a part and blind himself to the appalling value structure its policies reflected. The Eichmann case is an extreme one, but, like many polar cases, it reveals the significance of an element of normal behavior that is not readily apparent.

The converse also holds. To speak and write in fresh or unconventional terms while jargon swirls all about one in an organization is to state definitively that one is not buying the accepted values and not docilely conforming to authority. The difference in the two modes of expression is partly a question of how much information is conveyed. Jargon is largely ritualistic and predictable. Its audience gets no surprises. The ratio of information to number of words is low, for it consists chiefly of the ritualistic incantation of values, beliefs, and procedures that are accepted and es-

---

[10] George Orwell observed in a perceptive essay that political speech consists largely of stale phrases which dull the critical faculties of speaker and audience. See his "Politics and the English Language," in *A Collection of Essays* (New York: Doubleday, 1954), p. 172.

[11] *Eichmann in Jerusalem: A Report on the Banality of Evil* (New York: Viking, 1963), p. 63.

tablished. Its function is less to find optimal solutions to current problems than to promote the stability and integrity of the established organization.

The person who is searching for solutions to problems rather than reaffirming his organizational loyalty must communicate in language that is not ritualistic and has a high information content.[12] In large organizations it is assumed that some kinds of specialists will, in fact, behave and communicate in this way in their professional work in order to solve problems. It is also assumed, however, that in their nontechnical communications the same specialists will retreat to the accepted jargon, thereby reassuring their superiors that there is no threat to their status, that loyalty is the watchword. In solving technical problems the specialist can focus on the pertinent facts and use a language style, verbal or mathematical, that is appropriate for such focusing. In dealing with values he is expected to avoid independence and create a symbol of personal loyalty to the established order.[13]

Apart from the message it conveys, administrative jargon is a particularly striking illustration of the reflection of ambivalence in language. Like other metaphors, it masks what one does not wish to face. If bureaucrats deal with "personnel" rather than "people," they find it easier to deny their clientele's claims or to rebuff them, for the petitioners have become abstractions rather than humanity. If Pentagon pronouncements speak of structures in Vietnamese villages, people feel better than they would if they read that huts or houses were being destroyed. At a more basic level, administrative jargon helps its users and its audiences to avoid facing the fact of their uncritical acceptance of the organization's values and their unwillingness to assert their own values. Such political metaphor suppresses recognition of the reality of subservience or conformity while at the same time signaling the suppression.

Language styles serve in the same way to signal conformity or rebellion in social groupings generally, though the style that is banal in one group may be fresh and innovative in another. In any army barracks, the man who lards his speech with conventional profanity, slang army terms, complaints about army life, and fantasies about sexual exploits is signaling to his listeners that he is the conventional soldier, willing to play his assigned role and not likely to recognize it as corny, confining, or demeaning; but the college professor or student who uses the same style in class signals

---

[12] In a review of my book, *The Symbolic Uses of Politics* (*The Annals* 361 [September 1965], 142–43), Warren Bennis suggested that scientific language is a distinctive form of political language. His comment led me to the analysis in this section.

[13] On this point see Victor A. Thompson, *Modern Organization* (New York: Knopf, 1961), pp. 147–51.

himself a rebel against the established academic order. In a Rotary or Kiwanis meeting stylized jocularity and stereotyped, rhetorical questions and responses about business, the weather, one's family, one's sex life, and politics signal conformity. The Kiwanian who began talking in a sociologist's jargon would be regarded with surprise and suspicion, as is the sociologist who speaks clean prose.

Though people are not likely to be conscious of it, they accept language styles as signals of conformity or independence and play their own roles accordingly. Because the pressures are strong to conform to the conventional language style of whatever group one is in, innovative and rebellious behavior is rare. Ordinarily, people do not consciously decide against being innovative or rebellious. The language they speak makes it unlikely that they will even think of it. Their forms of expression both reflect and determine their personalities. The conforming bureaucrat thus has a message to convey that is incompatible with some of the strongest cultural norms—such as rugged individualism and self-reliance—and he is bound to be ambivalent about such hidden incompatibility. What most vividly characterizes his role, his identification with the parochial values and perspective of the particular organization or subunit of it, is exactly what he cannot explicitly proclaim. But he does it implicitly through his language style. He fills his sentences with peculiar terms that are more ambiguous than the common ones and that, at the same time, identify him as a member of a particular ingroup. The awkwardness in the style apparently evokes metaphorically the tension and anxiety in the organization, which are occasioned by the pervasiveness of role defenses and of trained incapacity to find innovative ways to achieve the organization's objectives or to question the objectives.

Noam Chomsky's distinction between surface structures and deep structures in grammar[14] furthers this form of analysis. Surface structures are phrasings a native speaker recognizes as grammatically correct (and which may or may not be meaningful). Deep structures are the meanings conveyed by surface structures. These need not correspond logically or by any rules we can identify to the phrasings, yet are suggested to all native speakers by particular phrasings. A wide range of alternative phrasings may convey the same meaning at the deep structural level. At issue in this conceptualization of grammatical forms is the link between mind and grammar.

The surface structure itself, as distinct from the conventional definitions of the words employed, conveys identifiable information peculiarly relevant to political conformity and opposition: information about statuses,

---

[14] Noam Chomsky, *Topics in the Theory of Generative Grammar* (Mouton, 1966); *Language and Mind* (Cambridge, Mass.: MIT Press, 1968).

value structures, and ideological bents of people who use language and of audiences who react to it. In particular geographical regions, at different educational levels, in particular bureaucratic organizations and social milieus, phrasings convey such information, as do inflection, intonation, stress, and other stylistic embellishments that vary with the subculture. By identifying and highlighting social roles these facets of surface structure subtly but very powerfully influence mass audiences and the willingness of mass publics to adopt or resist particular political positions. They can also serve as empirical indicators of the boundaries between insiders and outsiders.

Deep structures, precisely because they have no empirical form, can convey politically relevant meanings only through their content. Here the metaphoric and other symbolic references discussed earlier are in point. So are denotative references to politics, of course, but because these evoke *conscious* agreement or dissent, they are less potent.

The possibility of divergent, even conflicting, meanings arising simultaneously from these different structural levels in the same language manifestly helps account for political ambivalences, cognitive confusions, and ideological manipulability. It may also help people reconcile their behavior with incompatible norms, as it did at My Lai; for people are apparently highly self-manipulable as to the kind of meaning upon which they focus and can, moreover, focus vividly upon several incompatible meanings simultaneously.

FORMS OF MYTHIC EXPRESSION

The student of political language quickly notices a striking disparity between conceptions held by the mass public and those held by social scientists regarding the influences that determine policy formation. The public accepts relatively simple forms of explanation. Social scientists, however, know that decisions rest upon an enormously complex, largely unplanned, tangled web of factual and value premises coming from all levels of complex organizations; that early decisions in some measure predetermine later policy directions; that there are significant constraints upon the possibility of rationality and planning; that changing economic, diplomatic, or other conditions have an impact upon decisional premises that is largely unforeseeable.[15]

---

[15] For extended analysis and demonstration of these propositions, see James G. March and Herbert A. Simon, *Organizations* (New York: Wiley, 1958); Herbert Simon, *Administrative Behavior* (New York: Macmillan, 1947). See also Thompson, *Modern Organization*.

For amateur political spectators, a small number of classic themes or myths serve repeatedly as explanations of what is shaping the political scene. In contrast to the complicated network of competing influences in the empirical world, the world of the myths is simple: It revolves around hostile plotters and benevolent leaders, and both factions carefully plan the future and can shape it in accordance with their plans. The language of political discussion, analysis, and debate frequently evokes these themes by personifying observed, feared, or desired trends into plotters and heroes.

The myths frequently evoke a strong emotional response, seemingly disproportionate to what the observer would expect. This helps account for their ubiquity in political explanations. If a few classic themes are surefire vehicles for engaging the emotions of large numbers of people, leaders will predictably interpret events in these forms, and their audiences will eagerly cooperate in creating the world in the same configurations.

What are the themes? One of them is the evocation of an outgroup, defined as "different" and as plotting to commit harmful acts. There frequently seems to be a strong element of projection in the specification of the respects in which a particular outgroup is malevolent. Policemen who are bewildered, nervous, and sometimes trigger-happy in the urban ghetto define the slum dwellers as disoriented in the city and likely to resort to violence. Subliterate "poor whites" define the Negro as subhuman. Russians who are sympathetic to preventive warfare suspect the Americans of intending to strike first, and vice versa. Invaders of a foreign country perceive the enemy as aggressors. Even when there is no apparent projection involved, however, the outgroup is classically perceived as different, homogeneous, highly potent or omnipotent, and conspiring to harm the ingroup.[16] When such a myth is offered as an explanation, anxious people prove eager to organize their perceptions of the world so as to reinforce the myth, and often do so with intense fervor. It is not easy to find an issue about which there is strong and widespread political concern without encountering wide acceptance of some version of this theme as the explanation—consider inflation, labor relations, subversion, and so on.

A second stylized myth, consistently offered to reassure those who are frightened by the first, is the view that the political leader is benevolent and is effective in saving people from danger. I have analyzed in some detail elsewhere the evidence for the proposition that an incumbent political leader benefits from automatic ascriptions of virtues to him by political

---

[16] Kenneth E. Boulding makes essentially this point when he observes, "Nations are the creation not of their historians, but of their enemies" (*The Image: Knowledge in Life and Society* [Ann Arbor: University of Michigan Press, 1965], p. 114).

spectators if he acts decisively, even if unsuccessfully.[17] If he seems to display the qualities of courage, aggressiveness, and ability to cope, he becomes a reassuring symbol. The zeal with which this attachment to the head of government is asserted is often impressive. Russian peasants suffering from the oppressions of the czarist regime firmly believed that their torments were the result of the plotting of evil administrative officials but that the czar would disapprove and correct this state of affairs if he were only aware of it. One similarly often hears followers of any American President attributing policies of which they disapprove to the misguided policy predilections of subordinates. The intense and universal sense of shock occasioned by the death of an incumbent President further illustrates this myth. Like the myth of a plotting outgroup, a Presidential death or assassination evokes emotions out of all proportion to the demonstrable importance for national policy of the event in question. The deaths of Garfield and Harding occasioned intense shock as surely as the deaths of Lincoln and Roosevelt, and did so both for the deceased President's political opponents and for his supporters.

Corollary to both these themes is the belief that a group—a nation, a state, a party—can achieve victory over its enemies if it will only work, sacrifice, and obey its leaders. In the context of a sense of crisis, which is always present for many, this appeal evokes a strong and enthusiastic response, even—perhaps especially—when the exact nature of the work, the sacrifice, and the obedience is left unspecified. Kennedy played this theme with impressive success in his Inaugural Address when he said, "Ask not what your country can do for you. Ask what you can do for your country," and in other parts of the address reiterated it. Anxious populations seem to want fervently to be exposed to this appeal and so it predictably is offered to them.

Psychological explanations for the passion in political responses of these types have frequently been offered. Lasswell wrote of displacement of private affect upon public objects, rationalized in terms of the public interest.[18] Smith, Bruner, and White similarly found evidence of projection of internal tensions in some political opinions.[19] There is reason to suspect that oedipal repressions and sadomasochistic impulses help explain the strong affective responses to the stylized myths that dominate political discussion,

---

[17] Murray Edelman, *The Symbolic Uses of Politics* (Urbana: University of Illinois Press, 1964), chap. 4.

[18] Harold D. Lasswell, *Psychopathology and Politics* (New York: Viking, 1960), pp. 65–77.

[19] M. Brewster Smith, Jerome S. Bruner, and Robert W. White, *Opinions and Personality* (New York: Wiley, 1956).

for the mythical themes involve identification with a leader, suppression of enemies, and self-sacrifice.

This concurrence of a restricted range of emotions, of mythic perceptions, and of linguistic expressions reveals much about the psychodynamic process operative in political cognition. Recall the suggestion in the last chapter that such emotions as fear and anger occur together with perceptions of vulnerability, frustration, and dominance and with self-conceptions that rigidly limit the perceiver to a particular political role. Empirically, emotion, cognition, and sense of identity are part of the same transaction in such situations, each a signal that the others are also present. A person experiences them as separate, however, and social scientists are socialized to analyze them as though they were *empirically* distinct.

Their phenomenological separation has powerful consequences for cognition. To experience the perception, the emotion, the sense of one's political role, and the linguistic expression as if they were independent of each other is to avoid recognizing that perception is in fact distorted or grossly simplified by ego needs, by intense feeling, and by a metaphoric description of the facts. The political actor therefore feels reassured that his perception is accurate, and he is strengthened in his zeal to act appropriately. Language, thought, feeling, and personality formation are integrated; but the temptation both of the actor and of the social analyst to treat them separately is a major source of illusion.

In their polar forms the myths make the world meaningful and rationalize conformity for those least able to assert, express, and identify themselves through innovative behavior or demonstrated political efficacy. They catalyze uncritical attachment to established leaders, regardless of the particular policies they pursue.

It is more important, however, that the same stylized myths serve constantly to promote conformity and bolster leadership on specific issues even among those who are not blind followers on all issues. It is apparently possible for one to become bemused with myths of antisocial plots, and of courageous political stances against such plots, among proponents of Medicare, among oligopolistic sellers, among foreign or domestic Communists, or among motorcycle riders—even if one usually behaves skeptically and forms independent judgments respecting other policy areas. The question always is whether people are responding to the special stylized world that is created and given meaning by a collectively held myth, or whether they are trying, as individuals, to observe and to verify their perceptions through free empirical inquiry.

Plots do sometimes occur and leaders are sometimes effective in countering them. Political responses are frequently not based upon empirical observation or rational inference from the observations. There is a basic distinction between (1) dispassionate organization of data and (2) observation only to persuade oneself and others that preconceived worlds exist; the possibility of creating ardent followings through reliance upon the penchant of the anxious for organizing their perceptions in the form of these myths is a major fact of political life.

Myth can be explained as an externalization of inner impulses and tensions. They are converted into events outside ourselves as a form of catharsis and, more important, as a means of establishing communication and mutual support with others. As Bruner put it, "the externalization of inner impulse in the form of myth provides the basis for a sharing of inner experience and makes possible the work of art that has as its objective to contain and cleanse the terror from impulse."[20] A shared belief in a plotting enemy, a benevolent and competent hero-leader, and a public willing to work, sacrifice, and conform to assure the victory of the right and the good enables people suffering from diverse sources of inner anxiety to assure each other that the fault is not their own but that of an identifiable enemy, and to reassure each other that the leader will save them if they will follow him. To become attached to this myth is, then, to assume a particular political identity or role: the uncritical follower. Because the myth is a means of succor against severe anxiety, it is strongly embraced and defended, and so it becomes the mold into which perceptions of political developments are organized. As its chief terms are unobservable motives, intentions, traits, and cause-effect assumptions, observation cannot disprove it, but can provide material that is perceived as evidence for its validity. Political leaders can, therefore, rely upon the ubiquity of anxiety and its externalization in the myth as an ever-present base for a following. By the same token, anxiety readily converts even implicit and metaphoric references to mythic themes into vivid and intensely held beliefs.

RHETORICAL EVOCATIONS

The successful politician is likely to employ particular linguistic devices to reinforce the myth, and especially to reinforce a popular belief in his ability to cope successfully with the exigencies of political life. A common device is the grandiloquent speech, ringing with memorable but ambiguous phrases. The audience is encouraged to realize its sometimes desperate wish to entrust responsibility to someone who can cope by finding in the striking rhetoric an assurance of clearsightedness and determination. Not everyone

---

[20] Bruner, "Myth and Identity," p. 286.

can say, "All we have to fear is fear itself," or "Ask not what your country can do for you. Ask what you can do for your country." When a head of state presents himself as the uncommon man who does find the striking phrase, he encourages his listeners to trust and follow him, both through his style and through what he says.

Phrases like these appeal to deep-seated and widely shared anxieties and impulses, such as the fear of personal responsibility and the wish to rely upon someone else to overcome the sources of threats; the need to be reassured that one's personal anxieties are also experienced by many others; the masochistic focusing on the nation as the symbol for which the individual enjoys making sacrifices and experiencing deprivations. Because such phrases do appeal to these strong anxieties, people are moved by them. They have no concrete referents, but they permit people to read into them what they keenly want to believe.

Still another reason for the intensity of the emotional charge such phrases carry probably lies in their syntactical form. Word orders like "Ask not what. . . ." are not used in ordinary conversation or even ordinary speechmaking. We associate the unusual deployment of verb, adverb, and accusative pronoun with biblical language and with eloquent oratory of the past, and we respond to the poetry of these associations.

Another classic rhetorical gambit is the public exhortation to sinners to turn to virtue. Heads of state and budget ministers appeal to management and labor to exercise restraint in raising wages and prices. The President appeals to Negroes in urban slums to avoid violence. This appeal carries many political advantages and offers few risks. The nature of its tie to public opinion and response is worth examining.

When making such public appeals, a politician's real audience is always much wider than his ostensible audience. When the President says he is addressing union and management officials, he is actually telling all consumers that he is espousing their interests against the threat of inflation. When in form his words are addressed to blacks, he is in fact reassuring all who fear violence that he stands with them.

To most of his audience he seems to be battling heroically for virtue against a visible enemy; but both the heroism and the battling evaporate when one examines the response of its *ostensible* audience, the allegedly sinning groups, to this form of speech. For one thing, they oppose the vice, too. Union and management officials recognize inflation as undesirable and hazardous and, like everyone else, in principle they applaud governmental efforts to avoid it. Like everyone else, however, they are ambivalent when those efforts touch the price of whatever it is they sell: their labor or goods. Similarly, urban Negroes are, for the most part, ambivalently favorable to an abstract argument against violence.

Exhortation, moreover, frequently carries the implicit message that only words and not forceful actions are being employed. When an official simply appeals to labor and management to show restraint, he is telling them that the decision is really theirs, not his, and this is a welcome and reassuring message.

Still other implicit, though misleading, messages are involved in a high public official's exhortations. His appeal misleadingly pinpoints the source of danger, ascribing it to a relatively small group. By personifying the threat, he appeals to the strong temptation already noted among anxious people to see conspiracies rather than complex causes.

Even more clearly he conveys a fictional impression of his own ability to help. His appeal is an implied assertion that he is keeping matters under surveillance and that he is a potent force for changing the plotters' behavior. Actually, the appeal is inevitably without effect where complex social and economic forces are at work. Exhortations for wage-price restraint are notoriously futile, and so are appeals to restive slum dwellers to respect law and order. Those who fear inflation or urban violence see the "virtuous" official, however, as their instrument for bringing about the state of affairs they want. The effect is to channel the anxieties of political spectators into hostility toward some individuals and political support for others, while the fundamental causes of the anxieties remain unexamined.

Both the ambiguous, grandiloquent political speech and the public exhortation to virtue encourage people to indulge their already strong impulses to avoid examining issues and to trust in an official leader. They distract attention from group conflict and focus it upon a personality, thereby hopefully bringing support—even from many opponents of the leader's stand on the issues. When he cannot avoid taking a clear position on a controversial issue, the incumbent official must be even more sensitive to public impressions of his ability to cope and to win. He must look potent, not stalemated. The shrewd official squarely espouses a controversial position only after he is fairly sure his position will win—after others have fought the battle through its uncertain earlier stages. Its political benefits flow less from the tangible benefits accruing to the winners on the issue than from the dramatic demonstration that the leader has matters in hand. The winnings are frequently tokens, in any case, so far as most of the voters are concerned.

It is no accident that William Jennings Bryan's celebrated "cross of gold" speech, which did take an unequivocal—and losing—stand on a passionately fought issue, was delivered by a challenger for power, not an incumbent. When a politician takes a clear stand upon an issue that so divides the country that it is doubtful he can win, his speech further polarizes public opinion. It intensifies the feelings of both his supporters and his opponents and it induces the apathetic and the fencesitters to join the fray. It therefore produces the opposite effect from that classically sought by incumbent officials, who do better when they promote consensus through ambiguous formulation of the issues and when they help the mass public to escape from wrestling with the issues and to play follow-the-leader. In a contest between a challenger who polarizes opinion on a key issue and an incumbent, the cards are heavily stacked in favor of the latter. Even as eloquent a challenger as William Jennings Bryan is likely to lose at this game. An incumbent is more effectively discredited when the public comes to believe he is unable to cope, not when the public is led to believe he copes effectively in what an articulate critic considers the wrong direction. Through their failure to understand this crucial fact, political challengers frequently enhance the public support of their incumbent opponents, even as they attack them.

There is, then, a systematic though unplanned dissemination of illusion and ambiguity through the language of government. To a striking extent we choose our significant political symbols and stances in a world of metaphorical and mythical cues. Because the political perspectives we create systematically take particular forms, their consequences for political institutions and political behavior also systematically take particular forms.

The causes and remedies of the depressions, inflations, wars, and riots that threaten the world are complex and they hinge upon the small and large decisions of vast numbers of people. Myths and metaphors permit men to live in a world in which the causes are simple and neat and the remedies are apparent. In place of a complicated empirical world, men hold to a relatively few, simple, archetypal myths, of which the conspiratorial enemy and the omnicompetent hero-savior are the central ones. In consequence, people feel reassured by guidance, certainty, and trust rather than paralyzed by threat, bewilderment, and an unwanted personal responsibility for making judgments.

Men's need to believe that their top officials can cope supplies reassuring meanings for ambiguous political phrases and provides personal followings, and so creates and sustains leaders. Charismatic leadership becomes a frequent possibility and a source of political stability in spite of failure and unrealized promises and hopes.

Together, these consequences of the language of politics often mean ineffective use of the energy devoted to public affairs and a bias toward continuing conformity to the norms, values, and goals of particular groups.

Chapter 6

· MASS TENSIONS

Data on racial tensions are available in abundance, and more can readily be found or generated. The problem is how to learn from them the character of the social-psychological and political processes that explain political arousal and quiescence. Chapters 1–5 offer a general explanation. The present chapter weaves back and forth between that explanation and data on particular instances of militance among the poor and the black, recent and not so recent, with a view to identifying meaningful patterns in relevant events and so elaborating the explanation.[1]

An observed sequence of social events and behaviors is, from an analyst's perspective, an amalgam of diverse social-psychological responses to different kinds of cues. The challenge is to identify and sort out the specific dynamic processes that explain the outcomes. This in turn involves mutual enrichment of theory and empirical observations: rearrangement of the observations so that they most neatly fit the theoretical categories, most sharply throw light upon the processes at work, and so refine and elaborate the explanations. Unless an analyst of complex semantic and emotional communications among political groups explicitly recognizes the focus upon explanation as primary and the analysis of empirical observations as a necessary means, his descriptions of observed sequences of behaviors or of other empirical observations will too easily postulate a mythical explanation.

Lévi-Strauss has provided one ingenious model of the necessary procedure in this sorting out of the diverse themes in myths: a sorting that violates the time sequences and the plots of the myths as stories but that facilitates identification of the meanings, psychological needs, and psychological effects involved in the perpetuation of the myths.[2] This chapter and the next place illustrative historical data, case studies, perceptions by observers in disparate statuses and settings, and some findings of survey and

---

[1] Eugene Meehan, *Explanation in Social Science: A System Paradigm* (Homewood, Ill.: Dorsey Press, 1968).

[2] Claude Lévi-Strauss, *Structural Anthropology* (New York: Basic Books, 1968), pp. 206–31.

laboratory studies into what are hopefully appropriate conceptual categories in the light of relevant theory, and at the same time try to refine the categories and their functions in the light of empirical observations. Evaluation of this enterprise must lie ultimately in how well the explanations fit future developments and in the conclusions of readers about the utility of the explanations it suggests and the additional hypotheses it generates.

The plan of these two chapters is to consider in turn the bearing upon political arousal and violence of: particular patterns of objective conditions; the evocation of diverse perceptions; the acceptance of political myths and associated political roles; organization and leadership patterns; the mobilization of public support; and the conditions under which violence is precipitated.

OBJECTIVE CONDITIONS

To recognize that it is the meaning to human minds of politically relevant situations and conditions, rather than their physical or objective characteristics, that influences political behavior is in no way to deny the central importance of such situations and conditions. Particular economic and social statuses catalyze particular interpretations of political acts and language. A mayor's declaration that he will employ whatever force is necessary to maintain law and order may be regarded among blacks and many upper middle class whites as a portent of racism and repression and by lower middle class whites as a signal that criminal lawless elements will be justly dealt with and democracy encouraged. Words and things, observable conditions and unobservable evocations, shape each other. The question is how far we can go in identifying the processes through which the mutual shaping occurs and the aspects of the interaction that are systematic.

Consider first what we know about the personal and demographic characteristics influencing militance and quiescence among blacks. The typical rioter in the sixties

> was a teenager or young adult, a lifelong resident of the city in which he rioted, a high school drop-out—but somewhat better educated than his Negro neighbor—and almost invariably under-employed or employed in a menial job. He was proud of his race, extremely hostile to both whites and middle class Negroes and, though informed about politics, highly distrustful of the political system and of political leaders.[3]

_____
[3] _Report of the National Advisory Commission on Civil Disorders_ (New York: Bantam, 1968), p. 111 (hereinafter cited as Kerner Commission report).

As for some pertinent beliefs and attitudes of the rioter, he feels he deserves a better job but is barred from it, believes blacks are in some respects superior to whites, is extremely hostile to whites, and is almost equally hostile toward middle class Negroes. The hostility, however, is more likely to stem from his social and economic class than from his racial identification. Rioters are substantially better informed about politics than nonrioters and highly distrustful of political leaders and of the political system.[4]

The striking pattern in this profile is the combination in the rioter, as against the uninvolved, of better education and better information about politics with underemployment and demeaning status. This is manifestly the combination of conditions that can be expected to produce a strong sense of relative deprivation; the attitudinal aspects of the profile reflect this sense. One would also expect these conditions to be reflected in hostility to all who are perceived as less deprived, whether black or white; and this too is the pattern that emerges.

The characteristics of counter-rioters fit this thesis. They combine better education with higher incomes than those received by *either* the rioters or the uninvolved,[5] so that there is little gap between expectations and perceptions of benefits actually received.

Cognitions, however, are rarely simple reflections of some one or two objective conditions. The conditions themselves become symbolic of beliefs about the past or the future or of beliefs about a different facet of the present. Though counter-rioters sense little deprivation, no particular combination of conditions can be counted on always to yield this cognitive outcome. On the contrary, the studies consistently show that the ghetto residents with better educations and better incomes have *supported* the riots in high proportions.

Color and economic status, both highly salient in American society, inevitably have an intimate bearing upon what it is that objective conditions come to symbolize. The underemployed and those employed at menial jobs, it has already been noticed, resent and distrust all with higher status, black and white; their sense of deprivation is fundamentally a *class* perception. Blacks with relatively good educations and relatively high incomes are likely to take whites with roughly similar educations and incomes as their reference groups: to expect the kind of treatment these whites receive and to perceive themselves as deprived in the measure that their status falls below this expectation. For most of them *color* is evidently a more salient basis for a perception of relative deprivation than income or education. A minority nonetheless become counter-rioters.

---

[4] Ibid., pp. 128–29.
[5] Ibid., pp. 111–12.

One study that investigated the relationship between contact with whites (social distance) and riot support and participation confirms and elaborates this conclusion. When appropriate controls (for socioeconomic position and life style) were employed, no relationship appeared between riot support and contact with white persons. This finding suggests again that it is the interpretation placed upon contact or lack of it, not its objective existence, that matters. One combination of conditions that apparently does give such contact some degree of systematic meaning is high social distance coupled with a high socioeconomic level, as the foregoing theory would suggest. The study found that only where this combination existed was there a significant relationship between social distance and participation in riots.[6]

Some empirical findings about the influence of education and of employment status upon Negroes' perceptions of discrimination throw further light upon the subtle links between reality testing and personality needs as elements in perception. Well-educated blacks are more likely than others to perceive police malpractices and discrimination against Negroes; but educational level is not significantly linked with consumer discontent.[7] Employed blacks feel more discrimination than the unemployed; but employment status is not significantly linked with either perception of police malpractice or consumer discontent.[8] These data suggest (1) that relatively good education increases sensitivity to discrimination more effectively than being employed, though both these statuses have that effect in some measure; and (2) we can identify a gradation of forms of perceived discrimination according to ease of perception; as we move from consumer discontent to police malpractice to racial discrimination it becomes increasingly easy to perceive the discrimination. Both employment and better education increase perception of discrimination against blacks; only better education increases perception of police malpractice; and neither leads to significantly greater sensitivity to discrimination in treatment of consumers. As there clearly is significant discrimination of all three types, the differences in perceptions seem to hinge not only upon the increased *expectations* produced by employment and education, but also upon ease of objective discrimination. In this respect the data confirm what one might reasonably expect. It is in fact hardest to know when a consumer is being discriminated against, though careful studies do show that the poor and the black "pay

[6] Raymond J. Murphy and James N. Watson, "The Structure of Discontent: The Relationship between Social Structure, Grievance, and Support for the Los Angeles Riot" (Los Angeles: University of California, 1962, mimeographed), pp. 103–4.

[7] Ibid., p. 63.

[8] Ibid., p. 63.

more."[9] Discrimination against blacks as a generic practice is easily identified, and so it is hardly surprising that education and higher socioeconomic
status increase sensitivity to it. Police malpractice clearly falls between the
two, requiring some study to confirm it, yet easier for the layman to perceive
than discrimination against consumers. Though the extant studies afford
this insight into the links between objective ease of perception and psychological need for perceiving discriminations, the particular areas of discrimination to which these data apply are certainly illustrative rather an exhaustive.

The linkages between objective demographic differences and perceptions of discrimination are certainly systematic, but also complex and
subtle, as some other kinds of data suggest. One study found that 36 percent of the nonwhite males in the $6,000 to $10,000 income range thought
the police in their neighborhoods were "almost all honest" while 21 percent
thought they were "almost all corrupt." For white males the corresponding
figures were 65 percent ("almost all honest") and 2 percent ("almost all
corrupt").[10] On both logical and empirical grounds it is evident that these
diverse perceptions must be based largely on something other than empirical observation and verification. There might, of course, have been some
observations of instances of police corruption, but these manifestly cannot
verify conclusions about "almost all" policemen either way. It is also likely
that blacks have more opportunity than whites to observe and hear accounts
of such instances. Clearly, then, the color of the observer was significantly
associated with the probability of a particular perception on this point,
partly on empirical grounds and chiefly through social cuing.

The same analysis applies to the finding that 17 percent of nonwhite
males in the same income bracket believed "the police did a 'very good' job
in protecting people in their neighborhoods, as opposed to 51 percent of
the white males of similar income,"[11] and also to the finding that Negroes
were more than three times as likely as whites to complain of being over-
charged in neighborhood stores.[12] In these cases the empirical component
of the cognition was very likely more salient; there is abundant evidence

---

[9] David Caplovitz, *The Poor Pay More* (New York: Free Press, 1963).
[10] President's Commission on Law Enforcement and Administration of
Justice, *Criminal Victimization in the United States: A Report of a National
Survey* (by Phillip H. Ennis) (1967), p. 57.
[11] Ibid., p. 54.
[12] Angus Campbell and Howard Schuman, "Racial Attitudes in Fifteen
American Cities," in *Supplemental Studies for the National Advisory Commission on Civil Disorders* (Washington, D.C.: U.S. Government Printing Office,
1968), pp. 44–45 and Table IV-k.

that police do protect white neighborhoods more zealously and that stores in the ghetto charge higher prices than the supermarkets most whites patronize.

Yet color is not the only significant factor in such perceptions. Young black people are much more likely to perceive police actions as prejudicial than older people are; but so are white youths as compared to older whites.[13] Here again, the perception is based upon both the greater sensitivity of the younger generation to discrimination and upon the greater likelihood that police will choose young people as the targets of discriminatory action. Manifestly, the cases cited here are only illustrative of a much larger class of actions and perceptions characterized by this same mix of empirical and nonempirical cuing.

Such cases help illuminate a fundamental social psychological process. Both the selection of empirical observations by participants (on both sides) in these encounters and the generation and acceptance of nonempirical signals reflect a patterned evolution in role playing and an escalation of conflict. When police actions, for example, provide empirical evidence for a belief that policemen discriminate against the black and the young, they create in the targets of their acts an expectation of continued and increased discrimination. The latter accordingly have wider and stronger support from others to behave in precisely the provocative ways which the police expect of them. By the same token the police have greater incentive and support for conforming to the role expected of *them*. In this way escalating expectations generate different perceptions in the adversary groups and quite different norms about what is proper and what is rational. The perceptions do not stem from the innate characteristics of the individuals who hold them, but rather from an identifiable and systematic form of social encounter.

All the studies find a strong relationship between age and approval of the riots. Young people are both more likely to participate in a riot and more likely to look upon rioting with favor, and this is true for both blacks and whites. One study notices a suggestive coincidence of responses:

> Youth apparently has the same effect as greater education in making the riots seem to be purposive protests rather than simply episodes of mass criminal activity . . . among teenagers and also among college graduates at older age levels, about the same proportion of whites and Negroes perceive the riots as protests. The young and the better educated of both races converge in their perceptions of the basic character of the riots.[14]

---

[13] Ibid., p. 43 and Tables IV-h and IV-j.

[14] Ibid., p. 50.

One study of the Watts riot found nonetheless that age apparently did not correlate significantly with a belief that the riot helped the Negro cause.[15] Both these findings suggest that for young people the decision to riot and support rioters is in part at least an expression of life style: an existential declaration of identity and of a form of sublimation less likely to occur among older people. This view is, of course, not incompatible with the position that relative deprivation is basic. It rather helps us understand how the age factor qualifies behavior and attitudes once a sense of deprivation is present. In any case all the riots have revealed, as one of their facets, some appeal as a sport: an opportunity for the rioters to behave without regard to some of the customary rules and to exhibit prowess in such behavior. It is strikingly clear to the rioters which rules are being temporarily discarded and what kinds of new rules are in force. For some participants riots may be partly a sport, but they are not breakdowns of all social constraints.

The perception among young people and the better educated that riots are protests rather than mass criminality, nihilism, or subversive plot can most parsimoniously be explained as a reflection of the relative freedom of both these groups from nonempirically based beliefs as explanations of riot behavior. The educated have been taught some of the relevant facts and so are, hopefully, closer to verifiable reality. The young have not been socialized into the mythic beliefs as long or as intensively as their elders, and in the 1960s have felt themselves deprived by the elite of cherished values, making them empathetic to the protests of other groups deprived of more material benefits.

Riot support or participation is, however, both a mode of self-expression and a source of self-definition, particularly for the young. To participate in a riot is dramatically to make the point, both to oneself and to others, that one no longer accepts the subordinate role and status defined for blacks by the prevailing belief in a symbiotic social order. Even while serving this function, riot participation realistically takes account of the objective limits upon behavior imposed by relative access to weapons and relative social support. The selectivity in the kinds of white property attacked inside the ghetto, the substantial concentration upon the destruction of symbols of the ghetto itself rather than of outside persons or property, and the relatively short time duration of the riots all reflect these constraints. To remain within them also serves to make "defeat" impossible. For the blacks themselves, as for whites, the very least the riot can mean is that Negroes are not behaving subserviently according to the accepted expectations of the elite and those who identify with them.

---

[15] Murphy and Watson, "Structure of Discontent," p. 82.

Additional insight into the effects of objective conditions upon perception of a partly ambiguous situation can be gained from survey research into Negro beliefs as to whether they have failed to share in progress. Combining some of the results of two Louis Harris polls[16] produces the following data showing the percentages of Negroes who believed they had failed to share in progress:

Non-South, low income (i.e.,
   from the ghettos):   20 percent "worse"
                              37 percent "same"
National totals: 5 percent "worse"
                              23 percent "same"

The discrepancy between the beliefs of blacks living in the ghettos and those living elsewhere is even greater than these figures indicate, for the national totals include the respondents from the ghettos. As suggested in chapter 2, this discrepancy tells us something crucial about the limits of socially cued perceptions. People who do not live in the ghetto are influenced largely by news of the enactment and occasional enforcement of civil rights and antipoverty programs. For ghetto residents unambiguous experiences with housing, jobs, consumer practices, police practices, and so on are typically more compelling sources of cognitions than the symbol of progress the federal legislation represents. In the sixties their cumulative effect began to peak for many blacks; the evidence appears both in their mass behavior and in their individual responses in surveys. The number of blacks expressing a feeling of powerlessness to influence the government increased 20 percent between 1966 and 1968.[17]

In identifying the range of functions riots serve for blacks, it is useful to bear in mind that there are always counterpulls and some measure of ambivalence. Human beings do not shift their perspectives completely and cleanly. Survey research inevitably produces less contingent responses than depth studies reveal; but even the surveys of black attitudes toward the riots show striking ambivalence in the respondents. One study summarized some of the evidence for such ambivalence:

> According to the opinion surveys, the black community's attitude towards rioting is ambivalent. Of the Negroes in Los Angeles interviewed by U.C.L.A.'s Institute of Government and Public Affairs in 1965, only one-third favored the rioting, yet

---

[16] Based upon *Newsweek* (August 22, 1966) and William Brink and Louis Harris, *Black and White* (Simon and Schuster, 1967), p. 230, Appendix D, Table 1(c).

[17] Jerome S. Skolnick, *The Politics of Protest* (New York: Ballantine Books, 1969), p. 207.

two-thirds believed that it would increase the white's awareness and sympathy and improve the Negro's position; only one-eighth thought that violent protest was the Negro's most effective weapon, yet two-thirds believed that the riots had a purpose and five-sixths that the victims deserved their treatment; three-fourths preferred negotiations and nonviolent protests, yet only one-fourth believed that there would be no more riots in Los Angeles. Of the blacks interviewed across the nation by Louis Harris and Associates in 1966, 68 percent felt that Negroes stood to lose by the rioting; yet 34 percent thought that it has helped their cause, 20 percent that it has hurt, and 17 percent that it has made no difference; 59 percent were confident that Negroes will win their rights without violence, but 21 percent were convinced that violence will be necessary and 20 percent were not certain; in any event, 61 percent predicted that there will be further rioting, 31 percent were not sure, and 8 percent predicted that there will be no riots in the future.[18]

The fact of ambivalence hardly lessens the significance of the wide difference in attitudes and behavior that correlates with color. If both races are ambivalent, it is with a radically different mix of cognitions. According to the Murphy-Watson study of Los Angeles, 74 percent of the whites thought the riot would hurt the Negro cause, 19 percent that it would help. Among the Negroes 43 percent of the men and 35 percent of the women thought it would help and 20 percent that it would hurt.[19] Similarly, in a study done for the Kerner Commission, 60 percent of the white sample but only 18 percent of the Negroes perceived a rise in anti-Negro sentiment as a consquence of the riots of 1967.[20]

The underlying circumstances for such significant differences have already been explored. A closer look at some of the objective conditions that help explain *white* cognitions is now in order. Two of the most influential conditions, age and educational level, have some of the same effects upon the cognitions of whites as they do upon the cognitions of blacks. The study for the Kerner Commission of "Racial Attitudes in Fifteen American Cities" found a clear and consistent tendency

for the younger age cohorts to express a stronger appreciation of the discrimination to which Negroes are subject and to accept the presumption that Negro disadvantages in jobs, education and housing are primarily the result of this discrimination. The folk belief that Negroes "are born that way and can't be changed" is

---

[18] Robert M. Fogelson and Robert B. Hill, "Who Riots? A Study of Participation in the 1967 Riots," in *Supplemental Studies*, p. 242.

[19] Murphy and Watson, "Structure of Discontent," p. 37.

[20] Campbell and Schuman, "Racial Attitudes," p. 49.

accepted by very few people but by a much larger proportion of older people than younger.[21]

Among whites above the age of fifty, where this last belief is most prevalent, about twice as many men as women think Negroes are born inferior and cannot be changed.[22] This disparity by sex within the older group may well reflect a stronger feeling of threat from blacks among the men and a consequent stronger need to define blacks as inferior and thereby rationalize repression and discrimination.

The same survey found a consistent, though less marked, tendency for younger white people to react more favorably than their elders to a series of proposals to improve the conditions of urban Negroes: governmental action to provide jobs, improve schools, improve slum housing, increase spending and taxes to help Negroes, and otherwise improve conditions for Negroes.[23]

In young people, but much less clearly in whites over forty, college education produces significantly more support for egalitarian norms. Campbell and Schuman conclude:

> (1) In the older generation educational level has a consistently weaker relationship to racial attitudes that it has in the younger generation, and (2) in the younger generation attitudes of people of various educational levels below college do not vary greatly but there is a strong swing among college people toward clearer recognition of racial discrimination, greater acceptance of racial integration, and stronger support of Negro civil rights.[24]

Most of the educated people probably grew up in middle class families in which egalitarian norms and beliefs were voiced ambivalently by their parents and received with much less ambivalence by the children.

Negro geographic and occupational mobility has been a particularly critical influence upon the cognitions of white people by creating or reinforcing expectations of a new pattern of black political and economic threat to established status relationships. In 1919, 81 percent of American Negroes lived in the states of the Old Confederacy. By 1960 the figure was 52 percent, and there were fourteen metropolitan areas with Negro populations of between 200,000 and 1,500,000. This migration was especially heavy in the 1950s and the first half of the 1960s. Together with public policies in the fields of civil rights, welfare, and police administration it

---

[21] Ibid., p. 31.
[22] Ibid., p. 32, Table III-g.
[23] Ibid., p. 38.
[24] Ibid., p. 35.

evoked the diverse sets of perceptions and beliefs that have fueled the racial conflict and urban riots of the sixties.

Mobility probably functioned as an even more direct stimulus in the earlier period of riots initiated by attacks on Negroes by whites. In his analysis of the riots of this genre in East St. Louis in 1917, Chicago in 1919, and Detroit in 1943, Rudwick documents the steep increases in the black populations of each of those communities in the years immediately preceding the riots.[25] In the minds of working class whites the population trend lines apparently threaten to extend into a future characterized by black political domination and Negro takeovers of their jobs. An increase between 1940 and 1960 of the proportion of the Negro population in the middle class from 5 to 25 percent aggravated these fears in whites, even while it created resentment by lower class Negroes of the enlarged black middle class and thereby intensified the identity problems of blacks. For lower class blacks the key dimension in such circumstances is apparently class; for lower class whites it is race; for both it certainly moves between one and the other as new cues and symbols evoke different perceptions of future threat. The possibility of mobilizing mass support for hostile gestures and actions is therefore strengthened.

Where white aggression against blacks has occurred in America, a shared fear of job displacement or of another specific economic or political threat to the whites has consistently been present, although the concrete threat is also consistently translated into a more widely evocative vision of race war or degradation of the social order. A manifest difference either in color or in subculture apparently changes economic competition that occurs regularly in many contexts, and that is ordinarily perceived in highly realistic terms, into a myth of manichean confrontation. This is a pattern that has early roots in American economic history. Competition for work on the riverboats between blacks and Irish immigrants led to violent rioting in Cincinnati in 1862, and less severe riots occurred during the Civil War in Newark, Buffalo, and Troy. Hostility to the war and the manifest example of civil conflict the war presented apparently helped suggest the violent form which the economic conflict would take and probably deepened the conflict as well.

In East St. Louis in 1917 white riots against blacks occurred in a context both of job threat and of fears that the large influx of Negroes from the South was a plot to take over control of the Republican Party in the area.[26] Other examples of the pattern can be found in this and the

---

[25] Elliot Rudwick, *Race Riot at East St. Louis, July 2, 1917* (Carbondale: Southern Illinois University Press, 1964), pp. 3–17.

[26] Ibid., pp. 10–15.

next chapter. Such a sense of economic or political threat is spread through reference groups, even when a local economic conflict is a general and persistent issue and not centered upon a particular plant or employer, or upon a particular point in time. As such it helps explain mass support of whites for repressive police measures in those riots in which it is chiefly blacks who destroy property, as in the ghetto riots of the sixties.

Sometimes threatening economic conditions create sufficient fear of the future to evoke rioting against symbols of authority even when physical or cultural differences in a target group do not help define another mass public as the enemy. Generalizing from his careful historical study of crowd behavior, Rudé defines the necessary conditions for the occurrence of food riots. He concludes that food riots were consistently the direct product of price rises and shortage of food stocks, especially during a trade depression. They do not necessarily occur when prices reach a peak. What is critical, rather, is a sudden sharp upward movement in food prices, leading to panic buying and shortages.[27] In this situation, too, expectations seem to become alarming faster than objective conditions do. The dramatic threatening trend, in a context of anxiety, is projected into a disastrous future. In consequence riots against food stores or the government occur. A faceless enemy manifesting himself through sharp increments in alarming trends is apparently as threatening as a specific enemy with alien physical or cultural traits.

Barrington Moore has offered a hypothesis about revolt that helps place many of these observations about the function of objective conditions into perspective. He suggests that breakup of daily routines contributes to susceptibility to mobilization for revolt.[28] The theory offered here helps explain this effect. It is apparent that daily routine involves a focus of attention on the banal elements in the environment. Such a focus both reflects and encourages the expectation that the adjustment one has made and the status he accepts will continue. A change in routines, especially if it occurs suddenly, evokes anxiety about future status and threats. Sudden food shortages and price rises, a rapid immigration of blacks, new behaviors and values in college students, rioting by police: all of these dramatically destroy old and comforting banalities and create anxious uncertainty that threats will continue to be limited and achieved statuses honored.

Consistent with this view, Moore further suggests that participants in riots and revolution seem more strongly motivated by threats to their

<hr />

[27] George F. Rudé, *The Crowd in History* (New York: Wiley, 1964).

[28] Barrington Moore, Jr., "Revolution in America," *New York Review of Books* 12 (January 30, 1969), 6–12.

interests as consumers than by threats to their interests as producers. The opposite, I suggest, is true so far as mobilizability for *ritualized* conflict is concerned. Workers, corporate managements, physicians, and other organized groups grow restive and actively seek new forms of accommodation with each other when their interests as producers are threatened. Indeed, it has become a commonplace of social science theory in analyzing political conflicts of this latter kind that it is difficult or impossible to organize people to promote their interests as consumers.

The critical difference lies in the symbolic meaning of the activity, for the two modes of mobilizing people involve the difference between a focus upon status and a focus upon money. Where money underlies the interest groupings, the producer role is crucial. Serious, new, and seemingly long-term and cumulative threats to consumer interests, however, come to be perceived as status degradation, making accommodation through negotiation impossible and escalation of conflict likely.

PERCEPTION

Though particular objective conditions influence the forms perceptions take, the link between the two is far too complex to express as a simple cause-effect tie. Further examination of the forms particular selective perceptions have taken in the process of escalation of political conflict reveals something of (1) the characteristics and forms myths regularly take; (2) the links between the formation of crowds and the growth among their members of common cognitions; and (3) the resort to forms of behavior that purport to deal with "realities" but serve to reinforce mythical perceptions.

Perhaps the fundamental tendency in political perception is to attribute unwelcome developments to the deliberate planning of particular people. Regardless of the character of the psychic appeal of such beliefs, they unify disorganized masses politically. Every daily newspaper offers examples of the phenomenon, and it apparently has always been so. Beginning with Louis XV there was a wide and persistent popular belief in France that a deliberate *pacte de famine* to insure widespread starvation had been devised. A similar belief was widely held in England in the middle 1890s.[29] By the same token workers suffering from wage cuts, rising prices, a bad harvest, or other deprivations do not perceive incremental policy change or multiple causes: the conclusions of the social scientist. Rudé documents the consistent predilection in such circumstances

---

[29] Rudé, *The Crowd*, pp. 223–27.

to blame "clearly identifiable villains in the shape of the individual employer, merchant, forestaller, baker, landlord, or official."[30]

The same response is repeatedly evident today, as it has been in other historical periods. Sometimes "administered pricing" or other deliberate plans make the perception partially valid. It is nonetheless a predictable popular response, whether or not it is valid in a particular instance. In any case the local merchant or landlord is rarely the plotter even when plotting does occur at some level of the polity or of an economic institution. The perception of a plot by identifiable people serves to make feared events understandable and even to offer a possible way to remedy them through an attack upon the plotters. Threatening events that are uncontrollable and possibly random and accidental are more to be feared. Little wonder that the conspiracy perception is a recurrent response.

It is not only threat that is personified: so is reassurance. Where people are baffled by complex and threatening events they cannot control, they need to believe that the highest official of the state is both benevolent and able to cope.[31] This response has also recurred throughout human history. Rudé's summary of the phenomenon is instructive:

> In countries of absolute monarchy . . . the King was both the symbol and the fount of all justice and legislation, and the belief in his paternal benevolence persisted through periods of revolution and peasant revolt, when the King's ministers may already have been long discredited and the royal power itself was on the wane. Folk myths abound about the kindly concern for their people of Emperors, Sultans, Tsars, and French Kings from St. Louis to Henri IV and Louis XVI.[32]

The projection upon the ruler of the need to believe that underlying disorder and threat there are meaning, benevolence, and the possibility of control is a fundamental source of legitimacy in all polities. The findings of contemporary socialization studies about the perception of the American President as a benevolent leader,[33] the consistent ambivalence of opposition to chiefs of state,[34] the shock and grief experienced by political opponents of assassinated chiefs of state all point to this conclusion. At

---

[30] Ibid., p. 241.

[31] Cf. Murray Edelman, *The Symbolic Uses of Politics* (Urbana: University of Illinois Press, 1964), pp. 77–81.

[32] Rudé, *The Crowd*, p. 228.

[33] Fred I. Greenstein, *Children and Politics* (New Haven, Conn.: Yale University Press, 1969), p. 32.

[34] Rudé, *The Crowd*, p. 229; Dean Jaros, Herbert Hirsch, and Frederic J. Fleron, Jr., "The Malevolent Leader: Political Socialization in an American Subculture," *American Political Science Review* 62 (June 1968), 564–75.

least as revealing is the frequent inclination to blame subordinate government officials for disliked policies while assuming the chief of state is ignorant of their misdeeds or innocent of culpability. Critics of contemporary public policies frequently blame the CIA, the Joint Chiefs of Staff, the Secretary of Defense, the Federal Reserve Board, the FBI, and so on while assuming that the Chief Executive to whom these agencies are responsible is either keeping them in check or only waiting to be made aware of their wrongdoing: that his motive, unlike theirs, is to promote the public interest, and that he will do so once he learns all the relevant facts. The instrumental consequence of this pattern of cognitions is, of course, to make rebuff or repressive acts more acceptable to the deprived, even while it maximizes the maneuverability and policy discretion of the regime. To personify both the threat and the reassurance is to make both understandable and potentially subject to control and influence.

This pattern of perception of public officials by discontented masses is mirrored in the perceptions of discontented publics by public officials and elites. When they feel threatened, the empirical facts are translated into the forms that provide acceptable meanings and justify action to retain privileges. All in authority, Rudé points out, whether "aristocrat or middle class, conservative, liberal or rebel" attribute riots to "the machinations of a political opponent or a 'hidden hand.' "[35] In the East St. Louis riot of 1917 prominent Negroes were arrested without any evidence that they had been involved on the assumption "that as political leaders they must have promoted dissatisfaction and participated in the alleged plot."[36] The reactions of officials and elites to more recent race riots exhibit the same premise repeatedly.

What the policeman sees as he patrols ghetto areas is far more a function of preconceptions inculcated in his own social milieu than of empirical observations in the ghettos themselves. Both the policeman's anxieties and common police department policy serve to screen out observations that might challenge the preconceptions. "The patrolman comes to see the city through a windshield and hear about it over a police radio. To him, the area increasingly comes to consist only of lawbreakers."[37]

Police routines guarantee that this perception will be reinforced. Random searches of residents, including respected members of the community, define everyone as an actual or potential lawbreaker. The common practice of frequently changing the areas policemen patrol also guarantees that policemen will not come to know people except as illustrations

[35] Rudé, *The Crowd*, p. 215.
[36] Rudwick, *Race Riot*, p. 88.
[37] Kerner Commission report, p. 305.

of their preconceived typifications.[38] The reassignment policy is itself a systematic consequence of prevailing cognitions in the police bureaucracy, stemming from the fears, anxieties, and discontent of policemen charged with patrolling ghetto areas. A tight and mutually reinforcing circle of cognitions, role expectations, and bureaucratic policies thus makes change in any of these difficult and unlikely.

To a large proportion of the white population even nonviolent protest demonstrations define the demonstrators as lawbreakers. Campbell and Shuman found that to 35 percent of the white population there is "no real difference" between nonviolent demonstrations and riots. Respondents justify this view with explanations that the demonstrators are "just plotting up a riot" or "looking for trouble."[39]

In the personification of events symbolizing immediate threat or reassurance there is a strong predilection both to waive empirical evidence and to shape cognitions so as to minimize psychic tensions.

THE PRINCIPLES OF TRANSLATION INTO MYTH

Analysis of instances of political myth generation reveals that it is not a random or haphazard process or a manifestation of unconstrained irrationality. It is rather a systematic process whose basic principles are these: (1) a group interest in money or status is perceived and expressed in different terms from these; (2) the terms into which the political conflict is translated identify as the enemy or as the savior that group or individual that will mobilize a wide affective response and therefore broad political support; (3) in the choice of mythical enemies the most vulnerable politically is therefore selected.

The history of race conflict and of class conflict exemplifies these principles, and the most revealing cases are those incorporating both the race and the class components. The East St. Louis riots of 1917 provide almost a laboratory situation, so clear is the tie between the various tangible interests on the one hand and the corresponding mythical translations of them on the other. Key elements were a large migration of blacks to East St. Louis from the deep South, a job shortage, a housing shortage with consequent rent increases, and a disposition for the Negroes to vote Republican. White labor leaders and Democratic leaders saw and portrayed the problem as racial and resorted to blatant racist propaganda to win support for limiting the migration, thus protecting jobs, housing, and

---

[38] Ibid., p. 304.
[39] Campbell and Schuman, "Racial Attitudes," p. 51 and Table V-i.

Democratic election victories. Beginning in 1916 Democrats charged that Republicans were "colonizing" Negroes to influence elections. A Negro Republican leader in East St. Louis was linked with a plan to "vote 1500 colonized Negroes in Southern Illinois," and the metaphor of "colonization" was taken so seriously that the Federal Department of Justice, then Democratic, interrogated many Negroes on the reason for their migration.[40]

Corporation executives, who benefited from the migration, wanted no limitations upon it and had in fact encouraged it. In the tense spring of 1917, with a riot shortly to break out in East St. Louis and the United States a new combatant in the war on Germany, management spokesmen charged that labor leaders were in the pay of the Kaiser.[41]

In this milieu both the instrumental and the symbolic components of the issues are evident. The former include both income and status for the white workers of East St. Louis and strong economic incentives for local employers and landlords. The latter include a threat of black encroachment upon the established social order and a threat of treasonous plotting with an enemy country. Both these reformulations were clearly of a kind that would evoke wide and intense support for the economic interests involved. It is particularly instructive that the white labor leaders and their followers defined blacks as the adversary even though it was the corporation executives who instigated the conflict over migration and who benefited economically from it. Similarly, by perceiving and portraying the ultimate enemy as the foreign foe in a major war, employers mobilized support from people who would not become involved in an ordinary labor-management dispute. Pervasive racist sentiment made the blacks a highly vulnerable target even while pervasive free enterprise ideology made corporation executives highly invulnerable ones. Manifest and latent social support are critical variables in the politics of conflict escalation.

In a secular age in which class divisions are vague it is doubtful that racism and nationalism can be surpassed as potent symbolic issues. Religion has often served the same symbolic function at other times, as it did in the Thirty Years' War. Reminding us that concern for bread prices was a constant in the French Revolution, Rudé declares that "the shortage and high price of bread and food appear to have acted as a stimulus to popular participation in movements that were ostensibly concerned with other objects and issues."[42] These were fundamentally social class issues.

Divisions based upon race, nationality, religion, and clearly demarked class or caste evoke the most sensitive and cherished anxieties regarding

[40] Rudwick, *Race Riot,* chap. 2.
[41] Ibid., pp. 16–26.
[42] Rudé, *The Crowd,* pp. 219–20.

self-definition and survival. For a nation, a community, or a subculture, therefore, such translation is equivalent to minimizing the multifold, criss-crossing tangible interests that bind a society together through their over-lapping. It catalyzes a coalescence of many groupings based upon different interests. Their common enemy threatens to destroy people's very identities through attack upon the role and status structure that gives them their self-conceptions and sense of worth. The fact that rumors of sexual assault upon women of one's own group so often escalate hostility or help precipitate violence between the antagonists is a further clue to the manner in which myths about social conflict and ego and role definitions of the individual constitute the same phenomenon viewed from different perspectives.

THE INFLUENCE OF PUBLIC POLICIES UPON PERCEPTIONS

A central theme of this book is the impact upon people's perceptions and beliefs of formal actions of governmental bodies and of the public speeches of public officials. This cognitive influence of public policy is ultimately its fundamental influence, for it determines public support and opposition and gives leaders their maneuverability and constraints.

Frequently governmental actions generate cognitions regarding issues and situations in which there are few or no competing cues available to political spectators. This kind of monopoly is most evident in international affairs. The negotiation of alliances or the erection of defenses and the speeches of officials against an enemy country are the strongest, and sometimes the only, signal to mass publics that the target country is potentially hostile. In this case, as usual, actions are more persuasive generators of opinion than speeches.

Similarly, when police officers arrest or beat blacks, the poor, or students in neighborhoods bordering a university campus, the action is taken by a high proportion of the public who hear or read about it as prima facie evidence that the targets of the beatings were violating a law and required forceful restraint.

A second reason governmental acts are powerful shapers of perceptions lies in the legitimacy of the regime: a legitimacy derived from early childhood socialization processes and from such recurring legitimizing rituals as elections, appeals for support, justification of official actions as reflecting the will of the governed, and the political myths that define leaders as benevolent protectors of their constituents. A third and related reason lies in the intensity with which the state becomes for many a symbol of identity and self-definition: a part of the ego, making it a matter of pride and self-protection to give it credence and loyalty.[43]

The influence of political actions upon cognitions is certainly far from total; credibility gaps and challenges to official dicta appear. Under what conditions? As suggested earlier, a major condition is exposure of people to dissonant information when they have a strong interest in accepting the dissonant view. Where no such strong interest exists, dissonant information will be ignored (for reasons explored in chapter 3) even if it is demonstrably valid. Where it does exist (as in the case of ghetto Negroes who see evidence of lack of progress toward equal opportunity and potential draftees and their families who see news reports of corruption in Saigon and military stalemate or defeat in Vietnam), ambivalence, distrust of the regime, and dissent appear. Nonetheless, much of the population fails to perceive such information, even when it is conspicuously available.

A related limit upon the potency of signals from official sources is a dissenting view by another legitimate source. In this case the dissonant information may not be verifiable or unambiguous, but the legitimacy of the source creates a strain toward its acceptance, especially for those who would benefit materially from its acceptance. The long history of conflict in some countries between church and state is a classic example of such play for public support by competing legitimate sources. Here the monopoly of the government over relevant information is destroyed.

Sometimes the competition takes place within the government itself. It reflects rival beliefs regarding the meaning of an issue and it occurs so long as adherents of one belief are not forcefully suppressed as subversive or traitorous. The contemporary American division of opinion regarding the causes and remedies of restiveness among the poor illustrates the situation. Those who see the causes as subversive agitation and the cure as suppression are reinforced in their perception by recurring actions of local law enforcement officers, the FBI, and the House Internal Security Committee. Those who see the cause as economic and social deprivation and the cure as an end to the deprivation are reinforced in their perception by activities of the Office of Economic Opportunity and some bureaus of the Departments of Labor and of Health, Education and Welfare. People expose themselves to that set of cues that is compatible with their established cognitive patterns on the issue; some compartmentalize their cognitions and adhere to both; and all are ambivalent in some measure.

When a pattern of perceptions and beliefs established by public policy

---

[43] For empirical evidence that legitimacy of the state and trust in it are widespread see Gabriel Almond and Sidney Verba, *The Civic Culture* (Princeton, N.J.: Princeton University Press, 1963) and Robert E. Lane, *Political Ideology* (New York: Free Press, 1962).

is challenged by clear counter-evidence from nongovernmental sources, a high proportion of the population remains oblivious to or unpersuaded by the counter-evidence. In March 1968, when the federal government itself began for the first time to issue signals calling its earlier premises about the Vietnam war into question, 51 percent of the American people were still opposed to stopping the bombing of North Vietnam, let alone withdrawing troops.[44]

A social scientist trying to devise a test of the potency of official cues when they are confronted by clear evidence from unofficial sources could hardly do better than invent a situation in which the counter-evidence consisted of at least three years of news reports showing that the South Vietnamese government had little popular support for itself and for the war, regularly imprisoned and intimidated its political opponents, and was corrupt; and of even clearer evidence that the escalation of American military efforts was futile or worse in achieving military victory. Even under these "ideal" conditions, close to half the population continued to support the administration, no doubt with ambivalence on both sides. It is sometimes suggested that the defection of part of the population from President Johnson, forcing him out of office, is evidence that governmental cues are powerless before the truth. To anyone who likes to believe that people rely upon empirical evidence, however, it is surely more impressive that half the population could remain oblivious to facts in a situation in which the evidence was clear and conspicuous and the painful consequences of ignoring it almost as clear. The election in 1968 of another president committed to the previous administration's foreign policies further reveals the potency of the conventional cognitive structure on this issue.

Outside the field of foreign policy it is difficult to find a controversial issue in which the activities of governmental agencies are not offset by counter-cues from other government agencies reflecting different group interests. Such offsetting is especially conspicuous in welfare and poverty policy. In this area, therefore, the significant observations are those showing which groupings of the population systematically follow the cues of which public agencies.

That there is a systematic self-selection of cues and consequent cognitive structures is a clue to the transactional character of the link between widely held myths and public policies. It is apparent that governments are not omnipotent in shaping cognitions. The powerful impact of governmental actions upon cognitions must conform to the constraints imposed by the patterns into which political myths fall. These appeal to different groups: not randomly, but to serve status and material needs. It is accord-

---

[44] Reported in a Gallup Poll (*The New York Times*, April 3, 1968).

ingly a mistake to conceptualize public policy simply as a "cause" that produces identifiable "effects" in the form of particular cognitive patterns. The evocation of particular cognitive patterns through governmental actions is one crucial facet of a complex transaction that embraces myths, policies, cognitions, and personality needs.

Conventional wisdom, popular belief, and a great deal of social science writing differs with this thesis not only in regarding public policy as the outcome of cognitions rather than an influence upon them, but also in assuming that the media of mass communication and primary group discussion are the paramount shapers of people's political beliefs and perceptions. The view presented here implies that communication media catalyze and reinforce cognitions selectively, but do not originate them. The two-step flow process and self-selection of messages, both well-established phenomena, are further evidence that both transmitters and receptors of the messages that flow through the media respond to more fundamental cues. What they transmit and receive is a selective function of their cognitive structures, not an independent molder of their minds. Both the choice of content for newspapers and for radio and television news and the choice by audiences of what to absorb and what to ignore are reflections of established beliefs, expectations, and perceptions. The media that reach white audiences chiefly reinforce the perspectives those audiences already hold.

PERCEPTION OF DEPRIVATION

The urban riots of the twentieth century, and especially those of the 1960s, are especially instructive as to the ways in which public policies have contributed to active discontent and escalation of conflict. A sharp increase in a sense of deprivation through public policies that raise expectations has been analyzed earlier. In the language of the Kerner Commission:

> The expectations aroused by the great judicial and legislative victories of the civil rights movement have led to frustration, hostility and cynicism in the face of the persistent gap between promise and fulfillment. The dramatic struggle for equal rights in the South has sensitized Northern Negroes to the economic inequalities reflected in the deprivations of ghetto life.[45]

---

[45] Kerner Commission report, p. 204.

An effort by the Kerner Commission to probe Negro grievances found that the three most intense grievances stemmed from political practices, unemployment and underemployment, and inadequate housing.[46] In almost all the cities studied the political structure itself was a source of grievance because of the absence of adequate representation for blacks, lack of response to complaints, and the absence or obscurity of official grievance channels.[47] It is understandable that failure to provide official channels for Negro representation and influence in government should be perceived as more degrading than economic grievances, which are not as directly or formally a symbol of lesser status and second class citizenship.

That ghetto residents see their neighborhoods as deprived as a consequence of their actual experiences and the reports of acquaintances is clear from survey evidence. A 1966 survey of residents of the 12th Street area of Detroit showed that of those interviewed—73 percent felt the streets were unsafe; 91 percent believed a person was likely to be robbed or beaten at night; 57 percent worried about fires; 32 percent said they owned a weapon; 78 percent believed police did not respond promptly when summoned.[48]

More specific policies frequently evoke more specific perceptions of deprivation, even, and perhaps especially, when they are formally justified as helping the poor. A study of Negroes in Los Angeles in 1966 found deep cynicism about the antipoverty program because its "goals are long-range and most of its important benefits are deferred." Respondents perceived the program as providing economic benefits for bureaucrats, social agencies, and researchers and political benefits for politicians.[49]

Such skepticism among their clients about the benefits of the programs they are administering, together with budgetary rewards for quantitative evidence of success, have encouraged administrators to concentrate their efforts on the blacks with the least serious problems, who could therefore most easily be cited as successful products of the program. Job placements thus mainly benefited those who were already qualified and lacked "police records, functional illiteracy, spotty work records," and low-skill levels and had personal characteristics employers liked.[50] This form of

---

[46] Ibid., p. 143.

[47] Ibid., p. 145.

[48] Ibid., p. 88.

[49] Paul Bullock, "Fighting Poverty: The View from Watts" (Los Angeles: University of California, Institute of Industrial Relations, December 29, 1966, mimeographed), pp. 11–12.

[50] Ibid., pp. 7, 11.

official discrimination among the potential black clientele conveys two discouraging messages: (1) that public officials (largely white) can act arbitrarily in granting and withholding benefits from the poor, who are at their mercy; and (2) that the programs whites see as genuine benefits to the poor and movements toward equality are in fact tokens and put-ons or worse. An urban renewal project may constitute a real tragedy to those who are displaced from a neighborhood and forced to find housing lower in quality, higher in price, or both. It cannot be irrelevant to these people, and to others who share their perspective, that urban renewal should be officially touted as a boon to the poor—a way of eliminating slums and urban blight—or that whites outside the ghetto should generally see it that way, implying and apparently believing that the former slum residents now inhabit the modern apartments that replaced the slums, or have found similar ones elsewhere. Such blatant contradiction between words and things itself generates cognitions, particularly when they seem to be part of a larger pattern of public policy contradictions. Those who receive this message learn to assume that political rhetoric serves a function, political action a different and typically contradictory one, and that the two together constitute a threat of deprivation to be feared and opposed.

Punitive police actions against ghetto populations also create common cognitions in the groups they attack and somewhat different cognitions in others. Analyzing the Chicago riots of 1919, Waskow observed that "angry whites took the behavior of the police as a certificate of permission for them to enforce their wishes by using violence."[51] The same pattern appeared in Madison and in Berkeley in 1969, local whites attacking groups of students while the police looked on without restraining the attackers after the police themselves had gassed and beaten students. Such police actions suggest to ghetto populations both that police (the state?) view them as susceptible to punishment without due process and that a combat situation exists, the police constituting an adversary that must be harassed to minimize further punishment to themselves. Police in riot gear have repeatedly attacked people indiscriminately in urban neighborhoods perceived as hostile, evoking escalated violence. If enough police are physically present to prevent violence and actually do prevent it rather than engaging in it themselves, the message and the results are of course different and pacifying. The conclusion is evident from these often repeated scenarios that the influence of various forms of police action upon

---

[51] Arthur I. Waskow, *From Race Riot to Sit-In, 1919 and the 1960's* (New York: Doubleday, 1966), p. 41.

expectations and perceptions is even more important for future political behavior than the immediate physical consequences of such actions.

A related effect of the presence of police has been the reshaping of alliances and lines of cleavage among ghetto residents. Divisions among blacks based upon income levels and economic considerations tend to fade before a sharpened perception of a common cause and a common enemy. In Detroit and possibly elsewhere as well there were also instances of cross-racial solidarity.[52]

Perception of deprivation, then, like all perception, is a function of social cues regarding what is to be expected and what exists; it does not correlate directly or simply with objective conditions or with any particular measure of them. To those with reason to expect a higher status in the future, existing constraints are more conspicuous and more frustrating.

A 1967 study of the attitudes of Negroes in thirteen cities found almost half the respondents saying they were more angry than they had been a few years earlier and only about one in ten less angry, even though—$\frac{3}{4}$ thought they were better off than had been true in recent years; $\frac{4}{5}$ thought they had a better chance of getting a good job; $\frac{7}{10}$ thought their housing conditions had improved; $\frac{3}{4}$ were more hopeful that the problems of blacks would be solved and only $\frac{1}{25}$ less hopeful.[53]

PERCEPTIONS THAT JUSTIFY PAST ACTIONS

Once a group of people have committed violent or aggressive acts they develop shared perceptions of a kind that justify their actions. Blacks who have rioted or supported violence become all the more highly sensitive to past aggressions and injustices and very likely exaggerate these at times. In the nature of the case it is usually impossible to assess or document such exaggerations, if they occur, for they chiefly involve unreported and unrecorded instances of police harassment, overcharges in ghetto stores, and so on. More readily documented are the *post hoc* exaggerations of law enforcement officials who come to perceive their violent actions as justified by aggressions of restive minorities. In every regard the official and journalistic reports of damage to property and to people turn out upon

[52] See Allen D. Grimshaw, "Three Views of Urban Violence: Civil Disturbances, Racial Revolt, Class Assault," *American Behavioral Scientist* 2 (March–April 1968), 6.

[53] Summary of report by Daniel Yankelovich, Inc., from a special issue of *Fortune*, in *New York Times* (December 26, 1967), p. 40.

careful examination to have been grossly exaggerated. Early estimates of property damage in the 1967 Newark riot ranged from $15 million to $25 million; a month later the estimate was $10.2 million. Early newspaper reports of damage in the 1967 Detroit riot placed it at $200–$500 million; the highest later estimate was $45 million.[54] Police on a riot scene invariably perceive sniping after they have fired their own guns; an exhaustive study concludes that sniping was nonexistent in most of the riots and rare in any.[55] Police similarly were convinced after the killing of students at Kent State and Jackson State colleges in 1970 that snipers had been present, while study commissions failed to find them. Such phenomena illustrate the predilection to generate and spread perceptions of events consonant with a favored definition of one's own role. These perceptions as they are publicized are similarly useful to masses of nonparticipants: politicized spectators who need empirical or pseudo-empirical support for their preconceptions and self-definitions.

That a sense of deprivation, frustration, and anger are created through a complex pattern of developments and cues is, of course, not typically realized by those who feel the deprivation and the anger. Discontented people also assume that others expect explanation in terms of obvious grievances. It is therefore hardly surprising that respondents to attitude surveys cite widely recognized grievances of a short-term nature as their chief complaints. A survey in Detroit found blacks most often mentioning "gripes against the local businessmen, mistreatment by police, lack of jobs, dirty neighborhoods, and lack of recreation facilities."[56] The same real conditions, in short, may or may not be perceived as serious deprivations and may or may not be regarded as grounds for resistance and violence. Once violence occurs it is certain that manifest deprivations will be perceived as grounds for it. Naive phenomenological notions that particular conditions have stable meanings or that causes and effects of behavior are separate and readily distinguished from each other are clearly invalid as *descriptions* of behavior but are equally clearly significant as part of the explanation of behavior, for perceptions of phenomena by those who act are a critical facet of the transaction to be explained. Indeed, once this distinction is recognized, we can advance a long way toward a systematic account of the process through which objective conditions undergo particular changes in meaning.

[54] *A Survey of Attitudes of Detroit Negroes after the Riot of 1967* (Detroit: Urban League, 1967); Kerner Commission report, p. 115.

[55] "Sniping Incidents—A New Pattern of Violence?" *Riot Data Review,* Lemberg Center for the Study of Violence, Brandeis University (February 1969).

[56] *Survey of Attitudes of Detroit Negroes.*

THE IDENTIFICATION OF THE ENEMY
IN RIOT MYTHS

Certain themes recur in the myths voiced and accepted by participants in riots and those who encourage them to participate, even though the accounts of participants in particular riots differ in the kinds of incidents reported, in their chronology, and in their casts of characters. It is important to identify the respects in which the themes that differ in detail are basically the same and to uncover the functions these themes serve for the individuals who accept them and for the organization of political support and the structuring of violent confrontations.

Consider the kinds of stories circulated in the East St. Louis riots of 1917, riots in which the whites chiefly played the role of attackers. Some of the stories defined the Negro migrants to the area as lazy, shiftless, and criminal.[57] Some recounted alleged Negro atrocities: a white woman slashed across both cheeks by a black; Negroes drilling in St. Louis to carry out plots masterminded by the IWW;[58] a plot to murder 25,000 whites.[59] The last was a banner headline in the *St. Louis Republican*. Almost every statistic construable as evidence of the extent of the Negro threat was exaggerated: the number of black residents, the number of strikebreakers, the number who fled after the July 2 riot. Some Negro writers regarded the riot as part of a German conspiracy to sabotage the allied war effort; others saw it as instigated by southerners determined to end black migration to the North.[60]

What is involved here is the perception of flesh-and-blood people who currently seem to pose an economic or status threat as identical with a symbolic enemy. The latter is not made of flesh and blood, but rather of a vision of a threatening future: a future characterized by black supremacy, Communist supremacy, Jewish supremacy, Popish supremacy, German supremacy, or hippie supremacy. The labels for the symbolic enemy vary by place, time, and culture, and always refer to contemporary threats that are widely feared. A recent study by Hobsbawm and Rudé of the wave of incendiarism and destruction of farm machinery by poorly paid and unemployed British peasants in the early 1830s notes the kinds of "explanations" that circulated then:

Following the July revolution in Paris and the first incendiary fires in Kent and Surrey, the air became thick with rumors of French

---

[57] Rudwick, *Race Riot,* p. 35.
[58] Ibid., p. 72.
[59] Ibid., p. 71.
[60] Ibid., p. 64.

and Irish agents and 'Itinerant Radicals', traveling round the country in gigs, starting fires and inciting the labourers to break machines. Among the conflicting rumours circulating in Kent, the press reported, were that fires and riots originated "with the smugglers—with the Papists—with the agents of O'Connell—with the agents of Government—with the bigoted Protestants—with the Radicals—with foreign revolutionaries."[61]

The emphasis, as it usually is in such nonempirically based perceptions, was upon strangers and foreigners. Many strangers were rounded up and these people were often alleged to be foreigners. As the laborers who set the fires and destroyed the machinery were certainly English yeomen, the avid insistence upon an alien inspiration for the threatening actions is particularly revealing.

The character of the basic paradigm whenever a mass public comes to share a definition of some other mass public as "the enemy" begins to emerge from these observations and from similar ones that might be made regarding thousands of other historical confrontations in which conflict escalated. How other groups come to be perceived as enemies is certainly a salient question for social scientists in view of the enormous suffering such definitions manifestly promote. There are frequent changes in definitions of who the enemy is, and there is great difficulty in identifying and explicating the process through which collective perceptions of particular groups as hostile or friendly are made. Some pertinent observations that fall considerably short of a full explanation are nonetheless possible.

Central to any analysis of the issue must be the observation that a perception of some specific group as the source of harm to oneself and to significant others may be accurate or it may be demonstrably inaccurate. There was no ambiguity about European Jews' perception of Nazis as their enemy, though there was sometimes some doubt about which individuals supported the Nazis. By the same token Americans for whom European Jews were significant others could accurately and unambiguously identify Nazis as *their* enemy as well. When slum landlords whose properties are a lucrative source of income raise rents to what the traffic will bear, or allow slum housing to deteriorate, their tenants can readily identify the source of harm.

When the perception of the enemy is based upon empirical evidence and is relatively noncontroversial, the incentive is to end the threat, not perpetuate it. It may, however, be tempting to exaggerate the threat, con-

---

[61] Eric Hobsbawm and George Rudé, *Captain Swing* (New York: Pantheon, 1963), pp. 215–16.

sciously or unconsciously, in order to marshal wider support for ending it.

Another kind of political enemy is not *perceived* differently by those who fear him but serves a different or wider function for his political adversaries. He helps them marshal political support for themselves and for political objectives they favor and confers an esteemed role, often giving meaning to people's lives. This kind of enemy may or may not present an actual threat to those who perceive him as an enemy; but because he serves a vital function for his adversaries, they have a stake in *perpetuating* the threat perception rather than in ending it. History unfortunately abounds in examples of "enemies" who do not seem to have been so in the eyes of an observer relying upon objective empirical evidence: Jews in the ghetto villages of Czarist Russia, in post–World War II Germany, and, indeed, in most of Europe throughout the post-Christian era; Christians defined as heretics by the Inquisition; Catholics perceived as traitorous agents of the Pope in the pre–Civil War Know Nothing (nativist) movement in the United States; American advocates of civil liberties in the early 1950s; people either under thirty or over thirty in the late 1960s; welfare recipients. To explain the perception of such groups as enemies one must examine the perceivers as well as what is perceived, and one must focus upon the political and status benefits the perception brings. If such enemies did not exist, they would have to be created; and they are indeed created.

The point is easier to understand for low-status groups than for those with high status, but it applies to both. Most blacks are demeaned repeatedly and are denied the money, status, and prestigious work that confer self-pride. The same is certainly true of a great many lower-middle-class whites. Some of these, like policemen, must constantly play a role that is unidimensional: suspect others and seek them out and prosecute them with minimal regard for the social conditions and the socially condoned temptations that help justify their misdemeanors; to serve a function during the working day equivalent to that of a machine, though less efficiently; to be highly susceptible to displacement from even this modest role by economic conditions or organizational decisions they cannot influence. For people constantly though indirectly taught by others they respect that they hold this lowly place in the social scheme, the new role of fighter in a battle against the would-be destroyers of the social order is a gratifying one: a source of self-respect and therefore a role to be cherished and acted out with resolution.

If roles are analyzed with some care, the same point applies to many who enjoy affluence and high social status. Many may applaud and approve their behavior; but if there is also widespread disapproval, the actor will still feel a significant measure of guilt, shame, and a lack of self-fulfillment. The businessmen who, in the 1930s, employed terrorism, intimidation, and discharges to discourage union organization of their work forces and believed unions and union members were the vanguard of international Communism are an example. Hawkish congressmen and businessmen benefiting financially from a war widely regarded as unjustified are another. To convert their ambivalence about their role into the belief that role is heroic, such high-status groups must come to believe that those they punish do indeed pose a clear and present danger to the community. People create enemies in respect to those public issues on which others cue them to feel some substantial measure of guilt. The lower-middle-class white creates an enemy of the black he represses. The civil libertarian, upper-middle-class white feels, and creates, little threat from the black; but he may do so for Jews, for Koreans, for Vietnamese, or for restive students or workers. The paradigm therefore appears to be that activities seen reflexively as neither admirable nor self-fulfilling evoke a need for a valued role on other grounds; hence the creation of an enemy which in turn creates for the self a role of protector against an enemy of society.

The role is neither built upon empirical observations nor destroyed by observations incompatible with its premises, for its function is to protect the self, not to help one understand the world. This psychological function of enemy perceptions must be understood as only one aspect of dynamics of enemy perception: an aspect that varies in salience from one instance to another and that sometimes is an insignificant factor. Nor does the fact that it may play a part in any way imply that enemies may not also be real threats. The political psychologist distorts whenever he dichotomizes enemies as real or unreal or those who perceive them as rational or irrational. A cognition is more like a cubist painting than like a picture postcard. It is not clearly one thing or another, but a montage that changes its perspectives and its proportions for different observers and different scenes, in a systematic fashion whose rules we can partially identify.

Because the psychological incentive to perceive another group as the enemy occurs in only part of the population, those who are moved by it display strong avidity for testimonials that their enemy is indeed what they say he is. They enthusiastically reward the alleged subversive who admits that he or his associates engaged in subversive acts, preferably violent, while they scorn or penalize those who deny it. Investigators of political subversion are often not looking for evidence of whether it exists but rather for confirmation of what they need to believe. Racists reward the black who acts out the role of shiftless incompetent, fit only for menial work and happy in his subservient role, while Negro achievements inconsistent with that view infuriate them. In the same way, the overseers of American plantations and of German concentration camps rewarded slaves and inmates who acted out the demeaning, subhuman image and punished those who displayed evidence of superior capabilities.[62] Guards and psychiatrists in mental hospitals have been known to reward patients who act out the symptoms they attribute to them.[63] Who is perceived as the enemy may thus depend less upon what the alleged enemy does than upon the status and ego needs of the perceiver.

People who violate a social norm against hurting or killing others must persuade themselves that many others also violate it: they must create doubt that it really is a norm. They therefore reward those who join in their persecution of an enemy and stigmatize and penalize those who refuse or are reluctant. The soldier who hesitates to treat Vietnamese women and children as his enemy, the liberals who are seen as soft on Communism, the trade union organizers in the thirties who were stigmatized as dupes or participants of subversive conspiracies, have all learned that people who refuse to assent to a dubious choice of an enemy experience hostility and persecution akin to what might be meted out to a primitive tribesman who failed to join in a war dance. In the measure that perception of an enemy is controversial or without empirical foundation, insistence is the more fervent that the perception be universal.

Neither physical characteristics nor demographic traits nor ideologies nor national or religious distinctions nor any other objective attributes consistently define the cleavages between allies and enemies. People who feel threatened in their employment or in their social status by another group sometimes find reason to define their potential competitors as enemies, but not all competitors for jobs or aspirants for higher status are perceived as enemies. A foreign country is often defined as the enemy, but many foreign countries are allies or neutrals. People who are thought to hold a different ideology, nationality, or religion sometimes become the enemy, but these distinctions often do not define lines of political and emotional cleavage.

Caste and slave systems comprised of people of the same color as their masters have been common in history; while color, even defined in terms of assumed ancestral lines, has often not been the basis of status distinctions.

---

[62] Stanley Elkins, *Slavery* (Chicago: University of Chicago Press, 1968), pp. 81–139.

[63] Erving Goffman, *Asylums* (New York: Doubleday Anchor, 1961).

THE DEFINITION OF AN ENEMY
THAT MOBILIZES ALLIES

Because enemies, whether demonstrably harmful or not, do help marshal political and psychological support for their adversaries, the choice or definition of who the enemy is reflects an anticipation of which choice of enemy will most potently create and mobilize allies. The operation, usually unconscious, of this form of social and symbolic interaction in the choice and perception of enemies is the critical political fact in conflict escalation among masses of people and the key to explanation of the dynamics of the process. At the same time, its functioning is systematically masked by the manifest need to believe that the definition of the enemy is based only upon the manifest threat of harm he presents. People define as enemies those groups who most readily and most widely arouse anxiety and anger among the population. A foreign power long regarded as hostile to one's country, the heretics under the Inquisition, the anarchists in the nineteenth and early twentieth centuries, the Communists after the Russian revolution (in the Soviet Union, the capitalists), the Jews, the yellow peril, the blacks: the function these and similar enemies served is that they easily aroused the apathetic to strong belief in their malevolence and evoked support for those in the heroic role of fighting them. The very ambiguity about the plots they symbolized made them eminently suitable targets upon which diverse groups could project their own fears—sometimes, of course, with good reason.

Thinking, as George Herbert Mead helped us to recognize, is so intimately a matter of viewing one's own contemplated actions from the perspective of significant others, that to adopt the mode of cognizing such a matter that creates a socially approved self is natural and inevitable. It is therefore not a matter of conscious scheming or deception, though it may sometimes be a kind of self-deception.

Definition of the enemy so as to maximize social support calls attention to the fact that most people who accept and support such a definition are not themselves directly involved in conflict over a particular issue, such as union recognition or civil rights policy. It is nonetheless gratifying for them to see themselves as participants in a meaningful struggle against evil and in behalf of their fellow men. Life takes on reassuring meaning; the struggle helps erase anomie, boredom, fear of insignificance, and a sense of anxiety about being part of a generation that has grossly mismanaged public affairs and left posterity in worse condition than themselves. If no malevolent plot on earth adequately impresses the mass public, unidentified flying objects signalling a threat from outer space may do, just as signs of the advent of the antichrist powerfully served a less secular European mass public in the twelfth, thirteenth, and fourteenth centuries.

The enemy themes that most surely and consistently evoke mass arousal and anxiety are those that make it hardest to take the enemy as a significant other: those that emphasize the respects in which he does not share our human traits and potentialities for empathy, for compassion, and for social attachments. The alien, the stranger, or the subhuman are the themes struck repeatedly. These typifications most efficiently symbolize resolute malevolence because by definition they cannot become part of the social bond, the symbols of community that induce other political adversaries to resolve their conflicts through ritualized procedures that legitimize the outcome. The outside agitator, the agent of a foreign power (secular or satanic), the representative of a social milieu fundamentally different from the one we know and understand, the subspecies or superspecies that is not really human: it is in some variation of these themes that we see, and encourage others to see, our enemies, for people can deliberately hurt and kill only what they do not see as an exemplification of themselves and a component in their own self-concepts.

The symbolic utility of this theme of the alien is impressive, for the constraints it imposes do not rest chiefly upon empirical observations or facts, but also upon the psychological needs of people for self-fulfillment. Men of the same nationality and color may be defined as aliens on the basis of their caste or strange social milieu and subservient behavior, as in the caste or strange social milieu and subservient behavior, as in the cases of Hindu untouchables or nineteenth-century Russian serfs. A color difference defines the alien when that satisfies the need, but not in other circumstances. A cat may be perceived as more human and empathetic than one's neighbors.

While some enemies hurt and some help, the two are of course not perceived as different types by people in their everyday lives. The two types of enemies are equally real and phenomenologically identical. In different contexts the same group focuses upon one or the other or upon both. Changes in social cues account for the changes in focus.

Chapter 7

DISORGANIZATION AND LEADERSHIP

Violent disturbances display quite consistent patterns in respect to the functions served by organization, by disorganization, and by leadership. The empirical consistencies make it clear, moreover, that the common popular and academic assumption that formal organization and a leader's direction initiate, intensify, and shape the violence is simplistic and usually invalid. The common belief reveals more about the triumph in man of reassuring meaning over dissonant information than it does about the natural history of violent confrontation.

The empirical record first of all calls attention to the central function served by the absence of organization, and of social disorganization in violent encounters between masses of people. Chapter 2 offers some examples from the early stages of major national revolutions. The same pattern characterizes the black ghettos that erupt into riots, peasants who join rebellious movements,[1] and the American rural communities that have, on occasion, violently challenged mortgage foreclosures of their land titles or the institutions that set the prices they receive for their crops.[2]

The American black ghetto is not a community deriving coherence from a salient and recent ethnic heritage, a common ethos, a common religion, and many overlapping social organizations—the characteristics that solidified earlier ghettos of immigrants in the large American cities and brought them roots and dignity in spite of poverty. These earlier ethnic ghettos of Jews, Irish, Italians, and others are sometimes offered as models of the inevitable course of social integration in store for blacks as well. They should rather highlight the radical novelty of the black ghetto in American history, for it lacks precisely those institutions that facilitated the social and economic success of the European immigrants.[3] Observations by

---

[1] Eric Wolf, *Peasant Wars in the Twentieth Century* (New York: Harper & Row, 1969).

[2] Angus Campbell et al., *The American Voter* (New York: Wiley, 1960), pp. 402–40.

[3] Cf. Lenora E. Berson, *Case Study of a Riot* (New York: American Jewish Committee, Institute of Human Relations Press, 1966), pp. 9–10, for a

Malcolm[4] and by Bullock[5] on the role of the hustler in the ghetto reveal something of the meaning to residents of amorphous human relationships and social divisiveness. What distinguishes the hustler is his effort to accumulate money as quickly as possible and so win higher status while remaining a resident of the ghetto and exploiting the wants and the anxieties of other residents. This ploy for success in a fashion other blacks can emulate, Bullock notes, makes the hustler a more salient success model than a Ralph Bunche or a Jackie Robinson, who attained success in fields in which most cannot compete. The hustler's operations, however, are divisive and alienating, for they succeed only in the degree that they exploit others quite openly. That they become the success model reveals the deep sense in which divisive and alienating activities are at the core of ghetto life. Socioeconomic differences are also divisive; the better off and less alienated "are as critical of the practices of their lower-class neighbors as are the Anglo suburbanites."[6]

Once a disturbance begins[7] and a militant crowd forms, its actions are focused, though not formally organized. Those observations of violent crowd behavior that have not been inhibited by conventional assumptions either that its members are wild and berserk[8] or that they are misled by scheming agitators, consistently reveal crowd action as focused and selective even when it is violent. Rudé documents the "remarkable single-mindedness and discriminating purposefulness of crowds, even those whose actions appear to be most spontaneous." He concludes that the pre-industrial crowd "rioted for precise objects and rarely engaged in indiscriminate attacks on either properties or persons"; and that riots rarely spread "to areas untouched by the grievances that gave them birth."[9] The Kerner Commission report and other studies of the American ghetto and student riots of the sixties reached the same conclusion, noting that the rioters selected as targets the properties of merchants they believed had exploited

---

discussion of the absence of social cohesion and meaningful neighborhoods in the Negro ghettos, and particularly in North Philadelphia and Watts.

[4] *The Autobiography of Malcolm X* (New York: Grove Press, 1965), pp. 109–26.

[5] Paul Bullock, *Fighting Poverty: The View from Watts* (Los Angeles: University of California, Institute of Industrial Relations, December 29, 1966, mimeographed), pp. 13–15.

[6] Ibid., p. 16.

[7] The conditions facilitating its precipitation are examined on pages 27–30.

[8] Gustave LeBon, *The Crowd* (New York: Macmillan, 1925); Sigmund Freud, *Group Psychology and the Analysis of the Ego* (New York: Liveright, 1922).

[9] George F. Rudé, *The Crowd in History* (New York: Wiley, 1964), pp. 253–54.

them and police they believed had demeaned and hurt them; just as, in *their* rioting, police focused upon those they defined as enemies of the social order, judging people to be enemies by their appearance or their presence among the suspect.

The belief that rioters strike out indiscriminately at anything in their path, unconstrained by goals or moral inhibitions, is manifestly a potent political justification for repressive action against them. It is nonetheless a view that is inconsistent with everything we know about social role taking and the individual's internalization of generalized norms, just as it is inconsistent with the empirical evidence. Members of a crowd do not behave in that role any more than in any other role as uninhibited indulgers in whims and passions. They act extralegally or illegally or in violation of conventional norms only when they believe they are furthering a mutually shared objective, such as resistance to repressive property laws[10] or repressive policemen.

A revealing form of crowd behavior occurs when policemen or other paramilitary groups abandon the constraints imposed by the formal rules of their organizations and adopt instead the constraints imposed by jointly shared crowd norms. The killings of blacks at the Algiers Motel during the Detroit riot in 1967 and the numerous other police riots of the sixties exemplify the phenomenon. Police behavior in such instances is certainly violent, extralegal, and often illegal, but it is not random, wild, or purposeless. Like all crowd behavior, it is structured by mutual role taking and implicit or explicit sharing in a common purpose, which may be the suppression of an empirically nonexistent plot. Paramilitary movements are sometimes held together only by such a sense of shared purpose, with little or no formal structure. A recent study of violence in America declares of the Minutemen:

> Their disorganized character is an important index of the nature of these groups and of their relation to the larger social and political structure. As one observer has suggested, "The Minutemen are more a frame of mind than an organization or movement." Put differently, these groups could be said to represent a frame of mind in search of an organization, and having little success in finding one.[11]

---

[10] Cf.: The argument that looting in riots is a form of rejection of property laws appears in E. L. Quarantelli and R. R. Dynes, "Looting in Civil Disorders: An Index of Social Change," *American Behavioral Scientist* 2 (March 1968), 7–10.

[11] Quoted in Hugh G. Davis and Ted R. Gurr, *The History of Violence in America* (New York: Praeger, 1969), p. 232. Original in J. Harry Jones, Jr., *The Minutemen* (New York: Doubleday, 1968), p. 410.

The purposefulness of the violent crowd is all the more impressive in view of the diversity of the specific frustrations that usually underlie riots. Where there is such diversity, where different people feel deprived of a significant place in the social scheme for an array of different reasons, a shared belief that they are fighters for a common and laudable goal does create for them the gratifying social role they need. They accordingly embrace such a goal when one that meets these necessary conditions is presented to them. By the same token they reject any goal that presents their violent behavior in a derogatory light, including one that denies it any purpose at all.

Rudé notes that once a militant climate of opinion existed, slogans rallied people "with widely varying motives and beliefs to focus their protests on a common target,"[12] particularly in political demonstrations where the issues were not clear. Examples of slogans that unified European preindustrial crowds are "Wilkes and Liberty," "No Popery and Wooden Shoes," and "Long Live the Third Estate." In American riots of the sixties "Black Power," "Off the Pigs," "Save the People's Park," and other slogans served the same function.

On the more general issue of purposefulness or its absence, a large proportion of blacks have defied the common social definition of the disturbances. The communications media and the authorities universally used the word "riot" to describe the Watts disturbance of 1965; but 38 percent of a representative sample of Negroes in Los Angeles described it as a "revolt," a "revolution," or an "insurrection," while only 13 percent of the white sample did so. Forty-six percent of the blacks used the socially sanctioned term "riot." Even these apparently used it largely because it was the easiest way to communicate, for a majority of the blacks said they saw the rioting as a purposeful protest.[13]

That violent crowd behavior is focused and its targets not randomly chosen tells little in itself about the underlying malaise the violence reflects. The choice of targets, like all mass political behavior, is shaped by anticipation of what a broader public will see as justifiable. It signals only that there is a deep sense of relative deprivation; it does not specify the respects in which each or all of the rioters feel deprived. Earlier sections of this study have examined the complex dynamics of that process. To assume that the targets of rioters define the problem is grossly to understate the problem. Lewis Coser is therefore accurate, if vague, when he writes of the violence

---

[12] Rudé, *The Crowd in History,* p. 246.

[13] David O. Sears, "Black Attitudes toward the Political System in the Aftermath of the Watts Insurrection," *Midwest Journal of Political Science* 13 (November 1969), 517.

of the poor as a form of communication: a "danger signal . . . perhaps desperate cries for help after other appeals had been unavailing."[14]

THE LEADERSHIP OF CROWDS

Leaders serve many functions, specific to the kind of group they "lead."[15] For violent crowds they chiefly serve the expressive needs of the crowd and the political needs of the adversaries of the crowd. The implication of this view of crowd behavior is that because the unstructured and volatile crowd generates shared understandings about its behavior and its targets, its "leader" achieves his position by ascription. This leadership function contrasts sharply with leadership in a highly structured situation, where an astute leader can devise tactics that give him broad leeway in coping with inhibitions upon his discretion.[16]

When a person is identified as the leader of a violent crowd, others ascribe actions and beliefs to him. Leaders often stand outside the crowd in the sense that they are already known and have a wide popular following. Their utility to the crowd lies precisely in their wider support: in their identification with a broadly supported ultimate goal. The prevailing assumption is, of course, that as leaders they directly influence crowd behavior. Observers have repeatedly noticed the disparity between their actual and their ascribed function and the anomalous conclusions it has produced both in speculative academic writers like LeBon and in political adversaries of the popular movements the leaders have represented. Rudé noticed that leaders of pre-industrial crowds were sometimes quite reluctant to play their ascribed role and occasionally renounced the leadership role entirely, as Martin Luther did when he condemned the German peasants rioting in his name.[17] Rudé further observes that "by his position 'outside' the crowd, the leader was always in danger of losing his control over a protracted period, or of seeing his ideas adapted to purposes other than those he had intended."[18]

---

[14] Lewis Coser "Some Social, Functions of Violence," *The Annals* 34 (March 1966), 15.

[15] For empirical explorations of the functions see Fred E. Fiedler, *A Theory of Leader Effectiveness* (New York: McGraw-Hill, 1967).

[16] For a perceptive account of Franklin Roosevelt's performance in this regard, see Arthur M. Schlesinger, Jr., *The Coming of the New Deal* (Boston: Houghton-Mifflin, 1968), chap. 32.

[17] Rudé, *The Crowd in History*, p. 247.

[18] Ibid., p. 248.

Both casual observations of modern and contemporary violent crowds and the studies of their dynamics make it evident that it was not leaders who generated either the crowds or the violence; in an important sense, rather, the crowds and the violence generated ascriptions of leadership. The Kerner Commission concluded after investigating "hundreds of rumors" that no empirical evidence existed of organized planning or conspiracy to produce the riots of the sixties. Research by the Brandeis University Lemberg Center for the Study of Violence reached the same conclusion for the racial disturbances of 1967.[19]

When crowd leadership is ascribed to a local rather than a national figure, the same dynamics are operative; but the absence of leadership activity by the same person in other circumstances makes it even clearer that it was not his charisma or his planning that incited the violence. In England, after the Bristol Potteries riots and "Swing" disturbances in the early decades of the nineteenth century, the "leaders" were transported to Australia, and not one of them is recorded to have engaged in political or radical activity there or back in England after their return.[20]

Those who fear crowds and oppose their political aims find it necessary to pin responsibility for violence upon a leader or an oligarchy of leaders. To find leaders who can be blamed satisfies the impulse to punish someone for disturbing their normal way of life and threatening the social order with which they identify, and it offers a welcome opportunity to assert their own role in defending that social order. More fundamentally, it reassures them and all others who are anxious that the crowd was simply misled; that it was not reacting to real and deep-seated grievances and inequities in the social order; that a normal situation can be restored by punishing the agitators who upset it.

Rudé's account of the disposition of law enforcement officers to find leaders of crowds will look familiar to observers of the contemporary social scene. He declares that where no leadership was apparent,

> the police or militia were inclined to arrest and cross-examine, not so much leaders in any commonly accepted sense of the term as those who momentarily gave way to enthusiasm, showed more spirit, enterprise, or daring than their fellows, were heard to shout slogans, engaged in more spectacular acts of violence, or happened to be picked out and informed against by their neighbors.[21]

---

[19] *The New York Times* (December 29, 1967).

[20] Rudé, *The Crowd in History,* p. 252.

[21] Ibid., p. 251.

Because militant crowds both reflect and arouse high levels of emotionalism, the politics of crowds is conspicuously an expressive politics. In this setting militancy and violence take on predictable, even stylized forms. The forms compellingly shape perceptions of leadership, of political goals, and of schisms and alliances. They condense a broad spectrum of discontents and aspirations into a small set of widely supported cognitions that justify the actions both of the crowds and of their adversaries.

VULNERABILITY

Defeatism about the prospects of success from militant political action inhibits mass resort to militancy, while optimism about the prospects of success encourages it. Perceptions of vulnerability to defeat may be accurate or not. They influence behavior in either case. Much of what follows deals with the conditions of their generation, which, not surprisingly, are often empirically inseparable from their impact upon behavior.

A fundamental distinction turns upon the scope of the time-space scene within which vulnerability of invulnerability is perceived. Sometimes we perceive ourselves as a part of grand-scale events proliferating far afield in space and in time. Polar examples are the participants in millenarian movements who see themselves as caught up in cosmic developments fated to end in a millennium but committing them meanwhile to exterminate the forces of darkness or of the antichrist who are delaying the advent of the Kingdom.[22] A more common and less polar political example are consumers who see the steady price increases they have to pay as imposed by remote economic forces they cannot understand or control or effectively combat. There is a strong temptation to assume that the outcomes of such grand-scale scenes cannot be controlled by the actions of the people one knows and sees: that they are either inevitable or manipulated by a remote and an invulnerable elite. There is accordingly a strong inhibition against fighting them and compelling incentive to fit into what is fated anyway. Cues that evoke a grand-scale scene, proliferating far in space and into the remote past or future, therefore evoke concurrently some measure of quiescent acceptance of the social order perceived as established and determined. By the same token they evoke the view that officials, policemen, crowds, and other people one confronts directly and in the present are not makers of policy, but only instruments in a larger cosmic design.

---

[22] Cf. Norman Cohn, *The Pursuit of the Millennium* (New York: Harper & Row, 1961).

Earlier passages of this book call attention to many forms of political action that evoke myths of remote causes and predestinations. Others just as surely focus attention upon decisionmaking at close hand: the administrative, judicial, and electoral procedures seen as responsive to the interests of those they affect. Here the political setting is small scale, and there is concomitant perception that people with similar interests who act concertedly can be influential. For that reason institutionalized procedures serve to resolve conflicts ritualistically. Where there is no way for particular groups to use the institutionalized procedures, they may express their wants and frustrations through noninstitutionalized militancy. In either case there is some hope that the public presentation of demands can influence outcomes. Both students who demonstrate or seize buildings to influence university policies and students who contest the legality of university policies in the local federal court have some measure of optimism that they can win; and both see their allies and their opponents as people in the immediate setting. Both their own actions and those of others they believe are influential focus attention upon the observable setting. Reality testing is more influential as a way to gauge support and opposition than it is for "participants" in a cosmic scene.

There is, of course, a mix of empirically and nonempirically based cues in both cases; but the proportions are significantly and systematically different. It is easier to elicit in political spectators a perception of progress in civil rights, in extrication from an unpopular war, or in meeting welfare needs without significantly changing policies or policy impacts than it is to elicit in student protesters a false belief that their university has broken off its ties to war industries or significantly increased its black studies curriculum offerings.

We can be more specific about some of the dynamic processes through which a particular mix of empirically and nonempirically based cues are influential. The contrast between the American North and the South in attitudes toward blacks offers a useful basis for initial assessment, for it is a contrast not so much in substantive attitudes as in degree of ambiguity about attitudes. For the Negro in the deep South in the era following the Civil War, status and behavior rules were clear and relatively firm, and so was white determination and white ability to maintain existing status and social discriminations. Whether whites were perceived as friends or enemies, they and the rules they enforced were invulnerable.

In the North ambivalence among whites about race relations was manifest and explicit in both rhetoric and behavior. Denial of equal rights and equal opportunity was not accomplished through law or formal rules so much as through evasion of the rules or through social and economic practices; and the denials were not consistent. With greater ambiguity about relative power and intentions, there is also greater uncertainty about self-definition and roles on the part of both blacks and whites, and a real possibility of gaining advantage through maneuver or militancy. It is to be expected, then, that restiveness and protest should be greater where repression is less consistent.

Ambiguity about the situation, associated with ambivalence in both superordinates and subordinates, increases as rumors of an impending riot occur and increase in frequency. The case studies of riots consistently note an increase in the frequency and intensity of the rumors before the outbreak of disturbances, whether the latter are initiated by whites or by blacks.[23] Such rumors mobilize wider support, for they increase sensitivity to cues of escalation; they heighten anxiety levels, threat perceptions, and the politicization of previously apathetic mass publics. By arousing fear or anger they encourage the perception of adversaries as nonpeople, as embodiments of malevolent traits, subhuman or superhuman abilities, and threats; but always the undercurrent of ambiguity about the degree of the threat and the degree of vulnerability remains and fuels the likelihood of confrontation that will resolve the uncertainty.

If we recognize, as this definition of the situation does, that lack of clarity in power capabilities politicizes people and widens the scope of conflict, we are no longer surprised by both historical and contemporary evidence that peaceful demonstrations by nonelites should alarm authorities and the wealthy about as much as violence does. Police departments worry about granting parade permits to dissidents and frequently deny them. The federal Department of Justice showed the same alarm about the peaceful October 1969 Moratorium demonstration against the Vietnam war. Rudé makes the same point about elite reactions to peaceful but massive processions of tradesmen and workers in Paris in August and December 1789, and at Peterloo in 1819.[24] To the authorities such mass demonstrations are signals that resistance may escalate: that their status and power are sometimes insecure; that a present attack or confrontation may be the prudent course of action.

Clarity and certainty in perceptions of vulnerability are also crucial factors in shaping the course of a riot once it is underway. Riots have been stopped quickly by bringing in large numbers of police when these clearly could suppress disturbances, though large numbers of police or troops sometimes remain vulnerable to hit-and-run tactics by small bands of

---

[23] Elliot Rudwick, *Race Riot in East St. Louis* (Carbondale: Southern Illinois University Press, 1964), p. 37; *Report of the National Advisory Commission on Civil Disorders* (New York: Bantam, 1968), pp. 217, 326, 364 (hereinafter cited as Kerner Commission report).

[24] Rudé, *The Crowd in History*, p. 239.

demonstrators. In these latter cases the deployment of large numbers has not worked, for it did not mean invulnerability. Withdrawal of police forces from a volatile area even more surely ends uncertainty about vulnerability and also ends a form of incitement. This tactic has defused riots—in Paterson, New Jersey, in 1966 and in Cleveland in 1967, for example.[25]

Patterns in forms of destructiveness by crowds are also most usefully explained in terms of perceptions of which kinds of acts will be popularly tolerated and which forms will evoke general outrage and support for repression. As noted earlier, modern urban rioters have selectively destroyed property, but have tried to avoid the destruction of human lives. The same was true of the pre-industrial crowd and of those peasant rebellions, like the "Swing" disturbances, whose objectives were limited to immediate economic demands. Such relatively few attacks on lone whites as did occur in the urban ghetto riots of the twentieth century took place "in the early stages of the riots before the full extent of anger and power and sadism of the white mobs became evident."[26] Similarly, in both the May and the July East St. Louis riots of 1917 the white mobs fell back whenever there was firmness in dealing with them.[27]

Masses of people have engaged in large-scale massacres, by contrast, in the course of millenarian movements, slave revolts, and jacqueries in which people were moved by a vision of a wholly new world or a radically reconstituted society, particularly when they were committed to a myth that destruction of the forces of the antichrist or of some other symbol of evil was a necesary prerequisite to the achievement of a millennium.[28] Belief in such a myth confers a sense of invulnerability. The urban rioter, however, is well aware that massacres will bring quick repression and not the millennium: that he is highly vulnerable. The gross contrast between massacres of people and selective destruction of property reflects perceptions of what will be tolerated; the different perceptions in turn flow from marked differences in perceptions of the scope of the scene of confrontation. In riots and in demonstrations by eighteenth- and nineteenth-century crowds the authorities frequently took many lives, a fact that fits this thesis; for the authorities have the power and the legitimacy to do so with relative impunity.

Grand-scale scenes can connote total vulnerability as well as total invulnerability. The cosmic scale facilitates the absence of inhibition either way. Visions of a utopia in an indefinite future have even more frequently

[25] Arthur Waskow, *From Race Riot to Sit-In* (New York: Doubleday, 1966).

[26] Davis and Gurr, *Violence in America*, p. 390.

[27] Rudwick, *Race Riot*, pp. 32, 79.

[28] Cohn, *Pursuit of the Millennium;* Rudé, *The Crowd in History*, p. 255.

rationalized quiescent acceptance of severe deprivation than they have justified violent resistance or massacres of an enemy. When the Black Muslims or others picture a future world in which Allah will bring about black domination and destroy the whites, they serve to accommodate to existing institutions, just as the Christian vision of the Kingdom of Heaven on earth after the Second Coming serves the same function. In such instances the message of the myth is both that what exists is divinely ordained and, as a psychological safety-valve, that it is destined to end—by divine will, not by collective human effort.[29]

So far as the immediate scene is concerned, it is of course not only the physical force available to rioters or to the authorities that shapes perceptions of vulnerability. The case studies show conclusively that the actual and potential size and resources of the protesters critically shape perceptions of vulnerability. One manifest reason for the virtual disappearance in northern American cities of the kind of riot, common in the early decades of the century, in which white mobs attacked local Negroes, is the marked change in the size of the black ghettos. The Negro residential areas in northern cities are now so large that white mobs can no longer burn them down or harass them with a large measure of impunity, as they did in East St. Louis in 1917 and in Chicago in 1919.

Even in 1919 a large black ghetto was safer from attack than a small one. In the Charleston, South Carolina, riots, initiated by attacks upon blacks by white sailors from a nearby naval training station, the local authorities acted to prevent violence by the sailors as well as by the Negroes. Waskow observes that the unwillingness of the police to act only against blacks was attributable, at least in part, to the fact that Negroes made up a majority of the city's population "and might have been uncontrollable if they had been goaded into attacking the police."[30]

The posture of law enforcement authorities toward black-white confrontations is manifestly a critical factor in perceptions of relative vulnerability. The behaviors of local police forces have taught both sides how much maneuverability and how much protection they enjoy. Where police showed themselves to be in effect part of the white mob, their behavior repeatedly turned initial incidents into serious white attacks on Negroes. The riots in the early decades of this century in Longview (Texas), Washington, Chicago, and Arkansas were of this sort. In Knoxville and Omaha police vacillation encouraged white lynch mobs to escalate to mass attacks on the Negro communities.[31]

---

[29] Davis and Gurr, *Violence in America*, p. 390.
[30] Waskow, *Race Riot to Sit-In*, pp. 14–15.
[31] Ibid., pp. 16–20, 209–10.

These observations help explain the behavior of people who are already firmly committed either to the demonstrators or to their official adversaries. Where a large part of the population is uncommitted or only weakly committed, a rather more complicated calculus applies. The critical question is then the effect of deployment of force upon their perceptions and upon the behavior of this uncertain group. If the authorities resort to brutality or any form of force widely regarded as repressive of a legitimate right to demonstrate, new support for the demonstrators is mobilized. Troops or policemen may themselves begin to sympathize with the demonstrators under these conditions. Similarly, violence by the demonstrators may evoke opposition from the previously uncommitted. At the same time a part of the uncommitted group can be counted on to base its perceptions upon the assumption that *anything* the government does is legitimate: that those the regime defines as malevolent are indeed so. Attacks upon ideological dissenters, even wholesale killings of them, define them as the enemy for that part of the population with few reservations about the legitimacy of the regime. Resort to violence by the authorities therefore wins support both for the government and for the dissenting movement. It transforms the issue from one that concerns only a segment of the population to one that mobilizes a high proportion of the public; by the same token, it heightens the intensity of feelings on both sides.

Clearly, these two kinds of political impact of the resort to force, working in opposite directions, present a problem for tacticians on both sides. Their success or failure has often hinged upon how clearly they recognized the dynamic implications and the potential unintended consequences of the forms of action available to them. Where all or almost all the population in an area is already polarized on one or the other side, all-out deployment of available force is critical. It intimidates not only physically, but psychologically as well by creating perceptions of invulnerability. Where, as is more often the case, a large sector of the population with some sanctions at its disposal is largely uncommitted, successful strategies must be geared to winning their support; and force they perceive as illegitimate will rally them to the other side.[32]

Sometimes resort to physical violence underlines the awareness of both the attackers and their victims that the latter are growing in power and support even though they are still vulnerable for the time being. In such a situation the attack becomes a signal of the attacker's fear and anxiety rather than of confident invulnerability, and it encourages the subordinate group to show defiance. Waskow claims that 1919 riots "gave birth to 'the new Negro'—the first generation of Negroes to win the ap-

---

[32] For historical examples see Rudé, *The Crowd in History,* pp. 262–63.

pellation."[33] In places like Chicago and East St. Louis, to which large numbers of blacks were migrating in those years, blacks seemed to threaten the jobs of some whites and to manifest growing political power. In such a context attacks by white crowds highlight the passing of the myth of a stable social order in which the Negro's subordination is unquestioned dogma. The attacks connote to both groups that whites see themselves as vulnerable and see the Negro as a threat; for in a really stable and accepted social order subordination does not depend upon physical intimidation.

By the early sixties black voting blocs in major southern cities sufficiently large to swing elections were inhibiting white resistance to Negro demonstrations demanding other civil rights in those communities. The Kerner Commission report concluded that the civil rights demonstrations of the early sixties were chiefly successful where Negroes voted and could decide election outcomes: in Atlanta, Nashville, Durham, Winston-Salem, Louisville, Savannah, New Orleans, Charleston, Dallas and other cities of the South and border states with large black populations willing to turn out on election day.[34]

GOVERNMENTAL VULNERABILITY AND GOVERNMENTAL MILITANCE

The link between perceptions of vulnerability and predilection to militant action holds for public authorities as well. This is a special case of the same principle, but it deserves special notice if only because of the more potent myths and mystifications that envelop the formal acts of governments; particularly, of course, the belief that the actions of public authorities depend upon the language of constitutions and statutes. When the Chicago and Oakland police departments or the federal Department of Justice create occasions to shoot or imprison Black Panther leaders, they are responding to perceptions of broad support from a "silent majority" that will outweigh the predictable protests from civil libertarians and dissenters. When the FBI displays great zeal in moving against political dissenters, especially during periods of McCarthyist hysteria, and minimal zeal in moving against organized crime syndicates, it exemplifies the same principle. When public officials ignore the dictionary meanings of prohibition laws, or "right-to-work" laws, or health and safety codes for slum housing, they are reflecting a perception of which course of action will maximize their support and minimize their vulnerability.

---

[33] Waskow, *Race Riot to Sit-In,* p. 10.
[34] Kerner Commission report, p. 231.

Such perceptions are subject to rather rigorous corrective feedback; they cannot with impunity be grossly inaccurate. Unless they are responsive to what concerned publics will support and to the sanctions these publics will apply, the authorities will themselves be discarded or immobilized: through elections, passive or active resistance, or the intervention of a more responsive set of authorities elsewhere in the government. This is not to say that the authorities in any serious sense necessarily reflect the "will of the people." On the contrary, it is to emphasize their need to take account of inequalities in ability among concerned publics to apply sanctions and the will to apply them. At the same time, a popular sense that governmental authorities cannot act for long without reference to the concerns and sanctions of interested publics is translated, with the help of the agencies of political socialization, into a belief that government operates by consent of the governed. Governmental sensitivity to the interests of the powerful thereby helps legitimize its actions for both the powerful and the powerless.

The authorities and private groups contending for position and benefits are continuously engaged in a subtle exchange of signals about the extent of their potential resources for exerting sanctions: evidences of public alarm or approval of new developments, demonstrations, opinion polls, instances of militancy or violence that suggest the presence of a wider proclivity to protest. These and similar cues are more direct and more potent regulators of public and private actions than the formal elections that are supposed to perform that function.[35] Public officials and private groups are effective politically in the measure that they accurately gauge and anticipate which people will feel strongly about past or contemplated actions, which will respond to tokenism, which will be less impressed with acts than with rhetoric; above all, which will be influenced in their perceptions and behavior by governmental action itself. In this game the temptation to resort to public relations ploys naturally grows as media for reaching mass publics become more readily available for use and abuse. The more blatant gambits of this sort are perceived as what they are, and perhaps all of them are so perceived before long.

The actual outbreak of a riot or an unscheduled violent demonstration at a particular time and place is a facet of the larger process of conflict escalation this whole study examines. The occasion of the outbreak cannot, however, be regarded as intellectually trivial (it is manifestly not socially

---

[35] For an empirical study concluding that elections have little influence as policy mandates see Marvin Weinbaum and Dennis Judd, "In Search of a Mandated Congress," *Midwest Journal of Political Science* 14 (May 1970), 276–302.

trivial) or as an inevitable development, once all the underlying conditions are present. Incidents of precisely the kind that occasionally trigger a riot occur hundreds of times every day without triggering one. The dynamics of the precipitation phase are the same as those of the larger process of which it is a part; they involve a convergence of developments and not a simple association between incident and outbreak. Precipitation of violence is a systematic social process, but it is not a unidimensional one.

Like all political phenomena, precipitation depends fundamentally upon the mobilizing of support and opposition: upon changing perceptions of threats and opportunities in a way that facilitates collective action. To pay attention only to those who at any particular moment are already mobilized in a fairly stable way is to focus upon the trivial: to overlook the *political* action and potentialities in a situation and to define the issue as psychological instead. Such static focusing upon leaders or active cadres is itself a tactic in mobilizing political opposition, though not necessarily a conscious or deliberate one. When a group of whites in East St. Louis in 1917 began marching through the downtown streets shouting that Negroes should leave the city immediately and permanently, that action both assured the ambivalent that if they rioted, they would have plenty of support and intensified the resolution of the people who were already mobilized for action. Soon afterward the crowd began killing blacks.[36]

We can list the forms of perception that seem empirically to be associated with outbreaks, then advance a thesis about the dynamics of their convergence that is consistent with our observations about riot precipitation.

Collective violence occurs only if there is a readiness to regard some other group as an enemy that may, or will, escalate its threats or its thwarting of one's ends.

There must be a perception that if some defy the laws, the authorities, or conventional behavior, others will join in the action and a still larger public will be supportive. Aggressive impulses stemming from frustrations occur frequently in everyone. Rarely do they eventuate in collective physical aggression. They do so when there is reason for people to believe that physical aggression is a norm, to be regarded by a large public—some present and some a reference public—as proper, laudable, or conventional behavior in the specific situation.

The cues that convey such a belief in public support apparently assume a range of forms. They do seem to have an important characteristic in common, and we very likely have seriously undervalued its prevalence: conditioning, by report of incidents elsewhere or by manifest appearance

---

[36] Rudwick, *Race Riot*, p. 44.

of weapons, to the ready possibility of resort to violence. On this point there is both experimental evidence and case studies of riot outbreaks.

That there is a strong "contagion effect" in the outbreak of riots is clear. They have occurred in temporal clusters, the chief concentrations in the United States having appeared in this century in the years 1899–1908, 1915–21, 1935–43, and 1964–70.[37] Within the time periods these larger concentrations cover, there are even more condensed temporal clusterings, such as the months of July and August 1967, and the riots that broke out in a large number of places immediately after the assassination of Martin Luther King in April 1968. The Kerner Commission report makes some observations about clustering as a function of both time and place during the year 1967:

> When timing and location are considered together, other relationships appear. Ninety-eight disorders can be grouped into 23 clusters, which consist of two or more disturbances occurring within two weeks and within a few hundred miles of each other.

> "Clustering" was particularly striking for two sets of cities. The first, centered on Newark, consisted of disorders in 14 New Jersey cities. The second, centered on Detroit, consisted of disturbances in seven cities in Michigan and one in Ohio.[38]

In view of the wide range and the mixed character of the social cues suggesting threat, escalation, and probable support for protest, every individual, no matter how alienated or outraged, is bound to experience a great deal of uncertainty about whether and when he is ready to begin a disturbance or participate in one. He is unsure what he can gain and what he might lose; but these are precisely the issues about which information is most ambiguous, conflicting, and incomplete. Nor can the potential rioter take it for granted that to do nothing is the strategy that will minimize his risks; for he feels deprived and fears worse in the future.

Far from being the resolute, monolithic, "dedicated" militants that are stock characters in the stylized scenario of their political opponents, potential rioters are peculiarly anxious to respond to any information that will resolve their gnawing uncertainty about their support and the risks they run. At this point again, then, large groups of people experience the combination of anxiety and ambivalence that has been noticed in earlier phases of the escalation process as a favorable milieu for change in cognitions. Stable cognitions facilitate planning, conflict resolution (sometimes, it is true, by formal warfare, though not usually so), organization, and social

---

[37] Davis and Gurr, *Violence in America,* pp. 1–100.

[38] Kerner Commission report, p. 114.

symbiosis. Instability and ready susceptibility to changed and changing cues make all these outcomes difficult or impossible; they heighten sensitivity to cues conveying to members of an amorphous crowd a belief that others in the crowd will be aroused to escalating violence or intimidated into docility. Rather than the mass irrationality or collective loss of normal inhibitions postulated in the explanations of crowd behavior of LeBon and Freud,[39] the basic dynamic is, as always, the acceptance of social roles and symbolic cues through role taking. In this context a major moderating influence and source of ambivalence is lacking: that stemming from an anchoring of the self in an organization or community. An event that all recognize as a strong and mutually shared source of anxiety can therefore evoke strong and mutually reinforcing and escalating response. It is often a widely reported instance of police harassment. Often it is news of another riot, especially in a nearby community. Each person recognizes the event as a cue to others who share his fears and his frustration.

The cue often has been the spectacle of readily available weapons, in a sporting goods store that can be looted or in the hands of a nervous policeman. We have both undervalued the conditioning effect of the sight of a symbol of violence and insufficiently explored the dynamic links among a sense of frustration, a symbol that conditions the observer to expect resort to violence from those around him, expectation of significant social support, and the conspicuous presence of a target symbolizing deprivation or frustration. Other people become such symbols. Inanimate objects, such as guns, ammunition, or symbols of a religion or a nationalist movement, also evoke the idea of violence and encourage violent behavior. On this point we have impressive experimental evidence as well.[40]

RIOT PRECIPITATION AS SOCIAL LEARNING

Militant political behavior, including participation in riots, reflects a complex and subtle form of learning: an apprehension by the actors of a complex set of subtle clues about potential participants' probable reactions.

---

[39] See note 8.

[40] Cf. Leonard Berkowitz and Anthony LePage, "Weapons as Aggression-Eliciting Stimuli," *Journal of Personality and Social Psychology* 7 (1967), 202–7; Leonard Berkowitz, "Some Implications of Laboratory Studies of Frustration and Aggression for the Study of Political Violence," paper presented at the 1967 Annual Meeting of the American Political Science Association, Chicago, September 5–9, 1967 (mimeographed); C. A. Loew, "Acquisition of a Hostile Attitude and Its Relationship to Aggressive Behavior" (unpublished doctoral dissertation, Ames: Iowa State University, 1965.

People anticipate the cognitive and behavioral impact upon those around them of past incidents, police harassment and brutality, police assistance to ghetto residents, arrests, new and old deprivations, news that conditions people to expect violence, real and symbolic concessions and indulgences, relatively stable feelings of deprivation in particular ghetto groups and in particular groups outside the ghetto, beliefs about future developments, and so on. Our explanations of mass political response have radically undervalued the ability of the human mind, through role taking and sensitization by exploratory emotions, to take a complex set of such cues into account, evolve a mutually acceptable form of response among a group of significant others, and thereby devise a form of action that will be perceived by others as politically feasible.

As a polar example, a person who heaves a brick at a policeman or through a window is ordinarily perceived as a crackpot or a highly deviant extremist. On some occasions, however, it is possible to anticipate with considerable confidence that the same action will be viewed by some sizable number of people, opponents as well as proponents, as *political* behavior and not as evidence of personal pathology. It will be seen as an understandable response to extant dissatisfactions, grievances, emotions, and sense of political legitimacy. Such learning is a *social* process, not a case of individual learning. It establishes and reflects a complex network of anticipations of the reactions of others to contemplated actions.

If everyone were equally sensitive to such social cues and fully able to adapt his behavior to them, the calculus of political conflict and conflict resolution would be rigorous and certain. The conflict would not have to take place; for its outcome would be perfectly anticipated and agreed upon. What lends uncertainty to this learning act and makes it a political as well as a learning process are (1) the highly unequal incidence in any random population of the capacity for receiving and correctly evaluating social cues; and (2) the ambiguity and informational deficiencies of the cues.

At any time and place in which some significant number of people anticipates the possibility of violence, there is bound to be a range of perceptions, and of degrees of comprehension, of the potentialities of the situation. We can partially explain the incidence of diverse capacities for evaluating the relevant cues.

The strategy for such explanation that is most revealing takes cognitions and self-conceptions to be a function of social interactions. Those people with the surest sense of which groups of people will condone or support which forms of action are also those with the largest repertory of roles: the widest flexibility regarding the roles they can take and the others from whose perspectives they can view the scene and the least rigidity regarding their own roles.

That a person holds extremist or militant political views does not mean he is inflexible. Studies of the correlation between deviant positions and the intensity with which they are held show a strong statistical association between the two;[41] but the two forms of behavior are different and sometimes do *not* occur together. Those leaders of extremist political movements who have been adept at looking at the political scene from the contrasting range of perspectives of their heterogeneous audiences have, naturally enough, been the most successful and effective leaders. Lenin, while both extremist and stable in his political aims, was more effective than the multitude of other reformers and radicals of early twentieth-century Russia because he was far more astute and sensitive than they in apprehending the tactics and the timing that would maximize Bolshevik support and minimize that of his opponents.[42] Hitler was phenomenally deft in the same way, though he apparently grew more rigid in the final war years.[43]

The appropriate test of a political leader's effectiveness obviously depends upon his aims. Both Lenin and Hitler gained power; but there are doubtless many situations in which no conceivable strategy can achieve that result for an extremist movement in the short run. A long-run strategy may nonetheless prove effective, as it did for Lenin after he began to pursue it in the early years of the century. While it is unlikely that any Russian could have foreseen the precise events of World War I or the Russian defeat in it, or that any German could have foreseen the extent of the Great Depression, it was virtually certain, given the social and political tensions and polarization in both countries, that some devastating crisis would soon occur that would make possible a high measure of predictability about the responses of various social groups to dramatic political tactics.

These observations about the ability of the sensitive aspirant to leadership of the discontented to learn and to teach the potentialities for mobilizing them politically should be juxtaposed with earlier observations about the need both of restive groups and of their adversaries to ascribe leadership to a particular person or to an oligarchy. Where there is a leader able to anticipate a followings' potentialities, he is also likely to be perceived as the creator of the discontent. This coincidence makes analysis more complex; but the social scientist should not share in the very confusion that serves political ends for followers and for their adversaries. His

---

[41] Robert E. Lane and David O. Sears, *Public Opinion* (New York: Prentice-Hall, 1964), p. 106.

[42] Sidney Hook, *The Hero in History* (Boston: Beacon Press, 1962); David Shub, *Lenin: A Biography* (Baltimore: Penguin, 1966).

[43] William L. Shirer, *The Rise and Fall of the Third Reich* (New York: Simon and Schuster, 1960); Alan L. Bullock, *Hitler: A Study in Tyranny* (New York: Harper, 1952).

function is to identify the separate functions the "leader" serves for the diverse groups of participants.

THE CONVERGENCE OF EXPECTATIONS

Anxious people are always alert for cues as to how those around them will respond to a contemplated course of action that is controversial: will it be supported or opposed, and with what intensity, and by whom? It is a recurrent observation of this book that a large part of the mass public arrives at the same conclusion about such a question when some conspicuous and dramatic event, usually a governmental act, conveys a particular cue very strongly; or when a sequence of events so infuse a large part of the population with the same beliefs and anticipations that they are fairly confident that others will respond to a precipitating incident in much the same way.

A strategy of explanation, then, cannot usefully rely upon correlations between the outbreak of disturbances and empirical events or conditions; such efforts have consistently proved futile, for reasons already examined. The requisite, rather, is to learn how events come, under some circumstances, to have common *meanings* for part or all of the people who learn about them or witness them; how, moreover, a general awareness arises that meanings are indeed shared. Given a background of anxiety it is clear that some events that perform no such function under other circumstances now become condensation symbols: symbolic forms that merge diverse anxieties and emotions with a shared expectation about the time, the place, and the action that will evoke common support and a common perception of an enemy.

The histories and case studies of collective disturbances and protests show that the incidents serving this symbolic function have run the gamut from explicit signals to highly ambiguous actions whose meanings become clear only as they are disseminated through gestures and tentative efforts at evoking a general response. After two evenings of disturbances in Washington in 1919, the *Washington Post* ran a prominent story that read:

> It was learned that mobilization of every available serviceman stationed in or near Washington or on leave here has been ordered for tomorrow evening near the Knights of Columbus hut on Pennsylvania Avenue between Seventh and Eighth Streets. The hour of assembly is nine o'clock and the purpose is a "clean up" that will cause the events of the last two evenings to pale into insignificance.[44]

---

[44] Waskow, *Race Riot to Sit-In,* p. 25.

Such a "news story" of course represents a polar case of explicit convergence of expectations. Not markedly different are widely disseminated rumors about a mobilization of rioters at a particular time and place.

In such an atmosphere a newspaper story like the one quoted here cannot be regarded as an independent or accidental decision by the reporter or the editors. There is strong psychological and economic incentive for a paper to cater to an intensely held public sentiment, and therefore a probability that some such signal will be published where public opinion supporting a contemplated riot is perceived as widespread and intense. The same incentive exists for politicians and aspirants to positions of political leadership; and so it is similarly probable that they will furnish some kind of cue suggesting wide social support and perhaps signaling a time and place for action.

The most common forms that cue a convergence of expectations and so contribute to the precipitation of a disturbance have already been noted; a prologue of publicized incidents that increase tension and threat expectations, followed by a report of an injury to someone or to several who are representative of the deprived group: an unjust arrest, an assault, any signal that repression has escalated. Such incidents serve to converge perceptions and beliefs because they fit the expectations an anxious mass public has already come to share. People who feel threatened look for, and are eager to believe, that reports of such incidents are true and that they herald harm and repression; for they recognize, though usually not consciously, that such reports will indeed converge expectations and win social support and protection for the militant actions the individual wants to pursue. When a policeman, or a protester, publicly commits a violent action, he greatly clarifies the situation for his ambivalent potential adversaries. He has defined his own role and legitimated a violent role for them.[45]

The course of a disturbance, and therefore its precipitation at a particular place and time, is in some measure also cued by beliefs regarding what has happened earlier and hence about what others expect now. Rudé makes a revealing observation in this connection:

> In some rural riots, as in the French of 1789, the path of disturbance actually followed well-trodden and traditional routes. Thus memory and oral tradition, as well as the material conditions or social relations of the present, served to perpetuate the forms of popular disturbance.[46]

---

[45] For a discussion of this point see William A. Westley, "The Encouragement of Violence through Legitimation," *The Annals* 34 (March 1966), pp. 120–26.

[46] Rudé, *The Crowd in History*, p. 242.

The forms of disturbance, including the occasions of precipitation and therefore of quiescence, are sometimes indigenous to a particular culture, as Rudé implies. The burning of houses, the smashing of machinery, breaking into shops, stopping work for short periods to demonstrate in the square, breaking windows, sniping, and killing people—each of these has been the dominant mode of militant expression at some times and places. The explanation for the particular form a disturbance assumes (or for the form the ritualization of conflict takes) must be in different terms from the explanation of the generation and escalation of conflict. It depends upon different events, less universal in character—more closely tied to the norms and legitimized practices of a particular time and place.

INFORMAL CONVERGENCE AND FORMAL ORGANIZATION

Resort to violence as a form of militant protest is apparently stimulated by the absence of formal organization among the disaffected, though it is widely supposed that the converse is true: that the unorganized are likely to be docile or ineffective and the organized a threat. Evidence for the thesis that violent outbreaks initially occur among the unorganized and that cooptation is a more likely outcome where protesters are organized is discussed in chapter 2.

An understanding of the convergence of expectations among potential rioters also throws light upon resort to violence by an unorganized, amorphous crowd. Where people who feel frustrated and deprived have joined an organization, they have reason to believe that they can pursue and protect their interests through such methods as organized lobbying, negotiation, and formal representation in governmental agencies. The observations in chapter 4 about the psychological implications of ritualization of conflict deal directly with the inducements to quiescence and acceptance of established procedures provided by formal governmental conflict resolution arrangements.

An unorganized group of people who share a strong sense of deprivation and an expectation of escalating threat cannot hope for change through such methods. The people in a crowd or an amorphous group who happen to be present in some urban neighborhood on a hot day may be intensely aware of the problems but are equally aware that they are not organized for lobbying and that government officials do not even perceive them as a "public" with strongly shared perceptions. For them, there is no personally and socially satisfying alternative to militant expression. The very uncertainty and ambiguity of their situation make expression through militance all the more necessary. Because they are uncertain and anxious not only about an external threat but even about their support within their own group, they need the social anchoring and reassuring sense of identity that militant action provides. By joining the action each individual tells himself and others in an unambiguous way what he wants and how he sees himself.

At the same time he commits himself publicly to this social and political role in a way that makes later repudiation of it difficult and perhaps impossible, for the act he publicly commits is defined as illegal. People who resort to this form of social action are thus repudiating a role of passive victim of exploitation. It is their only way to show themselves and each other that they do not accept the ascribed role of the indefinitely exploitable and expendable. To demonstrate that fact is vital to them, for they are anxious and not sure which of these roles they can play.

Riots usually do not occur when someone publicly urges violent action upon a presumably deprived population. Such explicit testing for support is certainly common, and it usually meets with no response. Even Rap Brown, already a symbol of militant protest, could not win a following when, in June 1967, he went into the Negro areas of Atlanta and called for a demonstration to protest the shooting of several blacks who had been sitting on the front porch of a house.[47] The most modest conclusion to be drawn from such cases is that the combination of deprivation with a clear signal to act is not in itself sufficient to precipitate violence. There must also be cues widely interpreted as catalyzing a general readiness to join in the action.

RIOTING DISTINGUISHED FROM ORGANIZED COMBAT

The role structures and significant symbols associated with both riots and formal combat become clearer when the two are carefully distinguished from each other; for organization, whether for cooperation or combat, involves a fundamentally different form of social interaction from rioting and is not an intensified or escalated state of the same phenomenon.

When an individual becomes part of an organization, whether it is an army or other private or public bureaucracy, he accepts an ascribed role. For that facet of his life he suspends his flexible responsiveness to others' cues regarding his part in the social milieu. Many members of an army are ambivalent, or even self-consciously unhappy and resentful of the role they are forced to play. The ambivalence or resentment rarely expresses itself,

[47] Kerner Commission report, p. 36.

however, in a change in self-presentation or formal role, as *typically* happens in the case of the rioter. For soldiers there are the most severe sanctions for desertion or even formal disobedience of orders; such behavior is regarded as deviant. Ambivalence or resentment most commonly finds expression in the form of ritualistic "griping." Not infrequently it takes the form of marked lack of zeal in playing the expected formal role and in evasion of expectations whenever the evasion can be accomplished covertly. A revealing, if atypically dramatic, example appears in the finding of Samuel Stouffer that a high proportion of American soldiers in World War II failed to fire their guns in battle and even more regularly evaded other army norms, rules, and bureaucratic expectations.[48] The key distinction is that between restriction to a narrowly prescribed role in a formal fighting organization and an anxious search for a form of behavior that will win social support in the course of a riot. Together with others who are similarly groping, the rioter may create a new and more respected role for himself and thereby achieve a new measure of dignity. His options are wider than they are for the soldier. The participant in a riot inevitably experiences some ambivalence about adopting the role of the rioter rather than his customary one or, possibly, other alternatives.

An organization, like the individual in it, must fit into a structure. It normally does so by becoming a part of a larger or adversary organization, as in cooptation. Occasionally it fits into a larger structure by explicitly assuming an adversary or belligerent posture and formally defining one or more outside organizations as the enemy.

While national armies represent the polar example of this last form of organization, rebellious movements that have developed a formal organization also exemplify it. The completeness with which the organization specifies the function of individuals and enforces the specifications can vary widely. Some degree of such organization and specification of roles is bound to appear in any active protest movement that lasts more than a few days, the normal duration of a riot; but it is not clear whether the fact of organization chiefly helps prolong the action or vice versa. In any event, the creation of an organization signals a changed role structure and an altered set of significant symbols.

The two situations discussed so far—rigid enforcement of role performances through formal organization and search for social support for new roles in an unorganized milieu—rarely appear empirically in pure form. Two- and three-day riots do come close to the unorganized polar form; but combat organizations never completely specify and enforce the

---

[48] Samuel Stouffer, *The American Soldier* (Princeton, N.J.: Princeton University Press, 1949).

roles their members play, and vary widely in how completely they do so. Military organizations enforce ascribed roles most completely on such ceremonial occasions as formal inspections, parades, drill, courts martial, and the public recitation of rules and other dogma. They permit a wider role choice and employment of individual faculties when there is useful work to be done and especially when people have to cope with complex and challenging problems, as in battle, movement through enemy terrain, and the fictionalization of records and reports to satisfy hierarchical superiors that orders are being followed and ascribed roles maintained.

There is typically an inverse relationship between the breadth and intensity with which cognitions and values are shared on the one hand and the rigidity of formal role specifications through organization on the other. Participants in a guerrilla movement normally share common values and cognitions respecting their cause to a high degree and can be counted on to use their faculties to realize their common objectives, flexibly adapting tactics and role performances to changing situations and to others' actions. We have already noted that riot participants do the same thing, though they are less sure than guerrillas which goals are commonly supported and therefore must also be responsive to new cues bearing on that point. At the opposite pole are soldiers who are disaffected, either because they do not support the war in which they fight or because they resent their roles and status. Whenever there is suspicion of such disaffection, as there normally is in national armies, there is certain to be emphasis upon ceremonial acting out of the roles, as in close order drill, and upon formal adherence to them.

Occasionally, probably rarely, military rank-and-file support of a national cause is so clear that ceremony and enforcement of ascribed role performances are lax and minimal. According to one study, the Israeli army exemplifies this state of affairs.[49]

The dichotomy analyzed here is pertinent to all collective enterprises, whether they involve overt group conflict or not. The particular mix of these two organizational modes that characterizes any collective enterprise is, moreover, a key influence upon the effectiveness with which objectives are realized. The dichotomy manifestly applies to operations in hospitals, research agencies, and governmental or private organizations with non-routine functions. It therefore applies to orchestras and chamber groups. Any group of musicians who uncritically rely upon the score and the conductor to program their behaviors will present performances that are mediocre or worse. The conductor who is an effective leader will somehow

---

[49] Rozann Rothman, "Education and Participation in the Israeli Army" (unpublished).

stimulate the players to minimize their dependence upon cues from the leader, reject the role of the robot, and employ all their faculties to respond sensitively to the potentialities in the score and to anticipations of other players' responses. For an individual player this may involve supplying leadership in the negotiation of a passage that would otherwise be banal. It may involve cuing a nuance in respect to speed, rhythm, timbre, or emphasis.[50] Such collective sensitivity to others represents the polar opposite of the form of "discipline" that denotes blind adherence to prescribed rule. The same point can be made of any nonroutine group enterprise. "Discipline," "organization," and "leadership" are ambiguous words, regularly used to connote either pole of this dichotomy as well as intermediate patterns.

RIOT PRECIPITATION AS SYMBOLIC RESPONSE

This formulation places the emphasis upon the meanings to participants and potential participants in riots of their observations and their cognitions. The alternative, and more common, form of explanation of riot precipitation looks for correlations between the outbreak of disturbances and such data as: the proportion of a city's population that is black; income levels and other indicators of absolute deprivation; the demographic characteristics of ghetto residents; and police actions. This latter approach has yielded few, if any, consistently significant correlations.

To study the conditions of change in meanings calls for more subtle and more complex methods and concepts. It calls for concern for the phenomenology of the whole situation from the perspective of participants and not only from the perspective of social scientists employing a limited range of tools and modes of observation. Our explanation amounts to a partial formula for specifying the particular perspective from which a group of participants will perceive the action: pseudospeciation into allies and enemies; humanizing contact with significant others; actions that commit actors to consonant perceptions; cuings about the range of roles that will be supported or penalized. While the explanation is incomplete, it suggests how to take account of the full complexity of the phenomenon to be understood; and what it suggests does conform to what observers and historians of riots see.

---

[50] This example was suggested to me by a conversation with John Garvey, director of the University of Illinois Jazz Band and violist in the Walden String Quartet.

Chapter 8

RITUALIZATION: INDUSTRIAL RELATIONS

In the highly industrialized countries labor-management relations exemplify an advanced stage of the ritualization of political conflict. Analysis of the dynamic undercurrents in such conflict, therefore, reveals much about contemporary politics. In this policy area the salient elements are: a high measure of agreement among management and union leaders about their relative vulnerability and bargaining resources; a set of stylized procedures that both signal aggression and reassure both sides that it will be held within acceptable limits, while at the same time they marshal the support of union members and of the mass public for the leadership and for the outcomes of bargaining. The routines that accomplish these functions embrace both governmental "interventions" into labor-management conflict and collective bargaining negotiations.

POLITICAL AND SYMBOLIC FUNCTIONS OF UNIONS

Major unions in both advanced and developing countries serve as an integrating link, helping to furnish political and organizational support for government, union, and business bureaucracies, and at the same time providing symbolic reassurances for the workers and the mass public. By supplying these diverse benefits for the groups composing the system of industrial relations decisionmaking, unions help to preserve the system and the established power and status relationships within it. This generalization is less significant for the social scientist, however, than a specification of the exact functions served and needs supplied by particular groups and activities on the industrial relations scene.

The symbiotic tie between political leadership and unions is the most characteristic and significant relationship unions sustain in our times; yet students of industrial relations have treated it extensively chiefly when they have been concerned with the underdeveloped countries. When dealing with labor-government ties in the industrialized countries, labor economists have usually concentrated upon labor's role in political parties and election campaigns while paying less attention to the more pervasive, more covert, and more influential ongoing relationships with political administrations while they are in power.

Obviously it is public support that political leaders need most: support for policies that are popular and support or acquiescence in policies that are unpopular or that hurt sizable groups of the population. Studies of nationalism and industrialization in developing countries suggest that the labor movements of these countries are often closely and formally tied to the nationalist movements and, after independence, to the governments: directly influencing policy, influenced by policy, a major source of political leadership, sometimes with the same individuals and groups supplying union and governmental leadership.[1] In these countries we recognize that political and labor groupings supply each other with a set of tangible and symbolic supports, even while evanescent conflict and tension (intra- and intergroup) continue. The tie of both to nationalized and governmentally controlled industry involves business management in the same symbiotic arrangement. This structuring encourages and makes highly probable the popular support or acquiescence of workers and nationalist masses for public policies that the government-labor-business complex administers.

In the advanced countries few studies have focused upon the underlying mutual supports that flow from the structuring of industrial relations decisionmaking; perceptions that are consonant with dominant myths are harder to recognize for what they are in one's own culture. Our conceptual frameworks are underdeveloped in the highly developed countries; but union-government-business maneuvering, conflict, gesturing, and bargaining buttress popular and worker support for political and union bureaucracies in these countries as well.

What are the explicit and the tacit bargains? The decisive resource government offers is its role as principal determiner of employment levels, of labor surplus or shortage, and therefore of the bargaining power of unions and unorganized workers; the propositions suggested here apply to the degree that government does play this role. Through arms, space, construction, stockpiling, welfare, and other expenditures that constitute the major components of the national budget and through fiscal and monetary policies that are the critical influences upon employment, price, and wage levels, it is government and businessmen acting in and through government that basically fix workers' standards of living. Compared to this considera-

---

[1] Cf. Bruce H. Millen, *The Political Role of Labor in Developing Countries* (Washington, D.C.: Brookings, 1963), chap. 5; Clark Kerr et al., *Industrial Man* (Cambridge, Mass.: Harvard University Press, 1960), pp. 215–26.

tion, the influences that have conventionally occupied the attention of labor economists are largely symbolic and in some cases trivial. Collective bargaining strategy, protective labor legislation, union security legislation, the friendly or distant posture of political leaders toward unions, and their pro-union or anti-union rhetoric have become economic froth when compared to the macroeconomic influences, though they remain politically and organizationally important.

For union leaders and for political analysts it is a cardinal fact that the union leadership is not involved in either a significant or a public way in the decisions that affect workers most: public contract awards, the formulation of the national budget, the shaping of monetary policy in central banks and treasury departments. In this organizational context union leaders must find subtler, less direct methods to justify their leadership to the rank and file than were necessary in the early days of unionism. This is all the more true because it is quite unclear to economists, and seems only a little clearer to others, whether and under what conditions unions even affect wage levels significantly.

Workers are likely to acquiesce without wide or deep dissent in the continued incumbency of their union officials as long as the economic benefits of an affluent society continue to roll in and as long as the union officials present an appropriate dramaturgical perfomance suggesting they are furthering the interests of their followers. In supplying both kinds of benefits, government can help union officials the most; and the latter accordingly have as large a stake as businessmen in the continuation of an economy based upon large government expenditures. The ready response of a part of the low income population to apparent foreign military threats gives union and government officials a further incentive to support such policies as a strategy for retaining their followings. It is therefore much too superficial to attribute the strong support of mainstream unions in major countries for tough foreign policies to the personal predilections of incumbent officials. Regardless of the verbal rationalizations, the reasons run deeper than leaders' personal values. There are systematic reasons why potential leaders with dissenting values find it hard to achieve or retain high office or significant influence.

By the same token it is clear what unions and workers generally have to offer public officials and business interests as their contribution to the tacit bargain: a following that is either actively supportive or acquiescent in the policies that give these groups their political power and their profits. This tie runs deeper than party affiliations or campaign rhetoric. It applies in the United States under Nixon or Johnson as much as in western Europe and the developing countries.

There is no intention here to suggest conscious conspiring for selfish ends. The argument is that economic structuring yields these behaviors as part of the rational working of the system. The men involved are doubtless sincere and patriotic, but their motivations are irrelevant as far as this analysis is concerned. They act rationally, given their roles in the organization. It is also worth noting that there is persuasive psychological evidence that people's perceptions of fact are influenced by their interests and motivations.[2] The economic interests of the groups involved in this decisionmaking structure are clear enough, and their perceptions of appropriate economic policy and foreign policy are doubtless conditioned accordingly.

When cold war allegiances and public values generally are divided or bimodal, the role of union officials is inevitably more complicated; but the function they serve in conserving established decisionmaking institutions is still clear enough. The CGIL (Confederazione generale italiana del lavoro) in Italy and the CGT (Confédération générale du travail) in France oppose American policy, but they are integrally involved in the economic policies of their own countries and provide necessary buttresses for them. Through collective bargaining and tensions over particular contract negotiations, they reassure their members that their interests are being protected and thereby channel the expression of discontent into these passing economic conflicts rather than into serious political protest or revolutionary activity. They thereby buttress the position of the union bureaucracies and also help provide the work force industry needs. They did this in Italy even in the 1950s when union wage push demonstrably had less influence than management wage pull in raising wages; with the subsequent decline in unemployment levels in Italy employers repeatedly declared they found it easier to bargain with the CGIL than with the Christian Democratic CISL (Confederazione italiana del sindacati lavoratori).[3] These unions have also been involved in economic planning committees in both France and Italy and thereby have further tied their members to established policymaking institutions.

The basically conservative function of CGIL and CGT activities must therefore be recognized as separate from their rhetoric, which continues to conform on occasion to the Marxist myths. A detailed study of the Italian Communist Party emphasizes both that the party has increasingly become part of the established Italian polity and now helps maintain it, and that the CGIL has played a conservative role in shaping party policy. Sidney Tarrow concludes that the Italian Communist Party has been concerned chiefly

---

[2] See chap. 2, note 1.

[3] Murray Edelman and R. W. Fleming, *The Politics of Wage-Price Decisions: A Four-Country Analysis* (Urbana: University of Illinois Press, 1965), pp. 36–38. For a discussion of wage drift in Germany, see pp. 115–18.

with winning elections and not with conspiracy or revolution and that the Italian political system would be unstable if the party did not play the role it does. He also points out that the CGIL, which is dominated by the Communist Party, has avoided the political strike weapon in recent years and concentrated on bread-and-butter issues and that the union federation has consistently been a conservative influence within the party councils.[4]

There are some revealing additional facets to the symbiosis when an administration friendly to labor is in power. Then governmental leaders receive overt political support from the union bureaucracy. This is not chiefly significant as a device for delivering a labor vote, which can seldom be done much beyond the extent that other conditions, such as high unemployment levels or political socialization processes, would have delivered it anyway. It has been more useful as a device for blessing political leaders with a liberal aura and thereby augmenting their support among liberals.

More important are the frequent attempts of governments friendly to labor to use their organizational ties to the labor movement to get cooperation in wage restraint programs. Under the British Labor government from 1948 to 1950, in the Netherlands for a time in the late fifties, in the United States in some industries in the early sixties, and doubtless in other places for limited times, this tactic has been fairly successful. It has also sometimes weakened the organizational positions of the union leaders who cooperated, and in both England and the Netherlands it contributed to the downfall or withdrawal from office of labor parties. This particular form of labor support for government has apparently fallen short of carrying the rank and file along except while inflationary threats or balance of payments deficits were dramatic and immediately ominous.

In general, union officials win more significant benefits from collaboration with friendly governments than do the workers. Some of the demands of the latter are likely to win nominal support, but friendly governments can typically count on the workers' continued political support regardless of whether their demands are actually met through legislative and administrative action. Consequently, prolabor policies are usually put into effect when one of two conditions prevails: (1) Business groups may favor them because they impose on a wide segment of the public the cost of a program which business would otherwise be under pressure to finance, as in the case of social security benefits. In all countries social security has been a form of political insurance for elites, and therefore has been favored or accepted by conservative as well as liberal politicians. (2) Some powerful business groups may favor protective labor policies because they force their competitors' labor costs up to the level of their own. In the United States, for example, a major reason for the passage of federal minimum wage laws

---

[4] Sidney Tarrow, "Marxist Parties in Dual Political Systems: Communism in Italy," *American Political Science Review* 61 (March 1967), 39–53.

was the support of New England textile interests worried about competition from unorganized southern mills. In contrast to these forms of governmental help for labor that are supported by business, note the purely nominal and unsuccessful support of Kennedy and Johnson for repeal of Section 14b of the Taft-Hartley Act authorizing the states to enact right-to-work laws; in these respects the American experience is paradigmatic for other advanced countries.

Union leaders, on the other hand, win important support for their organizational positions from friendly governments and sometimes from nominally unfriendly ones. Wide publicity is given to the fact that they are frequently consulted by the President, the political party leadership, and the Secretary of Labor regarding presidential nominations, important appointments in the labor field, labor legislation, and such nonlabor policy areas as civil rights and tariff legislation and treaties. They are also invited from time to time to official White House and other public functions. In return for the aura of popular support they confer on the government, they receive an aura of high influence and statesmanship which helps them in winning acceptance from the public generally and in retaining a union following. This exchange of quid pro quos is far less significant or vital than the bargain involving public contracts and economic policy; but it is a political catalyst for both sides and part of the same game, in its consequences if not always in its motivations.

If their governmental ties help union leaders win the status and the rank-and-file support they need, so does collective bargaining. Collective bargaining can seldom, perhaps never, be regarded today as either a major or an independent determinant of wage levels or worker income. At most it provides workers in some organized industries with somewhat higher wage levels than they would otherwise enjoy, though many economists doubt that it does even that much; and some eminent ones are sure it does not. In the most thorough review of the evidence on this issue H. Gregg Lewis reached the following conclusion:

> I estimated that unionism has increased the inequality of average relative wages among industries by about 8 percent. If, in addition, unionism has changed the average relative wage inequality *among workers within industries* by less than 5 percent, then I estimate that unionism has changed the relative inequality of the distribution of wages *among all workers* by less than 6 percent.
>
> I conclude tentatively that the impact of unionism on relative wage inequality among all workers has been small—under 6 percent. The direction of the effect, on presently available evidence, is ambiguous.[5]

---

[5] H. Gregg Lewis, *Unionism and Relative Wages in the United States* (Chicago: University of Chicago Press, 1963), p. 295.

In some other countries, as already noted, there is persuasive evidence that wage pull on the initiative of the larger and more efficient industrial concerns has been a far greater influence upon workers' earnings than collective bargaining.

In the United States and abroad it is increasingly apparent that collective bargaining is serving political and organizational functions even though its economic functions are difficult to demonstrate and are viewed with growing skepticism. The dramaturgy of militant negotiations and cliffhanger settlements does constitute an acting out of the union leader's posture of serving his constituents zealously and therefore bolsters their loyalty to him and to the union. To a lesser degree the negotiations serve the same organizational function for management bureaucracies. It seems reasonable to suppose that the need for the dramaturgy and the ritual grows as suspicion becomes more widespread that the influence of unionism upon wage inequality is small.

Even more clearly, collective bargaining rituals serve another function for the total decisionmaking system and directly for management. In accomplishing this second function they are aided by widely publicized governmental mediation, arbitration, and exhortations to settle conflicts. These activities legitimize the imposition of greater burdens upon consumers through higher prices or taxes. Regardless of the precise economic leeway for administered pricing in particular industries, it is essentially a political tactic in the sense that it requires the acquiescence of the public: its willingness to pay more without resorting to political protest, demanding governmental intervention to keep prices or rates down, or fighting higher subway fares or taxes. Such public acquiescence is frequently bought through militant wage bargaining, with threats to the public's convenience, comfort, and well-being. In the steel industry and in the New York transit system, the gambit has usually produced the desired results. This is, of course, not the only or the invariably successful consequence of wage bargaining, but it is a frequent and important function of such bargaining. There is good reason to suspect that it is a more vital function for the decisionmaking system than the instrumental influence of bargaining upon wage levels. The dramaturgy of militant bargaining bolsters the public's belief in wage push; and it is this widely held belief, and not the demonstrability of wage push, that helps management raise prices without witnessing adverse political effects.

The ritualization of labor-management conflict is of course a conclusion of the social scientist or historian who examines behaviors and their net consequences, but does so in retrospect. The actors in everyday life see not ritualization but conflict. Reinforced by signals from the adversary parties, the government, and the communications media, they focus their attention upon differences in positions, which are systematically exaggerated and publicized in the early stages of negotiations. The hardships strikers experience during a strike and the anticipation of them before a strike further underline the seriousness and the reality of the conflict. This perception promotes intensified rank-and-file support for leaders in what is perceived as a crisis and promotes mass acceptance of an array of deprivations, including the built-in limitations on economic and other benefits in the settlement.

Other deprivations that are built into the overall system of industrial relations decisionmaking, particularly fairly extended periods without work, are also made more acceptable by the dramaturgy of conflict. Analysts of strikes notice that they often occur when inventories are high; for managements then have added reason to "take a strike." In this situation the strike is in substantial measure a substitute for layoffs that would occur anyway. As just noted, it serves important functions for the union leadership as well. Seen now as part of a crisis tactic for winning an economic or status victory rather than as a simple deprivation, the hardship buttresses support for the union even while it helps resolve a management dilemma. This interplay is basically different from that between adversaries in international conflict, even though publicity to the other side's hawkish behavior mobilizes mass support in both cases. In industrial conflict in highly developed countries it is the appearance of escalation that serves a critical function and not the actual destruction of the other side. Only when the conflict is rigidly controlled are there mutual benefits. Phenomenological perceptions that flow naturally from the institutional arrangements evoke the mass supports necessary for the benefit exchanges analyzed earlier in this chapter.

The principal benefits to business from the total system, then, are lucrative public contracts, a high and growing level of status and influence in public policy information, legitimation for its pricing policies, legitimation for some of the subsidies it receives directly and indirectly from the public treasury, and public approbation for its posture of social and patriotic service. In return it contributes economic benefits to workers that may go well beyond the power of unions to require, especially in the measure that labor costs constitute a small proportion of total costs.

The system has also functioned highly selectively, however, to legitimize effective restraints upon wages and prices when strong military, business, or political interests demanded them. Such demands, naturally enough, are increasingly likely as the economy heats up, inflation threatens, or balance-of-payments deficits loom large. Under these conditions profits are likely to be high as well, so that restraint is not economically disastrous and not necessarily even serious except to those workers who remain unemployed for extended periods. Monetary controls and threats to dump stockpiled goods on the market make for price restraint and also legitimize a hard management line on wages and employment. These encounters between government and particular idustries bolster the government's support with that large part of the public concerned about price increases, and they sometimes help resolve some internal management conflicts: for example, among steel firms inclined to raise prices, yet also worried about competition from foreign steel and from substitute products. Even these instrumentally effective governmental maneuvers, therefore, have their politically reassuring and organizationally useful aspects.

Another form of labor conflict has come to have conservative political consequences in the years since this pattern of exchanges has become established. Relatively well-paid American white workers have felt threatened by the status aspirations of Negroes. That such concern about blacks existed among workers in the late sixties is suggested by various surveys—among them a Gallup Poll in September 1968 showing 15 percent of union members favoring George Wallace, a white supremacy advocate, for President; 42 percent favoring Humphrey; and 36 percent favoring Nixon. In the South, 50 percent of union members favored Wallace, 29 percent Humphrey, and 16 percent Nixon. At that time both Wallace and Nixon were taking stronger stands than Humphrey in favor of police action to curb restiveness, and there was little question that this issue was the salient one in producing a shift of union member sentiment from a mean of over 69 percent Democratic in the presidential elections from 1936 to 1964 (with a low of 57 percent in the Eisenhower election of 1956) to the 42 percent favoring Humphrey early in the 1968 campaign.[6] Gallup data indicate a significant shift in the voting, by party, of manual and white collar workers between the 1964 and the 1968 Presidential elections:

| | 1964 | | 1968 | | |
	D %	R %	D %	R %	Wallace %
Manual	71	29	50	35	15
White collar	57	43	41	47	12

The anxieties of white wage earners about Negro encroachment upon their status and their jobs have furthered conservative ideologies and policies in several ways. Tension has increased between some union workers and upper middle class whites who are more supportive of egalitarian

---

[6] *The New York Times* (September 11, 1968).

policies and whose own success looks the more impressive if they persuade themselves that opportunity is open to all. Politicians have tailored their appeals and their positions to the demands for law and order, and belief in the support of lower middle class whites has encouraged police forces to discourage or suppress protest and dissent. These effects of widespread wage earner sentiment regarding race relations and political dissent are the more potent, of course, because of the developments already noted: the growth of union influence through ritualistic conflict with management and a consequent union-management symbiosis.

As far as the rank and file are concerned, the chief needs are for status in society, assurance of support for wage increases, and job security. The decisionmaking system provides all these in diverse ways. Conventional focusing upon collective bargaining rather than the entire system obscures the degree to which governmental and business actions provide the reassurances for which we have commonly credited the unions and provide them for the unorganized as well as the organized. More important, it obscures the degree to which the reassurances are symbolic and rhetorical rather than tangible in character. In view of this ambiguous position of the worker, it is hardly surprising that the dual loyalty studies popular a few years ago should have reached the findings they did. What is involved, one suspects, is a diffused loyalty to a business-labor-government complex that increases as real wages and social status increase and as this happy state of affairs becomes more clearly attributable to public policies, including defense and war expenditures.

To behave in this way is to accept a particular political role and self-conception. When workers limit their aspirations to what government and management offer them with only ritualistic pressure, they accept such conformist behavior as legitimate, as serving the public interest, and as defining their own proper place and function in the social order. Their self-conception is of course cherished and defended. Because it involves a mutually beneficial exchange of benefits and supports with the economic and political elite, attacks either upon the established political order or upon the union worker's role in it are seen as attacks on a part of his own ego. The identification between the self and the established political order explains the zeal and the intensity with which some hard hats oppose those they see as seeking to destroy the political order. We have, then, another instance of linkage among a shared political belief, a definition of the self, and the expression of emotion which inhibits empathy with adversaries and flexible role behavior.

The argument so far adds up to two major themes. First, the various groupings discussed (business, labor, and related government agencies) are in an important sense components of a single system whose functions are (1) to ensure and promote a continuing demand for production and a continuing flow of public contracts and (2) to arrange a mutual exchange of economic and political benefits. Once all the major dimensions of the transaction are brought into perspective, the assumption that union-management bargaining is a critical forum for economic decisionmaking is no longer tenable. It becomes at most a short-run and derivative influence upon economic trends and frequently a ritual, though it continues to have a significant organizational and political impact.

Like some other forms of encounter between two of the systems' subunits, it creates threats to be appeased; and the inevitable resolution of such encounters constitutes reassurance that necessary minor adjustments in bargaining power have been made and that everyone concerned still has his attention focused on the main event—the demand for production from which all blessings flow.[7]

Second, those directly involved in the bargaining and the decision-making can act only when they win support or neutrality from a large public of rank-and-file workers and political spectators. Symbolic reassurances are partly what these large publics draw from the total transaction: reassurances that serve incidentally to tie them economically and psychologically to the political establishment and the status quo.

MAJOR STATUS AND POWER REALIGNMENTS

In relatively infrequent periods of major realignment in status relationships and bargaining power, quite different political and psychological mechanisms come into play, and conflict escalation may occur. Such realignments seem to be triggered by large discrepancies between widespread public values regarding labor's status and bargaining relationships and its actual status and bargaining relationships. When it became evident in the thirties that workers and unions enjoyed far more public support than was reflected in existing institutions for determining wages and working conditions, it was inevitable that workers would grow increasingly restive until new institutions and a major status realignment had occurred. Comparable periods of realignment in other countries are not hard to identify, and the

---

[7] The view taken here that conflict and bargaining are compatible with, and promote, basic common interests obviously owes much to the kinds of analysis suggested by Lewis Coser in *The Functions of Social Conflict* (Glencoe, Ill.: Free Press, 1956), and to Thomas Schelling's concept of the mixed-motives game in *The Strategy of Conflict* (Cambridge, Mass.: Harvard University Press, 1960).

same process has on occasion operated in other policy areas, such as civil rights. The trigger for such realignment is never repressive objective conditions in themselves, but rather a discrepancy between public values and the values realized through existing institutions. The point underlines the continuing need for decisionmakers to win popular support or quiescence.

In an analysis of the decolonialization process in Africa, Frantz Fanon suggests that violence is a key catalyst to such major realignments.[8] It is not so much the instrumental usefulness of violence to groups striving for higher status and more tangible benefits that matters. It is rather the impact upon public opinion of counterviolence by elites and the impact of militant self-reliant effort upon the personalities of members of the low status group that are crucial. A Republic Steel massacre symbolizes the divergence between existing power relationships and the growing consensus on what they ought to be and thereby solidifies and promotes broader support for union organization. The fight on the bridge in the 1937 Ford strike symbolizes a worker whose militance brings with it a new estimate of his own dignity and who will therefore behave with new independence and at a more demanding level in the future. The analogy to the civil rights revolution of the fifties and sixties is evident. The process is basically one of adjusting social norms to self-conceptions and personality formation; violence, militance, and counterviolence serve a crucial catalytic function in bringing about the adjustment.

THE COOPTATION OF UNIONS

While major realignments in status and bargaining power may occasionally occur, the studies and observations in the United States, western Europe, and the developing countries in the postwar years call attention chiefly to the overt and tacit exchanges of benefits with which most of this chapter is concerned. With respect to such key objectives as giving workers higher living standards, maintaining economic stability when it is seriously and obviously threatened, increasing GNP, and maintaining political stability there is a striking sharing of values among political, industrial, and union leaders. Nor can this be regarded as a deliberate tactic by any of them. It involves considerable internalization of the others' values, doubtless encouraged by the realization that social, economic, or political instability threatens the system from which they all draw impressive benefits. Within this context, hard bargaining and occasional strikes do not have the same

---

[8] Frantz Fanon, *The Wretched of the Earth* (New York: Grove Press, 1963).

symbolic significance they take on during major status realignments. They are manipulators of public arousal and support, including the arousal, quiescence, and support of the rank and file.

In a world polarized by a cold war, this situation has given the major influence in public economic policy to business management and assured the cooperation of other elites. Balance-of-payment problems, threats and fears of inflation, direct control of the mass communications media by business groups, and growing affluence in the industrialized countries all serve, through the needs for reassurance created by frequent crises, to tie labor and public officials to the management orientation. Unlike governmental and labor bureaucrats, business leaders have no public constituency. It is precisely their ability to attract public support that makes the cooperation of government and labor officials vital to the continued functioning of the system.

Chapter 9

ESCALATION: INTERNATIONAL RELATIONS

THE TERMS OF ANALYSIS

Man's attempts to curb the pathologies of international politics—war, nationalism, arms buildups, and restrictions on international trade—constitute a curious history of futility, in theorizing and in practice. It is likely that more energy, time, and speculation have gone into the practice and theory of international relations than into any other facet of public affairs. Yet we can neither explain nor control international conflict as well as we routinely explain domestic political and economic developments and can influence the latter. Wherever failure to find a solution to a problem has been so complete over so long a period of time, it is sound strategy to assume that the problem has not been defined so that it can be analyzed rationally: that the very terms in which it is posed are suspect.

The key term in discussions of international relations is "nation," and it is exactly here that an unconventional assumption may prove enlightening and point to analytical possibilities not inhibited by age-old semantic confusions. Is it really useful to take it for granted, as common sense suggests and as both the popular and most of the academic discussions of international politics conventionally do, that it is *nations* that are in conflict: that the nation is the unit that has adversary interests, bargains, and is therefore the appropriate unit of analysis?

Clearly, the nation is a gross entity. With respect to any issue occasioning international conflict there are readily identifiable group interests within the nation, some opposing each other and many indifferent or quiescent. If, as a long line of political theory in domestic politics suggests, we assume that it is the interests of specific groups with shared attitudes rather than a "national interest" that explain the course of affairs, some new perspectives, new lines of analysis, and new strategic possibilities at once come into focus.

Consider as an initial and basic example the group interests concerned with conflict and détente itself. The hawks in any country gain budgetary increases, status, and escalation through domestic politics fastest in the degree that their opposite numbers, the hawks in a potential enemy country, make the same political gains. The hawks in rival countries are therefore in a position to help each other; and regardless of their motives, their behaviors are cooperative in this pragmatic sense. Though open communication about such mutual help is typically not feasible and would be sternly abjured as unpatriotic, there is inevitably a kind of tacit bargaining here, if only in the measure that hawks in each country recognize that it is to their advantage to observe, to publicize, and to exaggerate hawkish behavior of their opposite numbers in rival countries.

Similarly, doves in different nations serve each others' interests, have a stake in publicizing and exaggerating each others' successes, and win what they are after in domestic politics in the degree that the mass public can be impressed with the influence of doves in other countries. The same relationship (a "mixed motives game" in the conflict theory of Thomas Schelling) holds for other groups concerned with international politics: the interests in restricting imports and in economic imperialism and those in freer trade, for example. In each of these cases the focus of attention is upon foreign policy; but the political gains or losses depend upon the outcome of the domestic political game, just as surely as this is true for domestic labor policy, civil rights policy, and the poverty program.

"Interests," it is worth observing, is the right word. It denotes the concerns of many ambivalent individuals respecting specific policy proposals and not only the formal positions of organized groups. The Pentagon generals may be among the least ambivalent of the hawks, but they are important politically only because hawkish sentiment is spread widely through the population. If there were not such mass support for them, cross-pressured and unstable as it may be, the generals would be seen only as cranks or crackpots. The same kind of patterning holds for the doves and for the interests in restrictive or free foreign economic policies.

To analyze the dynamics of international politics, then, it is necessary to learn how large groups of people develop into supporters or opponents of particular courses of action and the conditions in which they change the intensity or the direction of their support over time. Patterns of political support, opposition, and apathy are fundamental in international relations, as they are at every other level of political activity. To recognize this is not to suggest that the will of the people prevails or that public "demands and supports" are the "inputs" of the political system. On the contrary, it directs attention to the array of political devices, conscious and unconscious, for mobilizing and immobilizing mass opinion.

To see the politics of international conflict in this way is to recognize that it is a phase of domestic politics, romanticized and imaginatively projected into another forum of conflict where mass support is easier to mobilize. This does not make international conflict any less real or dangerous. It does have basic implications for how it can and cannot be controlled.

The official organs of the state make the formal decisions: the White House, the State Department, the CIA, the Pentagon, and so on. What decisions they make, however, what bargains they can accept and reject, depends upon the concerns and bargaining sanctions of changing group interests and does not depend upon any undefinable, transcendent "national interest." The term "national interest" serves a different function in international politics; it is considered below. An understanding of the dynamics of the bargaining must therefore begin with a hardheaded look at what it is that confers greater or lesser bargaining power upon particular groups of people with common concerns, including the help they receive from tacit and open bargaining with counterpart interests in other nations.

MYTH AND RITUAL
IN INTERNATIONAL POLITICS

The popular assumption that nations are the units in conflict and that they rationally oppose each other to further their separate national interests does have consequences, obviously, even if they are not the ones we take for granted. This cardinal tenet of our customary thinking about international relations creates for each person a world in which threat and potential aggression are omnipresent. It serves all the classic functions of "myth" as sociologists use that word. Like all myths, this one simplifies a complex world; it helps men to accept strain and deprivation; it promotes conformity to a particular pattern of thought and behavior; it furthers quiescent acceptance of the dominant and elite perspective. The myth is crucial to mass support for tough bargaining, military escalation, and restrictive foreign economic policies. It constitutes a major basis of the bargaining power of those who benefit from militant assertions of nationalism and ethnocentrism, for it conveys the message that these specific group interests are the "national interests": that the whole nation is involved in them and must patriotically support them.

Ritual supports the widespread and continuing acceptance of myth, in primitive societies and in modern ones, and this classic pattern holds in the present case. Whatever its other political functions are, the whole nation-state system, including its negotiating mechanisms, international organizations, and accompanying rhetoric, serves also as an intensely publicized rite. It is an acting out of the message, absorbed by mass publics

all over the world, that nation-states are the units in contention in international conflict: that the president, ambassador, foreign minister, or
United Nations delegate somehow transcends the conflicting interests of
domestic politics and speaks for the whole nation, which, in turn, negoti-
ates, resists, or fights other nations in defense of transcendent national
interests. In this ever present, continuously publicized, and deeply threatening drama of nations in temporary alliance, in cold war, and in hot war,
the myth finds its strongest psychological bulwark.

To suggest that the system of diplomacy among nations has this
powerful consequence among others is in no sense a statement about the
motivations of diplomats or political leaders, much less a charge that they
are deliberately deceptive. It is an observation about an unintended and
typically unrecognized effect of international political negotiation. Being
closer to it than most others, political leaders and diplomats are no doubt
even more involved in the symbolism of myth and ritual than their audiences, who participate vicariously.

Unless we get outside our own symbolic world and culture through
the works of a Malinowski studying primitive tribes or of contemporary
students of exotic foreign cultures it is hard to recognize how completely
actual and vicarious participation in ritual of this sort can channel people's
thinking, predetermining what is perceived and what is ignored and what
meanings and behaviors are elicited. The point is vital because it alone can
explain the millennia of futility of Homo sapiens in understanding and
controlling international conflict. Rite promotes joy in conformity and it
arouses mass support for the punishment of heretics. The solidarity of the
community in the face of an unknown and uncanny threat justifies acceptance of the official leadership and its policies. The formulation of issues in
dramatic, simplified, and ethnocentric or nationalistic terms and the acting
out of popular wishes lulls the critical faculties. In the face of disarmament
negotiations going on in Geneva or Vienna, who can doubt the regime's
desire for peace, especially as the government has participated in such negotiations for many years?[1]

People expect international organizations to serve the ritualistic function suggested here even though it is not their formally defined function:
they impose sanctions on participants who fail to play the expected role.
Even when an international organization is occasionally so set up that its
formal task is to deal with economic cleavages rather than nationalistic
ones, steps are taken to transform the organization so that it will become

---

[1] I. F. Stone, "A Century of Futility," *New York Review of Books* 14
(April 9, 1970), 30–33.

a forum for the expression of national rivalries. An especially clear case is the International Labor Organization. Set up with formal representation for management, labor, and government representatives and expected to deal with management-labor problems, it did so in a highly technical, somewhat desultory way between the two world wars, hardly noticed by the mass media or the public. It was established as a specialized agency under the United Nations after World War II, and was drawn into the cold war vortex, quickly becoming one more forum for cold war infighting. American and Russian union and management groups used it to attack their national rivals with far more zest than they used it to deal with their economic rivals. With newspaper and television reporters watching them, the ILO delegates had to play to a mass audience and had to follow the script the audience expected. Meetings are now reported chiefly to stress the cold war theme. A similar line of development is noticeable in the European Common Market and in GATT, though national differences have been formally emphasized in the structure of these organizations from the start, and it is French-German-British and similar rivalries that are dramatized.

THE FUNCTIONS OF ESCALATION

Given this combination of interest group politics and mass involvement in the symbolism of international conflict, support for escalation is more readily mobilized than support for détente in those countries capable of mounting serious military campaigns against potential rivals. In what respects is such a development systematic?

For any potential international conflict it can be assumed that most people are susceptible to influence to move from wherever they are toward either a hawk or a dove position and will remain ambivalent in some degree even after they take a position. Some groups are relatively committed as a function of their objective situations. This is likely to be true (to cite some polar cases) of high ranking, professional military officers, of members of minority groups oppressed in a foreign country viewed as a potential enemy, and of adherents of pacifist religions. For the large mass of the population, however, it is a question of whether domestic and foreign political acts create an expectation of foreign aggression or of international cooperation and coexistence; and such acts can be, and routinely are, manipulated, contrived, and interpreted so as to evoke mollifying or arousing cues. The publicized emphasis can be upon trade agreements, disarmament negotiations, cultural exchanges and agreements in principle or upon border incidents, espionage, subversive plots, and aggressive plans. News of governmental actions therefore influences popular expectations and evokes rationalizing ideologies. To a very significant degree ideologies are certainly the consequence, rather than the independent cause, of how the game is played. Men constantly create them to rationalize their behavior. They nonetheless become potent symbols once they are in existence, supplying gratifications, affect, and a justification for militancy on both sides. Yet in this vital respect newspapers and official statements routinely reverse the cause-effect relationships, presenting ideologies as causes that sway mortals. If Khrushchev says that Russia will bury us, his words and ideology are taken as iron fact, though his actions, which were often conciliatory, are somehow unreal, ephemeral, and not perceived as reliable predictors of future behavior. The manner in which diplomatic and military elites play the game creates widely shared expectations and perceptions of threat from abroad. Once this happens, consonant cognitions will predictably be created and political support maintained.

Allegations of the aggressive character of foreign countries regarded as enemies or potential enemies can take many forms. It can be current aggressiveness, as exemplified by American and North Vietnamese charges against each other in 1971. It can be future aggressiveness, as exemplified by repeated Chinese and Russian charges of Pentagon and CIA intentions to encircle them and subvert their allies and satellites. It can be stress upon manufactured aggressions, such as the Nazis created in the Sudetenland, Czechoslovakia, Austria, and Poland in the late thirties. It can be stress upon alleged past aggressions, as in Hitler's charges about the Versailles Treaty.

In every case this tactic, whether sincere or contrived, whether conscious, subconscious, or unconscious, has the effect of creating perceptions of threat and evoking mass support for a militant position.

Official policymakers have impressive incentives to perceive some foreign powers as hostile and aggressive, to act on that premise, and thereby evoke mass expectations of the same kind, legitimizing militancy and high armament levels at home. These incentives stem from advantages that accrue to a very wide range of groups in the domestic political conflict: advantages in money, status, and power for a business-labor-military-government complex that increasingly embraces a high proportion of the population in their roles as contractors, officials, policymakers, and employees. In this sense the President, State Department, Pentagon, and CIA are acting in behalf of a very broad constituency when they legitimize cold and hot war activities. This suggestion is not a charge of cynical opportunism on the part of these people and agencies. On the contrary, it means that they reflect their constituents' interests and that people's perceptions hinge significantly on their interests, a point further considered below. All who are involved in this interest complex are bound to be ambivalent about it in some measure, and a substantial minority of the population, notably the poor, the unemployed, students, and many intellectuals, are involved in it only minimally, adversely, or not at all. For these last groups the draft and the physical and moral risks of fighting are likely to be far more salient, for they and their children bear the brunt of these risks.

For those who do gain money and status from escalation, however, what is presented publicly as a national threat (the militaristic intentions and actions of other countries) is also an opportunity. The threatening behavior of hawkish groups in rival countries becomes the most potent bargaining counter in domestic politics. It provides the most telling justification for large defense budgets and relaxation of controls over how military appropriations are spent. At the same time it legitimizes reduced concern for civil rights and for welfare programs, keeps the economy buoyant, minimizes unemployment problems and the political threat they pose for the incumbent office-holder, and justifies increased controls over dissenting and protest activities. There is something for almost everybody and corresponding status benefits for those high in the political, industrial, military, and labor hierarchies.

This consideration is considerably more important in the world of the sixties than it was in earlier times, and it grows more compelling as private and public economic planning become important to an increasingly large proportion of the population. Our greater ability to control the rate of economic growth and distributive shares through fiscal policy and manpower and wage-price regulations is another pertinent contemporary development, as is the ability to interpret and manipulate popular responses to these centralized controls through a wider and more tightly integrated network of mass communications media. For these reasons escalation is more closely tied to the perceived interests of a wide range of groups than was true in the relatively decentralized economies and polities of the last century and the early years of this one. This is especially true, of course, of the large and highly industrialized countries, which engage in economic planning under a variety of labels. The peace advocate who posits a conspiracy of a small group of armament makers and brass hats as the cause of escalation not only grossly underestimates the problem but makes escalation politically more feasible. The millions of workers and public and private bureaucrats who share a perception that a serious foreign threat needs to be destroyed learn from the conspiracy charge that those who make it are ignoring them and misrepresenting the issue.

The psychologists who point to a tie between people's motivations and their perceptions furnish an important link in this explanation of what is involved, for this tie suggests the likelihood that hawk groups in rival countries will coordinate their expectations without open communication with each other. When it serves people's status or economic interests to perceive rival powers as contemplating aggression, such perceptions are likely to occur, especially in an ambiguous situation.

The fact that the coordination has to be tacit further encourages escalation, for, as Thomas Schelling persuasively remarks," if coordination has to be tacit, compromise may be impossible. People are at the mercy of a faulty communication system that makes it easy to 'agree' (tacitly) to move but impossible to agree to stay."[2] Even though various groups become alarmed at the crescendo of international tension, there is likely to be no way to exchange credible signals about willingness to stop or to compromise.

Still another key element in the bargaining mechanics is the status, and consequent ego stake, of leaders of organizations formally dedicated to promoting preparedness and the countering of threats from foreign powers. Some such organizations, like veterans' groups, are private; but the major ones are governmental. In either case their budgets, public support, and prestige depend directly upon widespread belief in foreign threats. This state of affairs makes retreat from militancy difficult, for it threatens both the political support and the self-conceptions of the leaders of these organizations.

Just as perception of the nation as the significant international unit masks perception of the real gains and real losses of specific domestic groups and of specific transnational groups, so does a derivative myth: that war is decisive in determining who gets what; that it is the ultimate method of settling conflict; that settlements reflect the balance of military power, for war is inevitable. In one national opinion poll more than 70 percent of Americans said they believe war is inevitable.[3]

These two myths depend upon and reinforce each other, for both divert perception from the concrete losses to large groups of people even in countries that win a war and from the grossly unequal incidence of gains and losses in status, money, and survival that flow from both cold and hot wars. They also divert attention from the more critical determinant of who gets what, both in peace and in war: political support and opposition. They reinforce the belief that military power will benefit everyone substantially and that military weakness will hurt everyone.

There are, of course, some influences making for détente as well, but

_____

[2] Thomas S. Schelling, *The Strategy of Conflict* (New York: Oxford University Press, 1963), p. 91.

[3] Otto Klineberg, *The Human Dimension in International Relations* (New York: Holt, Rinehart & Winston, 1964), p. 9.

they are not symmetrical with the escalating influences. More important, they become relatively weaker as the industrial and military potential of the nation grows. Among the most significant of these are the interests of exporting industries in foreign trade, including trade with potential enemy countries. Politically and strategically this calls for separation of the negotiations respecting foreign trade from those involving armament and nationalist rivalry. Trade agreements are typically arranged through narrowly based, technical negotiations, without wide mass involvement. Psychologically, trade agreements with potentially hostile countries involve toleration of some dissonance between economic and political beliefs, and the dissonance is naturally greater when nationalist rivalry is intense. The interest in expansion of foreign trade holds for only a fraction of a country's industries, in any case, while those attached to a great many industries have a contrary interest: in trade restrictions, protection against foreign competition, and expanding defense contracts.

Both the latter group of industries and the number of those who find the dissonance hardest to tolerate increase substantially as a nation's industrial and military potential grows. Such growth makes it appear more likely that military ventures will succeed, promotes a sense of invulnerability, and therefore encourages the adoption of diplomatic strategies that rely upon military power. The strong economic interest in military expenditures is a further incentive in this direction and helps shape perceptions of diplomatic situations so as to justify military solutions.

Once this trend has begun, a key sector of the economy acquires a vested interest in continued governmental purchases of its military and other output, further accentuating the trend. The work forces attached to these industries also share this interest. Indeed, the workers and their union representatives are often less able than business management to tolerate dissonance between ideological and economic objectives, so that they become still another key stimulus to escalation. It is hardly surprising that foreign trade negotiations have not proved to be a road to significant and lasting détente.

As weak a guide as foreign trade is in the search for détente it does at least evoke the efforts of an organized and sometimes strategically placed group of industries. The same is not true of the more direct promoters of détente, the doves and peace groups. Here is an ideology that is doubtless shared in some measure by everyone, including the hard-bitten military brass. For reasons already considered, however, it is substantially weakened or overshadowed by economic or status interests that weigh heavily with a very large share of the population; just as the consumer interest in low prices in domestic politics is normally relatively weak, overshadowed by the same people's contrary interests as producers in higher prices for whatever it is they sell: goods, services, or wage labor. What doves have to offer is appealing rhetoric and reason, but they can offer few bargains, tacit or otherwise, that are useful in political or economic logrolling. This is not to say that the universal interest in maintaining peace is without effect or negligible. It may well delay resort to military measures, especially in the interims when military establishments and associated industrial groups are doubtful that they can successfully carry through a strategy of force. The universal interest in peace also rationalizes the hesitancy of elites in pushing escalation to the point that the whole system, including its greatest beneficiaries, may be destroyed. These effects, however, manifestly have more to do with the timing than with the substance of policy.

It is even paradoxically true that the leaders and more active participants in the peace movement gain status as escalation proceeds; for the committed then see them as courageous nonconformists and heroes; and there is some chance that their support will widen as well as deepen; though we know little about the dynamics of that phenomenon.

THE CHARACTERISTICS OF COGNITIONS ABOUT INTERNATIONAL THREATS

The whole grand pattern of international diplomatic machinery conveys the message to those who observe it that nations are separate units in actual or potential contention with each other. This meaning is more compellingly presented through what is implicit in the words and acts of public officials than through declarations in the form of sentences, for it is less likely to be examined critically. The drama of nations in contention seems to be complete and manifest and is taken on its own terms. It creates its own symbolic universe or psychological space. If it is asserted in a sentence that nations are the units of international conflict, the proposition becomes one to be examined, debated, and criticized. To witness the continuing drama of international conflict and diplomacy, on the other hand, is to be impressed with a meaning that seems self-evident and that discourages critical examination rather than evoking it. It is for that reason that the whole spectacle constitutes a ritual powerfully supporting a myth. The very functioning of international institutions therefore mobilizes the mass public in support of particular group interests, for political spectators identify these interests with the nation they perceive as threatened by rival powers.

Because pseudo-speciation into rival nationalisms flexibly serves a range of psychological and economic needs for a wide and somewhat shifting portion of the population, it becomes the basic cognition about public affairs: generating, facilitating, and reinforcing consonant subcognitions of many forms. Children learn in their most susceptible years that national boundaries define the fundamental cleavages upon the world scene, that there is a transcendent national interest that has often been heroically protected and advanced through wars, and that the cause of international peace has been best protected by high levels of military preparedness and by wars against nonpeace-loving nations. Adults and children are socialized to identify greatness in historic figures primarily with their nationalistic and military accomplishments or with legends about such accomplishments. In perceiving history in this light people are of course defining a role and an identity for themselves, again illustrating the intimate link between myth and identity.

Even the celebrated historic figure whose achievement was cultural or artistic, transcending national boundaries and illustrating their artificiality, is perceived by the devotee of pseudo-speciation into nations as added evidence of the superiority of his own nation. That Goethe was German is evidence to the German nationalist that Germany should dominate people with inferior cultural genius. That great figures have appeared in a nation's history, becomes transformed into the postulate that all individuals of the nation are great and so have a mission to guide other nationalities, who are groping in outer darkness.

The empirical facts are not controlling in the genesis of such perceptions of history. Man's perceptions of comparative national accomplishments in the arts, politics, or war are chiefly a function of contemporary conditions and the need to justify current national acts and popular beliefs. Who invented the telephone, discovered America, won the War of 1812, or are ready for self-government depends less upon the dull facts than upon the consequences of one or another belief for status, political support, and foreign policy.

The very term "national interest" encourages people to redefine their concrete interests to make them consonant with the interests that are already strong in domestic political interplay. "National interest" is a totally ambiguous term in the sense that it can mean whatever an individual or group chooses to read into it, even though the various meanings are different and often conflicting. Its very semantic hollowness makes it all the more potent symbolically, however. Once an official governmental agency defines a policy as in the national interest it is endowed with compelling emotional affect flowing from the various social psychological processes just discussed. This effect is especially potent if the government defines the national interest by publicized action as well as by its words. This general interest is perceived as transcending the concrete interests of specific groups and so draws strong support even from some people who are hurt by it. Its lack of semantic precision enables it to condense for each person a set of empirically unobservable but emotionally compelling beliefs and meanings consonant with their perception of the national interest. To defeat a communist conspiracy against the free world sanctifies the deaths of civilians and soldiers and justifies other deprivations which, in a different context, would evoke strong and wide resistance and protest: price inflation, pollution of the environment, denial of funds to save cities from degradation, and alliances with venal and despotic oligarchies.

For the official policymaker the myth entails an even more flattering self-conception than it does for his followers. For him there is the possibility of attaining greatness, wide power, and influence, while furthering a noble cause. A perception of invulnerability is therefore likely to stir him to create a crisis, while he perceives and justifies his action as a response to outside events. The German invasion of Poland in 1939, the Cuban missile crisis of 1962, and thousands of other managed crises in the history of the world look different to uninvolved contemporaries and to later generations than they look to the policymakers and the politically involved whose ego needs and roles are tied to the myths that engage them.

For the mass public, then, as for those directly involved in policy formation, the processes promoting militancy in the contemporary world are increasingly more potent than those promoting détente. Doves and free traders can take advantage of no social psychological dynamism corresponding in potency to the ethnocentric response of those who can project their own hostilities upon potentially hostile foreign powers. They benefit from no combination of ritual and myth corresponding to those that constantly strengthen the idea of nationalism and the transcendency of national interests over cultural and economic interests. The strategy they espouse does not bring impressive economic and status benefits to wide groups of the population. In place of these appeals based upon profound wellsprings in the psyche and upon immediate economic advantages, the proponents of détente rely upon a widely shared interest that wins ritualistic asset as abstract rhetoric but is rarely compelling in a specific situation when confronted with the combination of escalating appeals that are always available. Advocacy of peace is therefore easily vulnerable to charges of lack of patriotism, cowardice, or special pleading by cranks.

There is a trait of the human mind that facilitates the organization of these several escalating appeals so as to make international politics the field in which organized mass conflict is most frequent and most prolonged when it occurs. Beliefs and perceptions about the hostile or friendly stance and potentialities of other nations exemplify better than other political cognitions that class of perceptions that is readily subject to change, quickly and in response to relatively few cues. Chapter 3 presents evidence that only cognitions that are held by a large population with relatively little dissent or controversy are readily changed, with relatively little dissent from the change. This condition is typical of perceptions of the posture of other nations. It is not typical of perceptions of domestic issues that arouse wide concern. On domestic issues controversy among large conflicting groups is normal. In international politics the same fears and anxieties can animate virtually everyone because the supposed threat is abroad; it does not come from another segment of the domestic population.

Although the proposition that consensually held cognitions change more easily than challenged ones seems paradoxical, it fits empirical observation and is consistent with pertinent theory. Quick changes in perception of a particular foreign country from ally to enemy or vice versa have often occurred. They are readily possible, as Orwell recognized in *1984,* because the cues upon which such cognitions are based are almost entirely governmental, with few counter-cues from other sources, and because deep and socially reinforced anxiety about foreign threats makes people peculiarly susceptible to these monopolistic cues. Where cognitions are challenged by organized interests or reference groups, on the other hand, the conflicting beliefs remain or escalate in intensity, as analyzed in the early chapters of this book.

Because of this notable characteristic of the mind and of public opinion, international threat is always present in constantly renewed and intense form. When the perception of the enemy changes, it does so for virtually everyone;[4] and the new foreign threat serves the same psychological and economic functions as the old while avoiding the diminution in intensity and the banality that might accompany lengthy focusing upon the same enemy.

The most striking and most systematically significant feature of the international political scene is its gross instability in respect to alliances and foreign and domestic support for policies. Diplomatic history chronicles a never-ending sequence of changes in definitions of the critical issues, in alliances, in public demands for war, in popular dissatisfaction with the current war, and in identifications of the enemy. The chronicle is at once an account of past instabilities and a symbolic justification of the contemporary instabilities of the chroniclers. If the change from eagerness to appease Hitler in 1938 to eagerness to fight him in 1939 chronicles the unstable attitudes of some people and of most officials in the late thirties,

---

[4] The Vietnam war exemplifies a relatively rare exceptional case. Here conflict about who the enemy is became a crucial issue in domestic politics. The conflicting beliefs accordingly are maintained or intensified.

it also serves to rationalize the switch in 1965 from limited American intervention in Vietnam to rapid escalation in Southeast Asia and the definition of Vietnam as the critical frontier of the free world. For other people the historical account rationalizes their opposition to contemporary escalation.

While only instability is stable in world politics, in people's minds the accepted explanations of international politics nonetheless focus attention upon stability. Power is balanced or tends to return to balance. Traditional allies confront traditional enemies. Nations find their proper positions in a bipolarized world in which the two superpowers fend off and stalemate each other's gambits. A single superpower or *pax romana* maintains peace. The metaphors vary by time and place; but governmental officials, mass publics, and academic writers are all socialized to see developments on the international scene in terms of them. The metaphors in turn catalyze confidence in official policies and justify resolute action, often by warfare, to restore or maintain the mythical stable norm.

In international politics, instability and perceptions regarding vulnerability or invulnerability feed upon each other and reinforce each other; they are facets of the same perception. The superpower, strong in military weapons and its officials therefore resolute in their assumption that military might is the ultimate sanction, predictably becomes obsessed with the need to destroy potential threats to its benevolent hegemony and police the world in the interests of peace, democracy, the true faith, or whatever other abstraction is currently fashionable. This course of action is highly destabilizing, for it evokes foreign and domestic fears, restiveness, and counteralliances among people who see it as a threat to the stable power balance and to their own rights and lives, rather than as benevolence. Overlooked or minimally recognized is the strong predilection of people imbued with a belief in their country's invulnerability to regard the politically powerless as expendable in war. Where people are aware of their country's vulnerability, on the other hand, they perceive a need for coexistence and are sensitive to the importance of political allies and support, abroad and at home. In international politics, as in all political conflict, perceptions about vulnerability are a major influence upon political strategy and especially upon beliefs about the need to fight.

STRATEGIES FOR PEACE

This view of the dynamics of escalation affords little support for the proponents of the popular strategies for maintaining peace and explains why those that have been relied upon most often are formulas for legitimizing escalation rather than for achieving détente. Military preparedness, deterrence through one or another threat, unilateral disarmament, and graduated tension reduction are much talked of. A key failing of all of them is their reliance upon the major premise that the decisive international bargaining is between national units, which decide through rational calculations what will serve their "national interests." This assumption encourages some ingenious planning of game theoretical strategies, but it has little bearing on the world we live in if the gambits of international politics flow from the interests of specific groups in status, financial gains, and survival, and not from an undefinable and empirically undiscoverable national interest.

Preparedness and deterrence have been tried with conspicuous futility since the dawn of the nation-state system. It is easy to understand both the reasons for their popularity and the inevitability of their failure. Both are rationalizations for achieving precisely what hawks always want: money, status, and bargaining power in domestic politics for themselves at the expense of rival claimants for these benefits; and they give militant groups in other countries the strongest possible justification for the same behavior. Following the principle pointed out by Kenneth Burke that political rhetoric "sharpens up the pointless and blunts the too sharply pointed,"[5] these strategies rationalize escalation in the name of peace. They can maintain a pretense that they are pursuing peace only because of the prevailing myth that nations as units make rational calculations as to what will serve their national interests in international politics. On this assumption of a world that never was, armaments deter rivals. If, however, we make the manifest empirical observation that specific groups benefit immediately in noneconomic as well as economic ways from armament production, then such production becomes the point of the game. It is not simply a means to a higher abstract goal, peace, as the myth would have it. In the real world the most dedicated hawks can never reach the point that peace rather than more arms becomes their concrete empirical objective. Such a result would violate their own interests; and it is obviously incompatible with the boost their arms buildups have upon the political bargaining power of hawks in the domestic politics of rival countries and therefore upon their own domestic bargaining power. The term "peace" in this context serves only, if potently, as a rhetorical rationalization and not as a designation of any behavior likely to come to pass.

The preparedness and deterrence theories do rest upon a peculiarly static and simplistic recognition of the influence of perceptions of vulnerability. Recognizing that those who know they are vulnerable will not at-

---

[5] Kenneth E. Burke, *A Grammar of Motives* (Englewood Cliffs, N.J.: Prentice-Hall, 1945), p. 393.

tack, these theories also assume: (1) that the powerful country, though heavily armed and invulnerable, will not itself become the aggressor, because it is benevolent and seeks only peace; and (2) that all rivals will complacently accept their own vulnerability as stable and tolerable. Although diplomatic history is a running commentary on the falsity of both these assumptions, the facts do not inhibit people with something to gain from perpetuation of the preparedness and deterrence strategy.

The strategies of unilateral disarmament and graduated tension reduction[6] are not based upon any such simple fallacy. They are clearly not rationalizations for the opposite of what they purport to achieve, and their logical and psychological assumptions seem sound. These strategies would probably work if they were seriously and persistently followed, but there are political reasons for doubting that they will be seriously and persistently tried. They call for the groups with most potent bargaining counters to throw away their strongest cards; for they misname the game that is being played.

If the view of international politics suggested here is correct, a student of the international scene has constantly to take account of three analytically distinct modes of political interplay which influence and complement each other. There is the political bargaining arena in which formal governmental organizations make policy respecting international affairs, but always in response to the demands and sanctions of interested groups which have something tangible to gain or to lose. There is the mass public of political spectators, to whose powerful influence the direct participants must always be sensitive, but who are mobilizable in support of particular positions, especially militant ones, or rendered quiescent through identifiable psychological and political processes. Finally, there is the bargaining, largely tacit, among group interests in rival countries, which is a major source of the *domestic* bargaining power of these interests.

In contrast to this multifaceted model of groups acting in accordance with rational and nonrational influences, the conventional view of international relations would have it that the world political scene is composed of national units working out subtle and rational strategies for besting each other, deterring each other, or cooperating with each other, always to serve an abstract national interest, and always seeing war as the ultimate sanction. This mythical model itself serves the interests of hawk groups in all countries, and the operations of our international organizations and

---

    [6] Proposed by Charles E. Osgood, graduated tension reduction calls for a single power unilaterally to take small steps toward détente at the same time maintaining enough military strength to repulse attacks on itself (*Perspective in Foreign Policy* Urbana: [University of Illinois Press, 1965]).

diplomatic machinery function as rituals that further support belief in the myth.

In the conventional view what a nation can get through international negotiations or war is the end-point of the whole game. In the view presented here international negotiations and aggressions are highly potent influences upon the future beliefs, perceptions, and bargaining positions of specific group interests. Their immediate outcomes are not ends in themselves.

The complicated international scene can be kept in perspective only by focusing upon the consequences of alternative actions for specific groups of people, and not by looking at how policymakers or others perceive, justify, or rationalize their behavior; for the policymakers, like everyone else, are caught up in the complex and powerful symbolism with which international politics are invested.

Chapter 10

HUMAN AND POLITICAL
POTENTIALITIES

Political analysis is ultimately adequate and enlightening in the measure that it takes full account of man's complexity and of his potentialities. It is a central theme of this book that political perceptions, beliefs, norms, and demands are multifaceted, ambivalent, and changeable; that changes are systematic and patterned; that careful attention to divergencies between the phenomenological perceptions of specific groups of people and the conventional observations of social scientists permits us to identify the respects in which changes in political cognitions and behavior are systematic. We are trying to formulate a model of the mind that enables the political analyst to explain and anticipate shifts in perceptions of interests, allies, enemies, threats, and reassurances. Such a paradigm facilitates analysis of the potentialities of political actions; it does not focus only upon its constraints; and it helps us understand why both the worst and the best possibilities are so frequently realized.

Although empirical observations and social psychological theory fully support the thesis that cognitions are complex and contingent, both everyday political talk and academic political science typically make the political world understandable and reassuring by postulating a high degree of stability in cognitions and in personality traits. It would be surprising if this were not so. In a world filled with uncertainties and threats it is reassuring to believe that Homo sapiens is normally motivated by persisting moral values, that he usually bases his beliefs on empirical evidence, and that he plans his acts to achieve his just ends. That some people behave in a way that strikes others as irrational or immoral intensifies the incentive to outlaw and repress them and to perceive them as exceptional and deviant cases: small minorities, outside agitators, or hard-core revolutionaries. To believe that perception and beliefs, as well as norms, are specific to particular social conditions and situations and that even the respectable will certainly deviate when placed in changed situations is to increase uncertainty and anxiety.

Both institutional and behavioral political scientists have embraced models of the polity that highlight the responsiveness of public officials to what are postulated as meaningful indications of mass wants and that subtly understate the shaping of wants by government, with elites and masses responsive to the same symbols. The metaphor of popularly controlled legislatures which mandate the carrying out of policy and the metaphor of "inputs" of demands and supports "converted" to "outputs" embrace the same basic conception. The difference between the two figures of speech lies in the kinds of empirical observations they call for; the similarity lies in what they imply for the legitimacy of political regimes and the stable and reassuring bedrock implied by "the consent of the governed," or "demands and supports." The respective models maximize the importance of observations about the formal acts of voters, legislatures, courts, and executives or they maximize the importance of observations about public opinions and attitudes; they thereby legitimize not only governmental regimes but conventional social science research. Systematically underplayed are the implications of the alternative and more holistic models that focus attention upon the conditions of change rather than the stability of political inputs: the work of the symbolic interactionists, the gestaltists and the phenomenologists, and the work of some novelists, film makers, and social critics. Both in everyday life and in the formulation of research designs this distinction is critical in the perceptions to which it leads and in the questions and hypotheses it generates. Either we ask how actions and developments do or might change people's beliefs and behaviors or we ask how people with postulated fixed perceptions and cognitions will behave or can be coerced or repressed. To direct one's attention to one or the other question is to predetermine both the forms of public policy that seem desirable and the kinds of empirical observations that seem pertinent to explanation and understanding.

This is in no way to deny that what people want and value often does persist in much the same form for long periods of time. So long as it does, that is an important datum and usually quite evident. Neither evident nor banal are the material, organizational, and symbolic conditions that systematically contribute to changed wants and values. That law enforcement officials are impatient with dissent; that young people oppose obstacles to their ready achievement of status and influence; that middle class Americans held their polity in high regard in the fifties and that Italians, with a much smaller middle class, did not are all data that are relatively true, relatively obvious, and in themselves relatively misleading about the bases of mass support and opposition to political regimes. If a social scientist does not link them to a full-blown, carefully tested set of general propositions about the conditions of cognitive change, they are of little use to him.

The propositions upon which this book draws stem from the view of social psychologists that only through interactions with others do people create symbols with common and compelling meanings and thereby create either common conceptions and beliefs about the external world or socially supported self-conceptions. Perception is always a selection and interpretation of observations consonant with more general cognitions and assumptions. These help anchor the self in a past and a future in a way that gives the ego a particular function and status. For some behaviors demonstrable effectiveness in action is critical to creating a gratifying identity. Under such conditions the incentive is strong to test perceptions empirically. The canoe builder, the natural scientist, and the arsonist are all in situations in which failure in action is readily and predictably ascertained and noticed. The range of examples also illustrates the fact that perception, and incentive to reality testing, occur as part of a hierarchy of cognitions and may take place at any level of the hierarchy; the arsonist and the canoe builder pursue their tasks as a function of more general cognitions about the consequences of their work.

For many behaviors "effectiveness in action" is not in point, not possible, or not verifiable. This is especially characteristic of the shared social objectives that become major political issues. Such political goals depend upon perceptions and beliefs that are not, and often cannot be, based upon empirical observation. Instead, they are socially cued by others who are significant to a person, creating faith in a belief that is not susceptible to empirical disproof and at the same time creating a valued self-conception for those who believe in the goal as well as for those who reject it. The man who sees himself as a fighter in the war against a Communist conspiracy, as a bulwark of the movement for civil rights, or as one who recognizes that welfare measures promote sloth and moral softness has strong reason to cling to the political role that is gratifying. He will shape and select other perceptions to accord with the central, salient one, and will seek out, emphasize, and usually exaggerate social support for his belief.

Government plays an especially salient function in the shaping of cognitions about political issues. On many of the most controversial ones the impact of governmental actions upon mass beliefs and perceptions is, in fact, the major, or the only, consequence of political activity. The conditions that facilitate governmental influence upon cognitions can be specified with some confidence and frequently occur: difficulty or inability to examine a source of anxiety empirically, often because it involves a situation expected to occur in the future (the expectation itself often cued by governmental action or rhetoric); avid search for information to resolve the uncertainty and anxiety, which is intensified by rumor and other forms of communication; conspicuous, publicized governmental action which either explicitly asserts or clearly implies a factual state of affairs that does resolve the uncertainty.

A legitimate government can make its actions potent condensation symbols that bring about such shared mass beliefs and perceptions about matters that evoke anxiety. Governmental officials present themselves as embodying the people's will; the mystical, nonempirical character of the assertion is not readily apparent to the political actor in everyday life, but only to the person who self-consciously looks for the bases of phenomenological perceptions. High officials are assumed to have special sources of intelligence not available to the naive observers themselves. The state, or its chief magistrate, takes on some measure of the protective and omniscient function of the primal father or the deity. Such cues, emanating from a governmental source, encounter no competing information bolstered by equally authoritative and legitimating symbols: often there is no competing information at all. Resolving uncertainty and anxiety and creating a gratifying self-conception, cognitions cued by governmental action often become paramount in the hierarchy of cognitions, screening out dissonant ones and generating subcognitions that are consonant and reinforcing.

The fact that religious authorities manifestly enjoy a similar power to generate and coalesce mass beliefs and perceptions in ambiguous situations in less secular cultures further supports this view of the cognitive function of governmental activity and helps to highlight its dynamics. Religious authorities or a legitimate church are assumed to derive their intelligence from God. Governments are assumed to derive theirs from the will of the people. Both sources are impermeable to empirical examination. Both allegedly draw intensity from oedipal projections. Both are therefore a source of powerful symbols that influence the behavior of mass publics. Such shaping of mass political support and opposition is the basic political phenomenon, underlying and constraining the actions of elites.

This view manifestly carries with it some important implications regarding the meaning of such concepts as "self-government," "the consent of the governed," and "political participation." If legislative, administrative, and judicial procedures significantly influence how people see leaders, issues, and themselves and therefore what they will accept, what they want, and what they demand, then those procedures are less likely to reflect the people's will than to shape it. More precisely, they reflect it only after they shape it, which puts the representation function in a rather different light. Usually the procedures legitimize the regime and help coopt potential dissenters; sometimes they help arouse dissent and protest. In either case they significantly influence people's roles, self-concepts, and willingness to accept their own statuses and the official rules. They affect not so much who gets what as who is satisfied or dissatisfied with what he gets and with who orders him around.

This definition of the functions of governmental acts does explain, as the conventional view cannot, the remarkable degree of support official

governmental acts and policies enjoy even when they bring serious deprivations to their supporters and to others: economic, welfare, civil rights, and
regulatory policies that are manifestly tokens or that perpetuate inequalities; virtually continuous wars fought in the name of a peace that
appears only intermittently and precariously. Those who look at such
phenomena outside the context of the conventional myths will feel the
need to explain support for regimes rather than to explain dissent—though
the latter is conventionally seen as the more legitimate function of a social
scientist.

THE DYNAMIC FORMS
OF POLITICAL CONFLICT

Both the escalation of political conflict to more militant behaviors and its
ritualization in governmental procedures that chiefly affect beliefs rather
than value allocations reflect the interactions of flesh-and-blood
people and nothing more abstract or more mystical than that. People
caught up in these processes nonetheless do explain and rationalize them
in abstract or mystical terms: the destruction of a threat to society, the
achievement of justice, the realization of the public interest, the equitable
weighing of claims. How people perceive the issues and how they perceive
themselves and their own social and political roles are integrally interrelated. These are not separate forms of cognition, but rather aspects of the
same cognitive structure, reinforcing and lending intensity to each other
and changing together. The alternative (and more common) assumption,
that particular people have aggressive traits, or law-and-order traits, or
innate perceptions of their political efficacy or of regime legitimacy, tells
us something important about those who hold these beliefs, but much less
about the people to whom they refer. Such beliefs powerfully rationalize
repression.

The processes of escalation and ritualization are highly patterned.
Political militance and violence, like political routine, has an identifiable
form of development and of expression, though its systematic and formal
character is also systematically obscured—both by the perception of
popular uprising and violent demonstrations as irrational, chaotic, and
purposeless and by the perception of protest organizations as potential
foci of rebellion. Escalation of conflict is basically a process through which
adversaries widen support for their opponents as well as themselves, each
act and gesture contributing to the translation of less salient policy conflicts into wider, more abstract, and more salient ones. Ritualization involves a tacit agreement regarding the terms of value allocations, rational-

ized in terms of the public interest through formal, and essentially banal, procedures and routines. Formal organization institutionalizes actions, formalizes signals of support and of opposition, reduces uncertainty about others' behaviors, and therefore inhibits individual search for cues and individual militancy, helping to furnish the conditions for ritualization and cooptation. Organization serves these functions at any level of violence. Nonritualized violence involves, as concomitants, the creation of perceptions of threat among potential adversaries and of increasing social support on both sides for militant expression of the threat. Escalating support for a possible antagonist sufficient to make him invulnerable inhibits counterescalation. The emotional concomitants of escalation are those that inhibit empathy, understanding, and mutual role taking; they chiefly are expressed as anger, fear, or hostility. These emotions are also associated with resolute conformity to a single role rather than with free exploration of possibilities and the flexibility to assume multiple political roles or to alternate among them.

In a politically significant sense, then, adversaries serve each others' interests. At successive developmental stages of both escalation and ritualization, moreover, the same formal processes recur. The critical characteristic of these processes is their generation through socially cued symbols that mask or displace empirical observation and reality testing, partially or completely.

Reality testing in its least contaminated form occurs in activities of individuals rigorously designed to achieve unambiguous objectives. By definition, these activities are nonpolitical; they are scientific, aesthetic, or technical in character. Carrying on overarching commitment to empirical verification that is also an overarching commitment to success, such work evokes the creative emotions that are associated with satisfying the expectations of the range of audiences that support one's work. Group activities that can be subdivided into individual tasks with unambiguous objectives may also approximate this empirically based model: the construction of a ship or a building, the performances of a symphony orchestra, the astronauts' trip to the moon. It is precisely when collective enterprises become controversial, i.e., political, that they grow heavily symbolic and begin to assume the forms of conflict that may escolate.

For some politicians and some spectators of politics a high measure of commitment to reality testing is also feasible. It stems, as in the nonpolitical examples, from a clear grasp of objectives and from the emotional gratification that comes from playing a range of political roles and feeling empathy with people with diverse political outlooks. This flexible form of political role taking diminishes in the degree that the inhibiting emotions prevail; in the measure, therefore, that status differences, domination, and threat are salient: for the poor and the rich, the elite and the nonelite.

People experience as separate phenomena their support or opposition to political movements, the roles they play, the emotions they feel, and the language in which political acts are described and justified. This book has analyzed all of these as key mechanisms that are integrally interrelated. Their very separation as subjective experiences reinforces the potency with which they shape political cognition and behavior.

IMPLICATIONS FOR THE ANALYSIS OF POLITICS

The model of political behavior discussed here furnishes scope for a rigorous political science that is at the same time imaginative and humane, for it examines the actual impacts of public policies upon specific people in the light of the symbolic forms that yield both unintended and intended outcomes. It directs attention to the social and the psychological processes through which the behaviors and the political outlooks of mass publics are shaped. It also directs attention to *meanings* of research findings: to the fact, for example, that survey responses are not necessarily stable, but rather instances among a range of possibilities. The crucial fact, then, is not the particular survey response, which is almost certainly ambivalent, but the contexts determining that one rather than another response occurs. By the same token, the substance of political demands and supports as of any particular moment or survey is not crucial, but only illustrative and possibly episodic.

To identify the mechanisms through which facile misperceptions occur regarding lines of political cleavage, alliances, and coalitions is to underline the importance of basing conclusions about these matters upon observation and verification. The boundaries suggested by formal organization and conventional or widely accepted definitions of allies and adversaries are themselves part of the strategy of conflict: part of the effort to win wider social support for particular group interests. The research scholar who takes them at face value embraces the very myths it is his function to identify and analyze.

This paradigm offers reason for profound skepticism about the responsiveness of government to the will of the people and also about the likelihood that governmental actions will effectively and rationally attack serious social problems. The justification of this pessimistic redirection in postulations must lie both in the persuasiveness of the evidence on which the book relies for its specific conclusions and in developments in public affairs and policies that can serve as indicators of governmental responsiveness and effectiveness in coping with problems.

SOME POLICY IMPLICATIONS

After an exploration of these complex and subtle interactions, it hardly needs asserting that no simple list of governmental actions or repertory of specific tactics can be counted on to eliminate or curtail violence against the poor or by them. This analysis nonetheless does have implications for what government might effectively do.

To be effective, public policies must be fashioned in the light of a realistic model of the generation and escalation of social restiveness and of the requisites of quiescence. A realistic model, however, is profoundly different in its dynamics and its implications from the view that seems self-evident to many people and that is most often supported. The latter, postulating that people who disrupt or destroy legal institutions are misled or subversive of the good society (unless they are public officials), prescribes that behaviors of large groups of people regarded as undesirable should be repressed, through stringent laws vigorously enforced. This position is plausible, simple, and demonstrably futile except for short periods of time and in a particular set of circumstances. If this were effective therapy for social unrest, the problem would long since have vanished.

Governmental actions inevitably affect what people want and how they think as well as how they are coerced to behave. To recognize this is to reject the view that individuals' political motivations and behaviors are fated and preprogrammed and that they can be changed or inhibited only by physical force or the fear of it. This implication suggests a wide range of policy responses that might be effective. Rather than weighing only the question how effective governmental threat or repression can be, the policy analyst can weigh a kind of question that is usually far more viable politically: How will each of the alternative policies available to government affect the dispositions of particular publics to behave in particular ways?

The difference between these two approaches amounts to a difference between what is politically viable and practical over an extended period of time and what is certain to be self-defeating. No public policy relying on physical repression of large numbers of people can succeed in its objective unless its targets are already psychologically disposed to cooperate in their own subjection. Repression, like any other public policy, can affect people's physical movements in the short run, but also shapes their political beliefs and expectations over a longer period. Its long range and more stable effect is to engender conflict escalation. This negative implication of the present study is one of its more practical ones and one of the most difficult for policymakers to accept when under pressure to react decisively to civil disobedience or disruption.

Policymakers should always be alert to both the physical and the cognitive impacts of their contemplated acts, but they must also shape their strategies in the light of predictable sources of instability in people's perceptions and beliefs. A belief patently contradicted by empirical evidence cannot long maintain quiescence or acquiescence if people can win money or status by heeding the evidence. Nor can a perception that is inconsistent with a myth long survive if the myth serves as a prop of a cherished political role or self-concept. Some forms of myth are therefore quite stable in spite of governmental efforts to dispel them or call attention to their invalid aspects; others are highly unstable in spite of governmental efforts to promulgate and perpetuate them. We know the key conditions that determine each form. Policymakers cannot ever hope to have before them a neat catalog of effective and ineffective specific courses of action. They can, however, learn how to analyze the probable consequences of alternative courses of action in specific situations.

Several more focused statements of policy implications can be listed; to some extent they recapitulate the observations just made.

1. Political arousal and violence among populations perceiving themselves as deprived or threatened are inevitable unless public policy or unambiguous events cue people either (a) to see their deprived status as inevitable or desirable; or (b) to perceive a closing of the gap between expectations and actual conditions. The proposition holds for policemen and low income whites who see themselves as deprived or threatened as much as for blacks, the destitute, and political dissenters.

2. The common and apparently growing American practice of adopting and publicizing public policies that are partly or wholly symbolic in character is a major stimulus to either violent or quiescent behavior because public policies powerfully influence both expectations and perceptions of actual conditions in ambiguous situations. Earlier chapters examine many specific sets of conditions under which one or the other behavioral outcome is probable.

3. When discontented people organize or are helped to do so by the government, the organization is more likely to facilitate cooptation to the existing order than to foment or catalyze violent demonstrations or rebellion against it. Continued symbolic as well as actual attack upon dissenting organizations does, however, facilitate conflict escalation.

These complex processes must be understood if the unintended as well as the intended consequences of governmental actions are to be taken into account in the planning of policy. Their complexity should not obscure recognition that the most efficacious, certain, and lasting response to popular unrest lies in substantial improvement in the conditions of the deprived so as to remove the reasons for their sense of deprivation.

INDEX

Whites, 63; attitudes toward rioting, 92; low income, 51, 77; perception of police honesty, 88; perceptions of demonstrators, 99; racial attitudes, 92–93, 123–24, 150–51
Whorf, Benjamin L., 66n
Wolf, Eric, 116n
Working class; *See* Whites, low income

World War II, changing perceptions in, 46–47
Wyatt, Dale, 8n

X, Malcolm, 117

Yankelovich, Daniel, 107n
Youths, attitudes toward rioting, 89–90